The Ancient Marir

SEAFARERS AND SEA FIGHTERS
OF THE MEDITERRANEAN
IN ANCIENT TIMES

Lionel Casson

Second Edition

PRINCETON UNIVERSITY PRESS
PRINCETON, NEW JERSEY

Copyright © 1991 by Princeton University Press
Published by Princeton University Press, 41 William Street,
Princeton, New Jersey 08540
In the United Kingdom: Princeton University Press, Chichester, West Sussex
Originally published by the Macmillan Company, © 1959 by Lionel Casson

Library of Congress Cataloging-in-Publication Data

Casson, Lionel, 1914–
The ancient mariners : seafarers and sea fighters of the
Mediterranean in ancient times / Lionel Casson. — 2nd ed.
p.   cm.
Includes bibliographical references and index.
ISBN 0-691-06836-4 (alk. paper) —
ISBN 0-691-01477-9 (pbk. : alk. paper)
1. Mediterranean Sea—Navigation—History.   2. Shipping—
Mediterranean Sea—History.   3. Mediterranean Region—History,
Naval.   I. Title.
VK16.C37   1991
387.5′093—dc20   90-47717

This book has been composed in Linotron Baskerville

Princeton University Press books are printed on acid-free paper
and meet the guidelines for permanence and durability of the
Committee on Production Guidelines for Book Longevity of the
Council on Library Resources

Printed in the United States of America

3   5   7   9   10   8   6   4   2

The Ancient Mariners

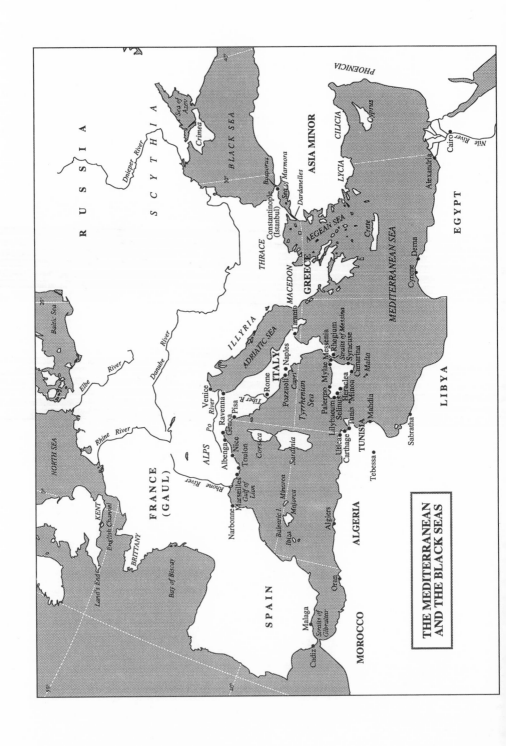

THE MEDITERRANEAN
AND THE BLACK SEAS

To my girls

———————————————

CONTENTS

ILLUSTRATIONS

PREFACE TO THE SECOND EDITION

Since *The Ancient Mariners* first appeared, much has happened to enlarge, change, and add detail to the picture it presented. Marine archaeology has provided a ceaseless flow of invaluable firsthand information about ships and their cargoes, even about their crews; new pictorial evidence of ranking importance has come to light; and authoritative new studies of various aspects of maritime history have been published. As a result, this book represents an overall exhaustive revision. Some sections are entirely new, many have been radically revised, and there is hardly a page that has not been altered in some way. The illustrations have been increased to include important discoveries of the past three decades (I am grateful to George Bass, Michael Katzev, and John Coates, who kindly supplied photographs). And the maps have been refashioned, by Paul J. Pugliese, to provide more detail.

The original edition supplied documentation for citations in the text and a selected bibliography for each chapter. To enhance the usefulness of the book for scholars, these have been replaced by a section (Notes) that furnishes comprehensive documentation keyed to the text by page numbers.

PREFACE

THE STORY of what the ancients accomplished on the sea has never been put between the covers of one book. A few episodes have been dealt with so often, in handbooks and histories, that they are as familiar as Caesar's assassination. But once off these well-trodden paths, searchers for information are forced to make their way through a miscellany of scholarly publications, more often than not articles in obscure journals, in a variety of languages; and they will find that there are some topics that have never been treated at all.

The present book is an attempt to fill this lack. I have tried to sketch, in a continuous narrative, the impressive record of the ancient mariner: how he perfected his trading vessels until from little more than rowboats they grew into huge freighters whose size was not to be matched until the eighteenth century of our era; how he perfected his fighting ships until from little more than oared transports they grew into mighty and complex rowing machines capable of carrying over a hundred marines, even of mounting artillery; how his maritime commerce progressed from timid coastal voyaging to an integrated network that stretched from Spain to Malay; how much that is popularly believed of him to his detriment—that he manned his galleys with slaves, that he could not sail against the wind, and so on—is utterly wrong.

Probably this story could not have been properly told until now. Up to a half-century or so ago we had only the writings of ancient authors to supply information. Today we can draw on the findings of hundreds of archaeological investigations; these have laid bare maritime civilizations hitherto unknown, yielded an infinite variety of objects of trade, and even turned up priceless written documents, from the official records of the Athens Naval Base written on imperishable stone to a tattered fragment of a maritime contract between some obscure businessmen on fragile papyrus. Moreover, in the last decade, the new science of underwater archaeology has enabled us to explore the actual remains of ancient wrecks. There are still gaps in our knowledge, but far fewer than there were fifty years ago.

The Ancient Mariners is addressed first and foremost to the general reader. Yet, since there is no other book in any language that covers the field, I have tried to straddle the fence and make it useful for scholars as well. . . .

Many people helped me in many ways with this book; I have space to acknowledge only my most important debts. A fellowship from the John Simon Guggenheim Memorial Foundation, by providing a precious opportunity to travel abroad for over a year, enabled me to investigate the sites of scores of ancient Mediterranean harbors, to search obscure corners of museums and come upon evidence that I would otherwise never have known of, and to use the unique facilities of half a dozen European libraries. I took particular pains to secure apt and clear illustrations; a number of institutions and individuals were of great assistance and their help is acknowledged at appropriate points in the list of plates. I must mention in particular Ernest Nash of the Fototeca Unione in Rome; I owe much to his eager and fruitful cooperation and to the splendid resources of the archive he heads. A number of the chapters have benefited from the remarks of my good friends, Professor Saul Weinberg and Professor Naphtali Lewis. Chapter 3 owes much to the generous cooperation of Fernand Benoit, director of the Museum of Archaeology at Marseilles. But far and away my greatest debt is the one I owe my father. He passed a careful and critical eye over the language and phrasing of every sentence in the manuscript; as a result, there is hardly a page in the book that has not profited from his comments and suggestions.

The Ancient Mariners

Chapter 1

DOWN TO THE SEA IN SHIPS

IN THE VERY beginning men went down, not to the sea but to quiet waters, and not in ships but in anything that would float: logs that could be straddled, rafts of wood or of bundles of reeds, perhaps even inflated skins.

But these were floats, not boats. The first true boat—something that would carry people upon water and at the same time keep them dry—was very likely the dugout, although experiments with bound reeds or with skins stretched over light frames must have taken place quite early too. And, when the desire or need arose for something bigger than what could be hollowed out of the largest logs available, the boat made of planks came into being. This was one of prehistoric man's most outstanding achievements; the credit for it probably goes to the Egyptians of the fourth millennium B.C.

As long as they stayed in shallow waters, men could propel their boats with punting poles. Farther out they used their hands—and this led them to devise the paddle, a wooden hand, as it were, and soon afterward the oar. They made impressive trips with these limited means of propulsion: as early as the eleventh millennium B.C. they were crossing from the mainland of Greece to the island of Melos to bring back the distinctive obsidian which is found only there; no doubt they hopped from island to island, but even so the voyage involved at least fifteen miles over the open sea. Then they hit upon something that revolutionized travel over the water: they learned how to use the wind. For the first time they harnessed a force other than their own muscles, their servants', or their wives'. It was a discovery whose effects reached down the ages: from this moment on, the easiest and cheapest way of transporting bulky loads over distances of any appreciable length was by water. This is the point at which the story of the ancient mariners really starts; the scene is again Egypt, or perhaps Mesopotamia.

In southern Egypt archaeologists have found a multitude of pictures of boats that, shortly before 3100 B.C., were drawn helter-skelter on rock outcrops or were included as part of the decoration on pottery. Among them are some that show, stepped amidships or forward of amidships, a mast with a broad squaresail hung upon it (Pl. 1).

No representations of sails discovered elsewhere come near to being as old as these. In Mesopotamia, a land where civilization began as early as in Egypt or even earlier, excavators digging in levels dating from about 3400 B.C. found a little clay model representing, to judge from its shape, what was probably a boat made of skins (Pl. 2). In the center of the floor, somewhat forward of amidships, is a sturdy round socket, and the hull at gunwale level is pierced by three holes. It is tempting to explain the socket as intended for a mast and the holes for a stay and shrouds, but, against this must be weighed the fact that sails are not otherwise attested in Mesopotamia until very much later. Perhaps the socket held a ceremonial pole and the holes were for cords by which the model was suspended.

Who first realized the potentialities of the sailing ship and dared to use it to strike out far beyond their own shores? For the age that predates history there is nothing to go on beyond what the archaeologists dig up, but this in most cases is ambiguous: save when islands are involved, you cannot be sure whether a prehistoric object of one country that turns up in another got there by land or sea. Yet, in the light of what follows (Chapter 2), it seems most likely that the first true sea voyages were made by Egyptians who worked northward along the coasts of Palestine and Syria or southward down the Red Sea, and by Mesopotamians and Indians who sailed between the Persian Gulf and the northwestern coast of India.

Egypt and Mesopotamia, then, had a head start over the rest of the world in the art of sailing as in so much else. But, as time passed, all along the coasts of the Mediterranean men started to go down to the sea. In the prehistoric age and long thereafter, these shores did not have the bare aspect they show today but in many places were mantled by forests that provided logs for the earliest dugouts and timber for the keels, ribs, and planks of their more complicated progeny.

How far did these primitive Mediterranean mariners sail? Did they by and large stick to their own shores or did they venture on long voyages? That their ships were probably quite frail need not have stopped them; Polynesian sailors covered impressive distances in boats that were very likely no more seaworthy. For long some archaeologists were convinced that certain beads and goldwork found in Britain came from Egypt and that a picture of a dagger carved in the rock of Stonehenge represented a type used in Greece about the middle of the second millennium B.C.; all this, they concluded, pointed to a trade route that led from the Mediterranean into far northern waters. Still others argued that doughty mariners of the age ventured to the northwestern coasts of Spain or even to Cornwall to bring back tin, that essential ingredient for the making of bronze, from the rich deposits there. But subsequent studies showed that all such claims are without solid foundation. So far as we know, the prehistoric sailors of the Mediterranean stayed by and large within the limits of their great inland sea.

Chapter 2

INTERNATIONAL TRADE BEGINS

"BRINGING OF FORTY SHIPS filled with cedar logs." So wrote an ancient scribe in listing the accomplishments of Pharaoh Snefru, ruler of Egypt about 2600 B.C. This handful of words brings us across the threshold into the period of history proper. The dim tracks of potsherds and other like objects are still important—giving them up is a luxury that the student of the history of shipping cannot afford at any stage in the ancient period—but now there exists, for the first time, the strong light of written words to serve as a guide.

As in the case of so many phases of civilization, the record begins in Egypt. Very little wood grows in the valley of the Nile. Cedar most certainly does not, and to get it Snefru had to look overseas. So he sent to Phoenicia where there was a famous stand on the mountain slopes of Lebanon. Snefru was blazing no trail, for Egypt had been in touch with this area even before his time. Archaeologists have found in the tombs of pharaohs and nobles of earlier dynasties jars and flasks and pitchers that were made in Palestine and Syria, and they have dug up in the latter countries objects that unquestionably came out of Egyptian workshops. Were these carried overland or by boat? Before the time of Snefru there is no way of telling. But the words of his scribe remove all doubt: some three thousand years before the birth of Christ a fleet of forty vessels slipped their moorings, sailed out of a Phoenician harbor, and shaped a course for Egypt to bring there a shipment of Lebanese cedar. It is the world's first articulate record of large-scale overseas commerce.

On the coast, not far north of where Beirut stands today, was the port of Byblos whose beginnings go back beyond recorded memory. It was here that, among other things, the timber of Lebanon in Snefru's day and for centuries thereafter was brought to be loaded for shipment, and copper from the rich deposits in Cyprus was ferried in for transshipment. So constant was the trade between this city and Egypt that from earliest times seagoing merchantmen were called "Byblos-ships" whether they actually plied between there and Egypt or not, just as in the nineteenth century "China clippers" and "East Indiamen" were used on runs other than those they were named for. Hundreds of years later, when Egypt's power had diminished and it could no longer maintain its overseas contacts, it felt the loss of this commerce keenly. "No one really sails north to Byblos," wailed one sage

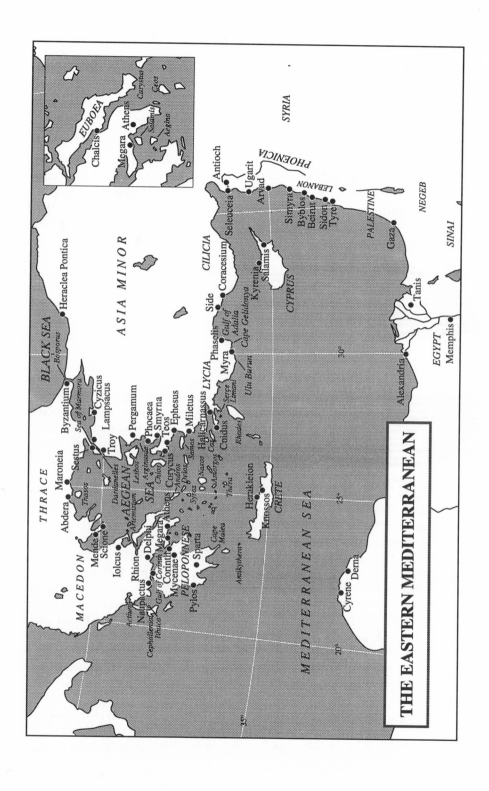

THE EASTERN MEDITERRANEAN

some four or five centuries after Snefru's time. "What shall we do for cedar for our mummies, those trees with whose produce our priests were buried and with whose oil nobles were embalmed?" It wasn't only the Egyptian shipwrights and carpenters who needed Lebanese timber; the undertakers depended on it too.

There was another important region which figured early in overseas trade. East of the Mediterranean, and separated from it by mountains, lay Mesopotamia, the land watered by the two mighty rivers, the Tigris and Euphrates. Here the ancient and highly developed civilizations of the Sumerians and Babylonians arose. Cut off as they were, their Mediterranean contacts had to be made through middlemen, probably the merchants of the coast, including, no doubt, those of Byblos. But, to the south, the twin rivers that formed their chief artery of communication emptied into the Persian Gulf, and beyond that lay the open expanse of the Indian Ocean. As early as the middle of the fourth millennium B.C., Babylonian merchants were either sailing these waters themselves or dealing directly with traders who were.

By the second half of the third millennium, the rulers of southern Mesopotamia, as we learn from written records found in the archaeological sites there, were importing for their statues the handsome black stone known as diorite from a place called Magan, either Oman on the Arabian side of the Persian Gulf, or Makran on the Iranian side, or perhaps both. Since Magan had a reputation for shipbuilding, most likely its people provided the freighters and did the carrying. From the same area came timber and, most important of all, copper. By the end of the second millennium B.C., trade in the Persian Gulf was thoroughly organized on a businesslike basis. On the island known today as Bahrein, a full-fledged port of exchange had been created. Merchants from Mesopotamia sailed there, carrying cargoes of textiles, wool, leather objects, and olive oil, and returned with their holds laden first and foremost with copper ingots but also with finished objects of copper, precious stones, ivory, and rare woods. Bahrein itself is bare; everything shipped out of it had first to be brought there. The copper poses no problem: written records reveal that it came from Magan, and there are copper deposits in both Oman and Makran, especially the latter. But the source of the ivory opens up interesting speculations.

In the ruins of the cities of Mesopotamia of the third millennium B.C., excavators have unearthed certain large conchs with a snow-white shell. These are examples of the Indian chank, which is found only in the coastal waters of India and Ceylon. They have discovered, too, beads of carnelian and of lapis lazuli; the first surely came from India and the second from Badakshan in Afghanistan by way of India.

The written records tell of a land named Meluhha, which supplied not only carnelian and lapis but also timber, gold, and ivory; Meluhha must be India, for all these materials can be found there. The implication is clear: even in this early period ships loaded with trade goods shuttled over the open waters of the ocean between the Persian Gulf and the northwest coast of India. The people on this coast who took part in the trade must have been the dwellers of the Indus Valley whose impressive ruins archaeologists have uncovered at Harappa and Mohenjo-Daro.

A great many details are known about the businessmen of Mesopotamia, for they wrote their correspondence and kept their accounts on clay tablets that are just about indestructible; excavations have yielded a multitude of them. All Mesopotamian import-export transactions were in the hands of individuals, not the state. The chief problem of the merchants, as their records show, was the same that faces their modern counterparts: where and how to get the capital to finance a voyage. Generally, a group of partners went into a venture together. They borrowed from a moneylender the cash to buy a cargo and guaranteed to repay the loan at a fixed rate of interest. Except for the usual hazards of credit, the moneylender was completely protected: if the vessel went down, the partners shared the loss among themselves. But if it arrived safely, they divided all the profits; the financier received only his original advance plus interest. Occasionally a less conservative moneylender took a flyer and had himself included as one of the partners, thereby sharing in the profits—or the losses. The clay tablets have even produced what is probably the earliest letter extant from a dissatisfied customer, one that dates sometime between 2000 and 1750 B.C. Ea-nasir, a merchant of Ur in southern Mesopotamia, had delivered a consignment of copper from Dilmun, as Bahrein was then called. The consignee was outraged at the quality of the shipment. "Who am I that you treat me in this manner and offend me?" he writes. "That this could happen between gentlemen as we both are! Who is there among the traders of Dilmun who has ever acted against me this way?"

For some reason this amazingly far-flung and highly developed trade died out shortly after 1750 B.C. and did not come to life again until almost a thousand years later. We must go back to Egypt to continue the record of what was happening on the sea lanes.

Egypt required imports for which it had to turn to countries other than Phoenicia. It needed myrrh for unguents and embalming mummies and frankincense as well as myrrh to burn on its altars. These products come from trees that grow in only two places in the world: in southern Arabia and in parts of Ethiopia and Somalia. Egypt derived

its supplies from a place that the pharaohs' scribes call Punt; this probably was the belt of land that runs from the upper Nile eastward across
northern Ethiopia to the Red Sea plus a strip that continued farther
eastward across the northern coast of Somalia. For centuries transport
was overland, taken care of by countless small traders who passed the
merchandise along from hand to hand with, presumably, an increase
in price at each exchange. The earliest pharaohs set themselves the job
of cutting out these middlemen. In so doing they created one of the
first great state-operated maritime enterprises.

The task was not easy. The only alternative to the overland route
was by water down the Red Sea. But Egypt's centers were all strung
along the banks of her life-giving river, separated from the Red Sea at
the closest point by an eight-day march across desert. On a barren
coast bare of shade and roasted by an ovenlike sun the pharaohs had
to set up shipyards, build a fleet, lay out harbors with all necessary
facilities, and, when this was accomplished, maintain and protect what
they had created. The easiest route from the Nile to the Red Sea was
along a gorge in the desert called the Wadi Hammamat. On the rocks
lining it at one point, Henu, minister of Pharaoh Mentuhotep III,
some two thousand years before the birth of Christ inscribed an account of his services to the state. In a few bald sentences he reveals
graphically the difficulties that faced the founders of such a trading
venture. "My lord sent me," he writes, "to dispatch a ship to Punt to
bring him back fresh myrrh. . . . I left [the Nile] with an army of 3000
men. Every day I issued to each a leathern bottle, two jars of water, 20
loaves of bread. . . . I dug twelve wells. . . . Then I reached the Red
Sea, made the ship and dispatched it." Henu was clearly a capable
man. There was nothing haphazard about his methods: notice how
each step was carefully plotted, especially the key one of how to supply
three thousand men with water during an eight-day trek. In his scrupulous attention to detail he even records the exact dimensions of the
wells he dug.

The Egypt-Punt trade was no sinecure, involving as it did carriage
by river, land, and sea, and the consequent transshipping of the loads
from riverboat to porter to ship and vice versa. Moreover, the sea voyage included sailing down the Red Sea and back. That body of water
was tricky to navigate, had few points where a ship in danger could
take shelter, and was the spawning ground of a virulent breed of pirate. (Pirates were a problem there right up to the middle of this century.) It is no surprise that it furnishes the scene for the earliest report
of shipwreck that has been preserved.

The story is told in the first person. The narrator is a sort of Egyptian Sinbad, for his tale is at the same time the earliest sailor's yarn that

we have; many centuries must pass before we meet a sober eyewitness's account of shipwreck. "I had set out for the mines of the king," the anonymous storyteller relates, "in a ship 180 feet long and 60 wide; we had a crew of 120, the pick of Egypt." The mines must be those in the Sinai Peninsula, so the departure was made from some Red Sea port. The ship's size is imposing; it was no little coaster but a full-fledged cargo vessel. "A storm broke while we were still at sea," he continues; "we flew before the wind. The ship went down; of all in it only I survived. I was cast upon an island and spent three days alone; I stayed in the shade. Then I set forth to find what I could put in my mouth. I found figs and vines, all kinds of fine leeks, fruit and cucumbers. There were fish and fowl; everything was there. I satisfied myself and there was still some left over. When I had made a fire-drill I kindled a fire and made a burnt-offering for the gods."

So far, nothing we couldn't also find in the pages of Robinson Crusoe. But things suddenly change. "Then I heard the sound of thunder and thought it was a wave; trees broke and the earth quaked. I uncovered my face and found that a serpent had drawn near. It was 45 feet long and its beard was two feet long. Its body was covered with gold and its eyebrows were real lapis lazuli."

The serpent's looks, it turns out, were deceiving; it was a most considerate and accommodating creature. It took the sailor up in its mouth tenderly, carried him to its lair, listened sympathetically to his story and then relieved his worries with the news that, after four comfortable months on the island, one of the pharaoh's ships would come along, pick him up, and carry him home. In gratitude the sailor burst out with a promise to bring it thank offerings of all sorts of incense. "Thereupon it laughed at me. And it said, 'I am the prince of Punt and myrrh—that is my very own!'" As if to confirm these words, when the rescue ship as prophesied did come along, the serpent sent the sailor off with a full cargo of incense of every conceivable type. Two months later he was safely home.

Near the famous valley across the river from Thebes where so many of the pharaohs dug their tombs, stands the huge temple of Deir-el-Bahari, a monument erected shortly after 1500 B.C. by Hatshepsut, the first great queen of history. On its walls she carved a record, with detailed illustrations, of an achievement she was particularly proud of, a large-scale trading voyage to Punt.

Many years before Hatshepsut's reign, Egypt had fallen upon difficulties. Civil war had split the country, and the fragments were ruled by upstart princelings or by invaders. None was in a position to maintain a project as sizable as a Red Sea fleet. The shipping of incense, as centuries before, was once again carried on overland through middle-

FIG. 1. Hatshepsut's fleet at Punt.

men. But around 1570 B.C. a new dynasty arose which reunited the
country, established a firm rule, and inaugurated an age that was to be
Egypt's most celebrated. The fifth member of the line was Hatshepsut.
Among her important acts was the restoration of direct maritime connections with Punt.

   On one of the walls of the queen's tomb-temple, exquisitely carved
in the low relief the Egyptians used so effectively, is a unique series of
vignettes (Fig. 1). We see a fleet entering the harbor at Punt: three
sleek, clean-lined vessels are still under way, their great sails bellying
with wind, while two others have doused their canvas and are ready to
tie up. Next is the disembarkation: an Egyptian royal messenger heads
a file of men and offers a heap of familiar objects of barter—necklaces,
hatchets, daggers—to the king of Punt who advances to meet him, followed by an enormously fat wife, two sons, and a daughter. Then en-
sues a scene of frenetic activity as a long line of Puntites brings the
products of the country to the tent of the royal messenger, while another file carries jars and trees up gangplanks onto the vessels. Then
comes the departure, the ships leaving the harbor under full sail, their
decks piled high with cargo. Each scene has a caption to describe it
down to the minutest details of action ("Hard to port!" calls the pilot
of one of the ships as they maneuver; "Watch your step!" is carved
over the stevedores in the loading scene), and from them an almost
complete list of the cargo can be compiled. It is imposing: various

woods including ebony, myrrh-resin, live myrrh trees (clearly shown in the reliefs with their roots bagged in a ball as carefully as any gardener would want), various other types of incense, ivory, gold, eye cosmetic, skins, 3,300 head of cattle, natives and their children. And some souvenirs: native spears, apes, monkeys, dogs, even "a southern panther alive, captured for her majesty." The inclusion of myrrh trees is suggestive. Were they merely to decorate the royal gardens or did Hatshepsut have the shrewd notion of cultivating them in Egypt to reduce her country's dependence on a foreign source of supply?

The vessels shown on Hatshepsut's reliefs represent the high-water mark of the Egyptian shipwright. Yet, though they are fine-looking craft, their design had serious weaknesses and for good reasons was not to play an important role in the history of naval architecture.

In ancient Egypt, stretched like a ribbon along the banks of a river that offered a clear course of over four hundred miles, it was natural that the designing and sailing of boats would begin early and develop rapidly. The Nile offered the best and easiest form of transport. It was even blessed with a prevailing wind that blew from the north: one could sail upstream and drift downstream—or row without strain, if in a hurry. The tombs of Egypt have yielded pictures and even models of a bewildering variety of river craft, from tiny rowboats through swift yachts and dispatch boats to enormous barges that were built to carry huge obelisks, weighing hundreds of tons, from the granite quarries far upstream. Life on the ancient Nile must have been every bit as varied and picturesque as on Mark Twain's Mississippi. And as designers of river craft the Egyptians were unsurpassed. This was their weakness: when they turned to seagoing ships they simply constructed oversize Nile boats.

The procedure for building a wooden ship that has been traditional in the Western world, the procedure we know best, is to start with a skeleton of keel and ribs and fasten to this a skin of planking. The Egyptians, building for use on a river where there were no storms, no violent winds, battering waves, or ripping currents, constructed their vessels, even the largest ones, without keel and with few, very light ribs. The planks were pinned to each other rather than to an inner skeleton. The only stiffening provided beyond a handful of ribs consisted of beams run from gunwale to gunwale on which the deck was laid. This was adequate for a river. A good deal more was needed for a ship that was to sail the open Mediterranean.

About 2450 B.C. Pharaoh Sahure built a fleet of transports to ferry his troops to the Levant coast. He ordered his artists to carve a picture of the scene on the walls of his pyramid and thereby left us the earliest clear representation extant of seagoing ships (Pl. 3). So carefully did the artists execute their assignment that almost every detail of construction appears; we can see precisely what the Egyptian naval architect did to adapt for use on a sea a boat basically built for a river. Around one end of the vessel he looped an enormous hawser, carried it along the centerline above the deck, and looped it about the other end. By placing a stout pole through the strands of the hawser where it passed over the deck, and twisting, one could tighten the whole harness like a tourniquet. This was his substitute for internal stiffening; twisted until it had the proper tension, the hawser kept the ends from sagging when the vessel rode heavy waves. The architect further added an elaborate netting that ran horizontally about the upper part of the hull. Is this, too, an aid for holding the ship together, a girdle as it were, or is it mere chafing gear to protect the sides from rubbing? The architect could not use the ordinary single mast, for there was no keel in which to sink its end securely (the heel of a mast exerts tremendous leverage against its socket); so he designed a two-legged affair that distributed the pressure, and he stayed it carefully with lines fore and aft. On it a tall, slender squaresail was mounted, in a fashion peculiar to Egypt: two spars spread it, a yard along the head and a boom along the foot. But the ship was not solely a sailing vessel; when there was no wind or when it was foul, sail was taken in, the mast was lowered, and rowers sent it on its way. The Egyptian artists, in their scrupulous attention to detail, have added a homely touch that enables us to figure out what kind of stroke the rowers used. Oarsmen are always pictured with a special type of loincloth, one made of a netted material with a square patch of solid leather on the seat. This obviously was chafing gear: the rower must have handled his oar somewhat the way they did in the Middle Ages and later, rising to his feet to begin the stroke and dropping back on the seat with the pull; without a sturdy patch on his rear, he would have rubbed through his loincloth in short order.

A thousand years later naval architects were designing the ships shown on Hatshepsut's reliefs (Fig. 1). With lines that have the graceful curves of a racing yacht, they are cleaner and faster than Sahure's. The sail is much larger and no longer tall, but enormously broad instead; it is still spread by two spars, a yard along the head and boom along the foot. It is so wide that yard and boom are made each of two tapering spars with their ends fished together; this not only gave greater strength but was easier to construct, since a pair of saplings fastened together at their thick ends did the trick. The broad sail permitted the use of a much shorter mast, one that consequently exerted much less leverage, and the architect has accordingly given up the old two-legged arrangement for a single pole. But except for these—improvements rather than radical changes in design—almost everything else is as before. The keelless vessel with its handful of light ribs must still be braced by a heavy hawser looped about its ends and twisted to the proper tension. These boats were beautiful; unquestionably they were fast; but they sadly lacked sturdiness. We shall not see them outside Egypt.

The peak of Egyptian expansion was reached in the reign of Hatshepsut's successor, Thutmose III, perhaps the greatest of the pharaohs. It was he who extended Egypt's arm over Palestine and Syria and Phoenicia and even beyond to countries inland, and carried out his conquest and organization of the areas so thoroughly that his successors were able to coast for centuries on what he had accomplished. For the next three hundred years, until about 1200 B.C., Egypt's trade flourished as never before. Vessels from the Levant dumped on its quays everything from ponderous timber to the finest and most delicate objects of Asiatic craftsmanship. The pharaohs and their courts rode in chariots that were made in Syria, raised cattle that came from Asia Minor, ate delicacies that were grown on the island of Cyprus, and were served by swarms of Asiatic and Semitic slaves. Their wives dressed in gorgeous stuffs from Syria and scented themselves with the perfumes of South Arabia. Punt provided its stores of incense, ivory, and rare woods. Copper was brought from Cyprus and silver from Asia Minor. In return, Egypt sent out gold that was mined in Nubia, writing paper made from the fibers of the papyrus reed or cordage twisted from them, linen textiles, and the fine products of its workshops—beads, faience, scarabs, figurines. A king of Cyprus, who had supplied the pharaoh with copper and timber, writes to ask for horses, chariots, a bed of rare wood all goldplated, women's dresses, jars of oil of fine quality. In another letter he requests an Egyptian specialty that may not have been as unusual as it sounds—a sorcerer; this one had to be an expert with eagles. The tempo of trade was such that merchants from overseas established residences in Egypt. In the great city of Memphis a foreign quarter sprang up complete, as such places always are, with temples to the strangers' gods.

A picture can at times tell more than a bookful of words, and by great good fortune there is one to illustrate the commerce of this period. The business executive of today orders a photograph of his plant in action and hangs it in his office; the ancient Egyptian functionary commissioned a picture of himself in official action and had it painted on the wall of a chamber in his tomb. Kenamun was an official under Pharaoh Amenhotep III in charge of, among other things, commerce

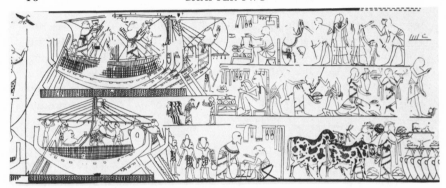

FIG. 2. Arrival of a fleet of Levantine vessels in an Egyptian port.

with the Levant. So he had painted in his tomb a picture, complete to the last homely detail, of a typical moment in an Egyptian harbor fourteen centuries before the birth of Christ (Fig. 2).

A fleet of ships has just arrived. You can tell where they come from by the dress and looks of the skippers and the mates, who wear gaily embroidered ankle-length robes and have full beards and prominent hooked profiles. They are unquestionably Semites; the vessels consequently must be from Syria or Phoenicia, perhaps even from Byblos itself. Are the ships, too, foreign or are they Egyptian? With their gracefully curved bow and stern and prominent overhangs fore and aft, they seem very like Hatshepsut's vessels. Yet they lack the telltale looped hawser. Perhaps it is the artist's fault: as an Egyptian he may have grafted a native look on to vessels that were really Levantine. He's a bit lubberly at best; no vessels could ride so high out of the water as his do. A number of them are already made fast, their sails furled, the boarding ladders lowered from the prows to the shore. Harbors were rough-and-ready affairs in those days; since there were no wharves, ships were simply run up on the beach. Other vessels are shown making ready to land. Sailors have sprung aloft to take in canvas, and on one the skipper stands in the bow carefully sounding with a long pole as the ship inches in toward the beach. On shore everything is bustling the way one expects when a fleet comes in. An Egyptian customs official, standing before an officer and file of men from one of the ships, is entering information about them on a tablet. One Egyptian tradesman is busy trying to sell his wares; he points with emphasis to his scale to assure prospective customers that it is accurate. Another is actually transacting a piece of business with one of the ships' officers. The latter is trying to sell a large jar, probably of wine or oil, for no good grade of either was ever produced in Egypt; behind him a file of hands from the vessel unloads more jars. A tradeswoman appears to be feeling the heat; instead of hawking her wares, she sits under slippers and other articles of clothing she has for sale and lazily fans the flies away. In the right-hand side of the uppermost panel a ship's officer seems to be asking a favor from an Egyptian official concerning two women and a child who precede him. Note the diaphanous triple-tiered dress that the women wear; we shall have occasion to refer to it shortly. In the panels below we see the procession before Kenamun himself: men from the ships stolidly file before him with wares of all sorts, while their officers grovel before the great man.

Active as Egypt's trade was, it had strict limits. Her lightly built ships raced south to Punt and north to the Levant but very likely not much farther. Many of the products the Egyptians imported and exported were carried in foreign bottoms, like those in Kenamun's picture. The distinction of being the first great traders of the Mediterranean goes to another people, a race of born sea sailors rather than rivermen.

Some decades before Kenamun sat in his office supervising shipments from the Levant, a noble named Rekhmire, vizier of Egypt and second in importance only to the pharaoh, ordered an opulent tomb to be prepared for himself. On its walls he commanded the artists to paint pictures showing all the world paying tribute to his master, the mighty Thutmose III. As in Kenamun's picture, there appear Semites from Phoenicia and Syria. There are men from the south, blacks from the Sudan, and people from Punt. Alongside these by now familiar faces suddenly appear others who are completely new. They wear unusually decorated kilts and queer sandals, and do their hair in a strange fashion. The bowls and other vessels they carry have unfamiliar shapes. "The People of the Isles in the midst of the Sea," the caption calls them. It has been one of archaeology's prime achievements to identify these figures.

"Minos is the first to whom tradition ascribes the possession of a navy. He made himself master of a great part of what is now termed the Hellenic Sea; he conquered the isles of the Aegean and was the first colonizer of most of them." So wrote Thucydides, one of the most sober and scientific historians who ever existed, in the fifth century B.C., some thousand years after the times of Thutmose and Rekhmire. As late as the nineteenth century, the statement seemed hard to believe: Minos, as far as anyone knew, was a figment of mythology, not a character in history. All that was reported of him seemed pure fancy: that he ruled the island of Crete, that he had built there a trackless maze called the "labyrinth" and kept in it the Minotaur, "Minos' bull," a mythical creature with the body of a man and the head of a bull; that he had the grisly habit of feeding it live mortals and for this purpose yearly levied seven young men and seven young women from Athens; and that Theseus, the legendary hero of the city, volunteered to be sent out, and with the help of Minos' own daughter, who had fallen in love with him at first sight, slew the monster and escaped safely.

In 1900 a British archaeologist named Arthur Evans started digging at Knossos, several miles in from Herakleion on the north shore of Crete. His results were spectacular. Within a few months he had begun to uncover the remains of a mighty civilization whose existence had hardly been suspected. He laid bare the foundations of an enormous palace, one that had so complex an arrangement of rooms and corridors that it resembled a veritable labyrinth. Everywhere he found the bull's head used as a sacred symbol. He found, too, a symbol in the form of a double-ax, and he remembered that Plutarch had once written that there was a non-Greek word *labrys* which meant "ax." In the ruins were a multitude of specimens of pottery decorated gaily in a unique style. On the walls were murals done in a charming naturalistic manner. He even uncovered clay tablets with two distinct forms of writing. Here, then, was a people with a fully developed civilization, their own art, architecture, and literature. What they called themselves Evans had no idea, for their writing was indecipherable. But the clues that connected them with the heretofore mythical Minos and his labyrinth and Minotaur were manifest. So he dubbed them the "Minoans" and so they have been called ever since.

As excavation proceeded at Knossos and other sites on Crete and more began to be known of these people, two features in particular came to the fore: first, that their pottery, so easily identified by its unique decoration, was to be found in many lands lying overseas, while foreign objects in abundance were scattered through the ruins of their cities; second, that their cities were completely unwalled. The conclusion was inescapable. Thucydides knew what he was talking about: the people of Crete, in an age remote even when he was writing, had been daring and active traders and the possessors of a great navy; Minoan towns needed no stone walls, for wooden ones, their ships, protected the island.

As far back as the days of Snefru and Sahure there was trade contact between Minoans and Egyptians. In the ruins on Crete, archaeologists discovered stone bowls that seem like types made in Egypt as early as 2700 B.C. Some seven hundred years later, when Pharaoh Amenemhet II was selecting treasures to be placed in his tomb, he included a group of silver bowls of a kind made in Crete. Did Minoan ships bring these objects directly to Egypt or did they carry them to the nearer coasts of Phoenicia or Syria, and did they then make their way to Egypt as part of the trade it carried on at all times with the Levant? There is no certain answer. Some of them may have, but not necessarily all. The sailors of Crete traveled to far more distant places; the direct voyage to Egypt could have held no terrors for them.

Minoan traders have left a trail of their pottery in Palestine and Syria and Asia Minor in the east. They reached north as far as Macedonia. Southward they knew other parts of Africa besides Egypt. One of the signs found among their carvings is a representation of a plant, highly prized in ancient days as a medicine and spice, that grew only in one particular spot on the coast of Libya, while a tiny seal found in their ruins has a picture that includes an ostrich feather. In the west they pushed as far as Sardinia and Sicily. Legend has it that Minos himself died on Sicily, and one of the Sicilian towns of later historic times was named Minoa.

The picture of what the objects of Minoan trade were is lopsided because the evidence is limited almost entirely to the sorts of things the archaeologist can dig up. Yet enough has been found to show that there was great demand in the outside world for the products of Minoan workshops. Among the highly civilized nobles of Egypt and Phoenicia and the semibarbaric chieftains of Greece alike, there were those who preferred to eat off dishes decorated in the Minoan fashion, carry Minoan-style weapons in battle, and wear Minoan jewelry and garments of Minoan textiles in court. Minoan women wore a tight bodice and bell-shaped skirt made up in a number of tiers; in an Egyptian tomb painting, a Semitic princess appears wearing precisely such a skirt, and it reappears on Semitic women in the harbor scene of Kenamun's tomb (Fig. 2). In return, the Minoans imported a good many things: gold, beads, faience, figurines, and probably papyrus paper from Egypt; copper from Cyprus; ivory from Syria. Amber, following prehistoric routes across Europe from the Baltic, made its way to their workshops.

The heyday of the Minoans' trade was from about 1800 to 1500 B.C., when they had connections with Greece, Rhodes, Cyprus, Asia Minor, and the Levant. It was in this period that their commercial and political leaders built the magnificent dwelling places, furnished in opulent and beautiful style, which the archaeologists' spades have uncovered.

Thanks to recent discoveries, we now know what the ships of the Minoan navy, that instrument vital to the protection of the island and its trade, looked like. Some seventy-five miles north of Crete is Thera, a small island distinguished by a large and vigorous volcano. Here a prosperous and sizable town stood until, around 1600 B.C., the volcano exploded in a mighty eruption that caused the whole center of the island to disappear under the sea, blew ash as far as Crete, and buried the town under a deep blanket of ash. In the early 1970s it was excavated, and in a room in a large, impressive house there was found a painted frieze, part of which depicts a procession of galleys and other craft (Pl. 4). The galleys are graceful, slender vessels, with handsomely decorated hulls and prows that jut forward in a gentle, elegant curve. The rig consists of a broad squaresail with yard along the head and boom along the foot; it looks much like the sails in the paintings in Kenamun's tomb (Fig. 2). The sails are furled since the ships are being driven by manpower, a line of twenty-odd paddlers. The use of paddlers on ships of this size at this time is indeed strange, particularly since other craft in the frieze are shown being rowed. Vessels propelled by multiple paddlers appear in Egyptian pictures, but these all date from almost a thousand years earlier. Very likely the Thera frieze portrays an age-old religious event featuring a parade of ships that, to suit the occasion, were propelled in age-old fashion. In another portion of the frieze (Pl. 5), unfortunately very fragmentary, we see these galleys in action, and here, as we would expect, they are being rowed. They have low parapets at bow and stern; on one a marine with a long lance stands stolidly behind the bow parapet. The vessels forge ahead through waters spangled with drowning men and abandoned weapons.

The nation that maintained the navy made up of these ships was the first great sea power of the Mediterranean, the first to explore in a fruitful way much of its expanse and to lay out trade lines that were destined to last for millennia. They were even the first—at least so far as we know—to depict the sea monsters that their sailors, like seamen everywhere, must have yarned about (Pl. 6). Must they not, therefore, be the "People of the Isles" on the wall of Rekhmire's tomb? The figures there wear their hair in the same manner as the men that appear in Cretan murals, and they carry vases shaped and decorated like those found in Minoan sites. Can we not conclude without further ado that these "People of the Isles" are from Crete? The problem is not quite that easily solved.

No more than a day's sail from Minos' palace in Crete lies the southern portion of the peninsula of Greece. Early in their history Minoan traders had made their way here. The effect of their arrival was startling. The local inhabitants gobbled up Minoan civilization as avidly as Japan in the nineteenth century did that of the occident. Their whole lives were transformed. They decorated the walls of their houses, their pots, and their dishware in the Minoan manner. They fashioned the same sort of seals and jewelry, wore the same sort of armor, dressed in the Minoan style. The women did their hair *à la minoenne*

and looked to Crete for their fashions the way we do to Paris and
Rome. Much of what was native disappeared under an overlay of culture from Crete. The phenomenon was so striking that some scholars,
viewing it, theorized that Crete had physically conquered the mainland of Greece and ruled it as a vassal.

But they had the facts somewhat twisted. A brilliant stroke of schol-
arship identified beyond doubt the people inhabiting Greece at this
period and straightened out the historical incidents of this remote age.
On the island of Crete, tablets inscribed in two types of writing had
been found. One of the two types reappeared on the mainland. In
1953 a British architect named Michael Ventris, who had as a hobby
played about with these inscrutable documents using pure crypto-
graphic methods, capped twenty years of work by breaking the script.
They were written, he determined, in an early form of Greek. In a
flash the picture became clear: the Minoans had carried their civilization to the mainland Greeks and, not long after 1500 B.C., the latter
had repaid them with conquest. That was why in the palace ruins on
Crete, along with the tablets—still undeciphered—written in the native Minoan language, excavators found writings of the new masters in
Greek.

With this act these early Greeks established themselves as the heirs
of the Minoans' maritime empire, and for some three centuries they
carried it on, from roughly 1500 to 1200 B.C. Their cities in the homeland grew rich, especially Mycenae where, according to Homer, King
Agamemnon once ruled; this was the first of their centers to be excavated, and as a result scholars refer to the Greeks of this time as Mycenaeans and the period as the Mycenaean Age. The rulers of Mycenae
and the other leading cities during this age included some who were so
wealthy and powerful and such redoubtable warriors that after they
passed away they—and their queens—lived on in men's memories
and, centuries later, were immortalized in Homer's great epics. "The
People of the Isles" of Rekhmire's tomb and of other Egyptian paintings may have been Minoans from Crete, but it is just as likely—the
murals all date in the fifteenth century B.C.—that they were Mycenaeans. The remains of Mycenaean jars and flasks have been found in
abundance in the ruins of the palace at Tell el-Amarna, a city built
from scratch about 1370 B.C. by Pharaoh Akhenaten as his capital; if
Mycenaean traders did not themselves get this far, then middlemen
who dealt with them certainly did.

A trail of pottery fragments dug up by archaeologists mark the
routes followed by Mycenaean traders. Their ships worked eastward
to the west coast of Asia Minor or southward to Crete, from where
they cut east by way of Rhodes and Cyprus to the cities along the Le-

vant. Here many unloaded and, letting Levantines transship whatever
was consigned to Egypt, picked up return cargoes that included whatever the transshippers had brought back from there. All papyrus
paper, for example, was manufactured in Egypt, but so much of it
came to Greece by way of the Levant that the standard Greek word for
the product was *byblos*, reflecting the name of the harbor at which most
traders from Greece must have taken on their cargoes of it. When
traveling westward, the Mycenaeans probably sailed to Crete to pick
up consignments of products from there, then up the western shore of
Greece and across the Adriatic to Sicily and southern Italy. The most
crowded ports of all, though, must have been those along the Levantine coast. Here ships from all quarters of the eastern Mediterranean put in: the Levantine merchant marine shared the quays with
vessels from Egypt, Cyprus, Crete, and Greece. The harborside of
Sidon or Byblos must have presented a scene every bit as polyglot and
bizarre as any of the modern international entrepôts. Along the docks,
vessels loaded and unloaded products that originated in various countries and ran the gamut from everyday commodities to precious luxuries. The proof is furnished not only by random statements in certain
contemporary documents or random finds in archaeological excavations but by the excavation of wrecks of ships of the time, one of which
may well have been carrying a cargo belonging to a king. The discovery and scrupulously careful investigation of this find in particular has
shed new light on the maritime history of the age, not only enriching
enormously our knowledge of its commerce but adding a vital detail to
our knowledge of the development of naval technology. Before going
into the matter, however, we must tell what made such a discovery and
such an investigation possible.

Chapter 3

EXCAVATING UNDER WATER

SHORTLY BEFORE EASTER in the year 1900, a group of Greek sponge divers, returning from their season off Tunisia, ran into a storm and took refuge in a sheltered cove on Antikythera, a little island off the southern coast of Greece. Just to pass the time, some of the crew slipped over the side. When, a few minutes later, one reappeared lugging the bronze arm of a Greek statue, marine archaeology was born.

Its babyhood was spectacular. The divers had had the astounding good fortune to stumble upon the wreck of a vessel that had been carrying works of art to Italy in the early decades of the first century B.C. when it went down. The Greek government undertook to salvage the cargo. The only personnel available were sponge fishermen who, though they found excavating statues on the seafloor a far cry from cutting away sponges, through herculean efforts managed to carry it off successfully. What they rescued was priceless: some fine bronzes, two of which are among the prize pieces in Athens' National Museum, magnificent glass bowls, even a bronze astronomical instrument, an orrery, with delicate and sophisticated gearing.

A few years later came another rare piece of luck, again involving sponge divers. A group that had been working off Mahdia on the coast of Tunisia circulated the story that they had seen a row of cannon on the seafloor. It came to the local director of antiquities, Alfred Merlin, and piqued his interest. He sent some divers down and quickly found out that the so-called cannon were a row of columns, part of the cargo of a ship that had sunk probably in the early part of the first century B.C. Merlin decided to carry out a full-fledged underwater excavation. He rounded up a squad of sponge fishermen, got the French navy to lend a hand by supplying a salvage vessel, and in 1907 began the first of a series of grueling campaigns. It was a fight against time and wind and weather—the navy kept recalling its ship, rough seas often prevented any diving, storms occasionally destroyed his markers, and the wreck had to be painfully discovered all over again—and, despite seven years of work, the job was never fully completed. But what he found well paid for his efforts. The vessel, in addition to the columns and other architectural elements, turned out to have been carrying works of art, and his divers rescued enough sculptures to fill half a dozen rooms of the Bardo Museum in Tunis.

The two discoveries naturally raised the highest hopes for the future. World War I interrupted things for a while, but prospects again brightened when fishermen, working in the strait between the Greek mainland and the northern end of the island of Euboea, brought up a superb bronze statue of Poseidon, now one of the treasures of the Athens museum. The wreck itself, however, was never discovered.

It was not until decades later that anything like the thorough investigation Merlin had carried out at Mahdia was again attempted. The fishermen of Albenga, a town on the Italian Riviera, had known since 1925 of the presence of a wreck with a cargo of amphoras—as the big clay jars used by the ancients for shipping are called—off their shores. In 1950 a well-known Italian salvage expert was persuaded to try his hand at it. He put one of his superbly equipped salvage ships at the disposal of archaeology and, by lowering huge mechanical jaws over the wreck, in twelve days his men managed to grub up seven hundred jars and some scraps of the hull and its fittings. These few days were all the vessel could be spared for, and the rest of the cargo, very likely over ten thousand more jars, had to be left on the bottom.

Excavation such as took place at Albenga and Mahdia had little future. The one had depended on the philanthropy of a salvage company, the other on sponge fishermen and a helping hand from the French navy. Even more important, at no time was the slightest effort made to follow proper archaeological procedures, to attempt to gain some overall view of what lay on the sea floor, identify even approximately the location of whatever objects were visible, record even approximately the location of whatever objects were removed. Marine archaeology had to find a totally new approach if it was to get anywhere.

The tool that led to such an approach was supplied by a French naval officer, Commandant Jacques-Ives Cousteau. An apparatus that did away with the need for the traditional heavy diving equipment, which involved pumps and crews, expensive diving suits and helmets, had been known in one form or another since as early as the 1860s. In 1943 the Commandant perfected a simplified version, now known as the Cousteau-Gagnon apparatus, which transformed diving from a strictly professional activity into one open to amateurs. Cousteau's creation consisted of one to three cylindrical tanks of compressed air connected with a mouthpiece and mounted in a harness that the diver strapped on the back. A big goggle fitting over the eyes and nose, and a pair of rubber fins that slipped over the feet, items for sale in any sporting-goods shop, completed the outfit. No longer were divers tied by an airhose, like an umbilical cord, to a pump on a ship's deck and limited in their range of activity; they could walk into the surf or dive from a rocky coast and spend half an hour or more under water, depending upon the number of tanks they carried and the depth they dove to. Today the apparatus has been so improved and refined, is so easy and safe to use, that SCUBA diving—that is, diving with the new Self-Contained Underwater Breathing Apparatus—has become almost as popular a sport as skiing.

It was the French who first went in for it in a big way. Hundreds of devoted afficionados would spend hours prowling about the seafloor off the southern coast, particularly the Riviera. Very quickly startling reports began to come in of the discovery of not one or two, but numbers of ancient wrecks. Soon they, as well as others infected by their enthusiasm, moved farther afield; and wrecks began to turn up along the Italian Riviera, in the straits between Sardinia and Corsica, off Greece and the Aegean Islands. However, unlike the first discoveries, none of these, it turned out, were carrying works of art. Like the one off Albenga, they had been loaded for the most part with amphoras.

The first extended investigation of a wreck using the new apparatus began in February 1952. A few miles outside the harbor of Marseilles lies a cluster of tiny islands which are little more than barren outcroppings of rock. Off one of these, the Grand Congloué, a diver had spotted in 1949 a batch of amphoras on the seafloor. The word subsequently reached Cousteau, and the idea came to him of excavating the site. It lay right alongside one slope of the Grand Congloué, so diving installations could be set up on the island itself. With Cousteau providing the technical know-how and Fernand Benoit, director of antiquities for the region, looking out for the archaeological end, the work got under way.

Progress was painfully slow. The divers were limited to twenty minutes on the bottom, including the time it took for them to get up and down; only two dives a day were permitted, and there were usually not more than two or three men on hand at any time. Often the weather stopped all work. Not only muck and marine growth covered the wreck but huge boulders had crashed down into it from the slope above, and the divers had to remove all this before they could get at the vessel itself. Moreover, since they were beginners, they had to invent the techniques of excavating under water as they went along. The ship—or, rather, ships; later investigation revealed there were two—proved to be freighters filled, like the Albenga wreck, with amphoras.

The excavation of the remains off the Grand Congloué exemplified marine archaeology in its infancy, when the archaeologist-divers worked—at least at first—with little more than their hands. Today they command a battery of sophisticated tools—powerful vacuum cleaners to suck away the sand that overlies a wreck, various lifts to bring objects to the surface, powerful lights to illumine the working area, even miniature submarines to extend their range of research and the length of time they can stay below. In its infancy marine archaeology was all too often little better than treasure hunting. Today its practitioners are as careful and exact in their methods as their counterparts on land. This was a development pioneered by American underwater excavators, notably George Bass, who was a trained archaeologist first and a diver second. Bass and his colleagues and students devised the procedures that are now standard in properly conducted digs: they start by erecting a grid over the whole of a site to provide reference points for the locating of every part of the wreck and every item in it (Pl. 7); they map and photograph the site before excavation and constantly during it; they pinpoint the location of every part or object and tag it; they photograph objects both before and after they are removed. As a result, they are able to determine the location of the various elements in a cargo, whether forward or amidships or aft. They can determine too whether an object came from the cabin area, and hence was not part of the cargo but belonged to the ship's equipment or to a passenger or crewman. They can often deduce from the disposition of the cargo and the remains of the hull how the ship struck when it went down.

By now hundreds of ancient wrecks have been located on the seafloor and examined to a greater or lesser extent. The majority are Greek or Roman ships dating from later times; we will deal with them in due course. But in 1960 a team headed by Bass began the excavation of a wreck that turned out to be far older than any found hitherto, dating to about 1200 B.C. It was a small freighter, perhaps thirty feet long, that was carrying a cargo of copper and bronze when it came to grief off Cape Gelidonya on the southwest coast of Asia Minor. A number of objects found in it make it almost certain that the ship either touched at or operated from the ports of the Levant; indeed, the owner of the cargo may very well have come from there.

Then in 1982 off Ulu Burun, just a bit west of Gelidonya, Bass hit the archaeological jackpot, the wreck of a ship even earlier in date, about 1350 B.C., and one that was a veritable treasure trove. The ship off Gelidonya was a tramp freighter shuttling along the coast with a cargo of metals. The Ulu Burun ship, to judge from the nature of the cargo, very likely was carrying a royal consignment. The major component was a batch of sixty-pound ingots of copper, some two hundred of them, carefully stowed in rows deep in the hull (Pl. 8). There were also dozens of ingots of tin; the smiths who would ultimately receive the shipment would mix the two to manufacture bronze. The second largest component was terebinth resin, perhaps a ton of it, packed in amphoras; such resin was used in making perfume. Then there was a collection of scrap metal intended for re-use—not mere copper or tin but fragments of gold and silver jewelry. There was a beautiful cup, in mint condition, made of solid gold. There were pieces of raw ivory, some hippopotamus teeth, ingots of raw glass, logs of African ebony, a consignment of Cypriot ceramics, eighteen pieces in all, carefully packed in a huge clay jar. The cargo reveals graphically how international was the trade of this period: the copper and ceramics came from Cyprus, the resin and glass from the Near East, the ebony and hippopotamus teeth from Egypt. Individual objects that were found underline the same point: Near Eastern cylinder seals, Egyptian scarabs, a Mycenaean seal, and pieces of Mycenaean pottery.

The ship had loaded on the resin at some port on the Levantine coast. It may have also taken on here the Egyptian goods—or it may have made a stop at Egypt itself for these. It loaded the copper and ceramics at some port on Cyprus, and most likely was on its way farther westward from there, to the west coast of Asia Minor or the Aegean islands or even Crete, when it went down. At least one Mycenaean was aboard, the owner of the seal, but this does not mean that the ship was Mycenaean; he may have been a passenger, not the owner. The vessel could just as well have been the property of a businessman or a consortium of businessmen from some port along the Levant.

A vivid picture of the trade of these times is not the only contribution of this extraordinary wreck. It makes yet another, equally notable, to the history of naval technology. For, burrowing through the layers of cargo, the excavators came upon the planking of the bottom of the hull; the overlying cargo had saved it from destruction. And this revealed a fact of paramount importance: the ship had been built in the distinctive fashion that, as we know from wrecks of a much later date, was the hallmark of the ancient shipwright. We had for years theorized that the technique was very old; the Ulu Burun wreck furnishes proof positive.

There are, basically, two ways to construct a wooden boat. The one we are familiar with, because it has been standard practice in the Western world for centuries, is to set up a skeleton of keel and ribs—or frames, to give them their technical name—and then fasten to this a skin of planks. The other method, favored in Africa, Asia, and certain parts of northern Europe, is just the reverse: first a shell is erected by pinning each plank to its neighbors, and then a certain amount of framing is inserted to stiffen the shell. In northern Europe planks are

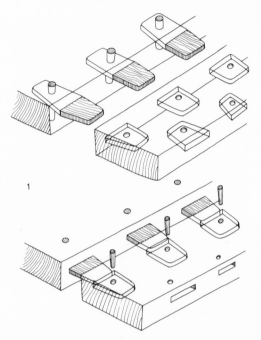

FIG. 3. Joining strakes by means of mortises and tenons.

set to overlap each other and pinned together by driving rivets through where the thickness is double. Elsewhere planks are set edge to edge and are held together by pegs or staples or nails or are even sewn together with twine made from coconut husks or split bamboo or whatever fiber happens to be available.

The ancient shipwright, it turns out, used the second method—but with a refined technique unmatched in the subsequent history of ship-building. Indeed, it was more cabinet work than carpentry. For he locked the planks of his shell together not with pegs or staples or the like, but with mortise-and-tenon joints placed as close to each other as in a piece of furniture, often even closer (Pl. 9, Fig. 3). In addition, he transfixed each joint with dowels to ensure that it would never come apart. Then, into this tightly knit structure, he inserted framing wellnigh as complete as in hulls made with a pre-erected skeleton. And he used this demanding and time-consuming procedure for craft of all sizes, from seagoing freighters to mere skiffs.

Until Bass's discovery, we had no sure clue to the age of this method of building a ship, to how far back it went. A passage in the *Odyssey* (p. 41) indicates that it was in use when Homer was writing, and his *floruit* is usually placed in the eighth century B.C. The Ulu Burun wreck reveals that it goes back certainly to the fourteenth century B.C. and very likely much before that.

What did the Ulu Burun ship look like? Our only clue to the appearance of seagoing merchantmen of this age are the Levantine vessels pictured on the walls of Kenamun's tomb—whose cargo, as it happens, includes the very same kind of amphora found in the wreck. These were deep-bellied freighters with curved ends terminating in short straight stems and sternposts (Fig. 2). Flush decks not only covered over their ample holds but, girt with high railings, permitted them to add a liberal deck load. The ships were driven by broad squaresails, which in shape and rig greatly resemble the Egyptian type and may have been modeled on it. As on Hatshepsut's vessels, the sail is bent to two spars, a boom along the foot and yard along the head, and there is a web of lines running from the upper part of the mast to the boom; these supported it so firmly that deck hands were able to walk along it. From written records of the age we know that Levantine merchantmen could run to great size, to no less than 450 tons in carrying capacity. From underwater finds we know that they could carry anchors weighing up to half a ton.

We have far less to go on for the merchantmen used by the Minoans, merely tiny pictures engraved on seals (Pl. 10). They show hulls that seem to be rounded and roomy, and the number of lines that the artists drew running from gunwales to mast would indicate that they used sails large enough to require considerable staying. As on Egyptian and Levantine vessels, there is a spar along the foot as well as the head. For the freighters of the Mycenaeans we have no evidence whatsoever. Quite possibly they borrowed the types they used, as so much else, from the Minoans.

The lords of Mycenae, like their Minoan predecessors, were wealthy and powerful men. They were able to build for themselves grand palaces to live in and sumptuous tombs to be laid away in. In these, excavators have found evidence that reveals how fabulously rich were the trappings of their daily life. They fought in beautifully wrought armor, drove in handsome chariots, and dressed themselves and their wives in style. They ate off magnificent dinnerware and drank from superbly decorated golden goblets. The age was a great one, great enough to linger in men's memories long after it had come to an end, for it was of the last part of it that Homer sang. But Homer is a poet of warriors, not traders, and his heroes, the soldiers of the sea, deserve their own chapter.

Chapter 4

WAR ON THE SEA

FROM THOSE EARLIEST DAYS when Egyptian merchantmen first sailed down the Red Sea and traders from Crete and Byblos made their maiden voyages in the eastern Mediterranean, the freighter had to share the seas with the man-of-war.

When the warship made its debut in history, it was not the stripped-down platform for mounting attacks against an enemy ship that it is today. It was far more prosaic. The first vessels used in warfare were merely an adjunct of the army, transports to ferry troops. There was no distinction between ships of the naval arm and freighters at the outset: the commander who conceived the idea of water-borne transportation almost certainly carried it out by expropriating available merchantmen.

The idea was thought of at least as early as ca. 2450 B.C. Egyptian records reveal that at that time Pharaoh Sahure used a fleet of transports to ferry an army to the Levantine coast (Pl. 3 and cf. Chapter 2). Some two centuries later, Uni, Pharaoh Pepi's able commander, rushed troops by boat to quell a rebellion, probably along the Palestinian coast. But the master of the technique of transporting soldiers overseas was Hatshepsut's successor, Thutmose III (Chapter 2), Egypt's outstanding figure in so many of the arts of war. The great general fought eighteen campaigns in Syria and, from at least the sixth on, moved his troops there by water. His first step was to secure undisputed control of the harbors along the Phoenician coast. He then placed them in charge of vassal local princelings who had strict orders to keep these all-important facilities in top-notch order and fully provisioned. Each year he made a personal tour of inspection to make sure his instructions were carried out. The details of this enormous project are all lost. From a scanty allusive line such as "Every port town of His Majesty was supplied with every good thing . . . with ships of cedar loaded with columns and beams as well as large timbers," we must imagine the ring of hammers and axes, the grunting of oxen, the shouts of carpenter and rigger, and the other varied sounds of a shipyard as quays, warehouses, repair shops, and the hundred and one other requirements of a naval base were set up. Thutmose carried it all out so rapidly and successfully that his military victories may have come about more from the quickness and ease with which he got his soldiers to the theater of combat than to their prowess.

But the troop transport was not the only type of man-of-war to sail the seas in earliest times. There were also the ships of the sea rover, slim clean-lined vessels, always driven by oars as well as sail, and built first and foremost for speed and maneuverability. Actually they were useful for missions of peace as well as war: they not only could attack an unarmed merchantman or partake in a lightning raid on an undefended coastal town, but they could deliver urgent dispatches in the shortest time possible. The sea rover's ship may be just as old as its slower brethren, but it made its debut on the stage of recorded history relatively late, not until the beginning of the fourteenth century B.C.

From 1379 to 1362 B.C. Akhenaten ruled Egypt, a young man who devoted himself to revolutionizing the religious life of Egypt as intently as his great ancestor had to building up naval bases and extending military conquests. To break clean with the past, shortly after ascending the throne the youthful zealot abandoned the old government center at Thebes with its traditional associations and built himself a completely new capital on a vast plain farther down the Nile. When, after his death, Egypt reverted to its old ways, his once fine city fell into ruins and was forgotten. And so it happened that in 1887, some three thousand years later, a peasant woman, digging in the area for dust to fertilize her garden, came upon what turned out to be part of the official archives of Akhenaten's foreign office, almost four hundred clay tablets containing letters that passed between him or his predecessor and various rulers of the Near East.

The Tell el-Amarna letters, as they have come to be known from the modern name of the place where Akhenaten built his new capital, are well-nigh unique in ancient history. Here for once we have before us not some carefully edited records left by a king with an anxious eye cocked on posterity or some second- or thirdhand report by a historian writing years or centuries later, but original documents, the raw material of history, comparable, say, to the records on file in our State Department.

A large proportion consists of letters written by the rulers in those very Levantine coastal cities that Thutmose III had molded into dependable naval bases. Times are very different now. A religious reformer and not a general sits on the throne of Egypt, and his correspondence is a graphic record of how these cities, once ruled so firmly by the pharaohs, are being picked off by enemies. In this drama Egypt is but the tragic victim; the villain of the piece is the sea rover. As letter succeeds letter, he enters the scene and gradually takes over the lead.

Here in these early records, sea rovers, formed into fleets, play some of the roles that navies were destined to play from this time on: grouping to enforce a blockade, preying upon maritime commerce, disrupting seaborne communications.

The chief victim was none other than Byblos, that city whose contacts with Egypt in this age were already over a millennium and a half old. Rib-Addi, a local princeling, ruled it and Simyra, its neighbor to the north. "Send me soldiers and provisions!" was the refrain of his earliest letters to the pharaoh, repeated as the years went by with mounting urgency. But then there came a time when the dispatching of mere men and food was insufficient: the enemy had massed a fleet, put it into action, and sea power was exercising its inexorable influence on Rib-Addi. He had foreseen the danger. The ships were being sent out from the key Levantine ports of Beirut, Tyre, and Sidon. "Put one of your men in each of these cities," he urged Akhenaten, "and prevent them from using their ships against me!" His plea had as little effect as his earlier ones for military reinforcements, and the inevitable results swiftly became apparent. "[The enemy] has placed ships . . . so that grain cannot be brought into Simyra. We can't enter Simyra," another letter reports. And Rib-Addi sums the situation up with a vivid simile, "As a bird that lies in a net, so is Simyra. The sons of Abdi-Ashirta by land and the people of Arvad by sea are against it day and night." The blockade was complete and Simyra fell. The enemy's forces on the water kept increasing. He grew bolder and no longer limited himself to blockade alone but went in for aggressive action. "Two of my ships have been taken," Rib-Addi wrote in desperation on one occasion and, on another, "[The enemy] has seized one of my ships and has actually sailed forth on the sea to capture my other ships." The contact by water between Byblos and Egypt was being severed.

But Rib-Addi wasn't the only one to suffer. Sea raiders were loose all over the high seas. "Ships from the Milim-people," he reports in a worried tone to the pharaoh, "penetrated into the Amurri [northern Syria] and killed Abdi-Ashirta [the local ruler]." We don't know who the Milim-people were specifically, but it is clear from Rib-Addi's lines that they were a dangerously successful group of hit-and-run sea raiders. But Akhenaten soon did not need reports of such activity; he felt the effects of it himself. Raiders from Lycia in southern Asia Minor, a region destined to achieve a great reputation in the grim history of piracy (Chapter 15), were bold enough to swoop down on the very shores of Egypt. The pharaoh wrote to the king of Cyprus accusing him of collusion, and the latter rushed back an aggrieved retort to the effect that, far from aiding Lycians, he and his island had been suffering their incursions yearly.

The warship, in a word, had come of age. Powerful naval units, massed in north Syria, could blockade nearby ports until they fell, disrupt Byblos' communications with Egypt, and prey upon the commerce between the two. Groups of raiders could sack cities on the Levantine coast, attack the shores of Cyprus, and even harry Egypt. The influence of sea power was making itself felt on history.

Things had not been thus a century before when Thutmose calmly shuttled his troops between Egypt and Phoenicia, and when Rekhmire, his vizier, filled his ledgers with lists of items brought overseas from Cyprus, Asia Minor, Crete, and Greece. Something existed then which was able to maintain peace on the seas and which now, at the opening of the fourteenth century B.C., was gone. It was not the Egyptian navy; their oversize riverboats were never intended for hard work on the high seas. It could only have been the fleet of Minos and his successors. Crete's far-flung trade and especially its unwalled cities presuppose the existence of a great fleet. "Minos is the first to whom tradition ascribes the possession of a navy," wrote Thucydides, as we noted before, and he had good reason for saying so. It was a navy that ruled the seas for centuries.

What happened to it? The archaeological record reveals that the Mycenaeans occupied Crete sometime around 1450 B.C. and made themselves the complete heirs of Minoan civilization: they took over its homeland, its trading posts, its commerce. Was the move into the island preceded by an all-out naval battle in which the Mycenaean fleet wiped out the Minoan? Had the Minoans, after ruling the waters uncontestedly for so long, grown careless in the upkeep of their ships and thereby opened themselves to easy invasion by the aggressively expanding Mycenaeans? Whatever the precise cause or causes, the Minoan fleet at this point vanishes from history.

"The northern countries which were in their islands were quivering in their limbs. They penetrated the channels of the river-mouths." So wrote the scribe of Ramses III in recounting a great victory of his king in 1190 B.C. Almost three centuries had passed since the Mycenaean navy had supplanted the Minoan, and over a century and a half since raiders began to disrupt commerce along the Levant. The age of flourishing overseas traffic was coming to an end, and the age of the sea raiders was beginning. The Mediterranean was infested with bands of rovers, not only Lycians and other peoples from the coasts of Asia Minor but also people from "the northern countries which were in their islands." They joined the Libyans in a savage attack on Egypt from the west in 1221 B.C. and again in 1194 and were somehow repelled both times. Four years later some reformed to attack again, by land and sea, from Syria and Palestine. In a great naval engagement, one which stands as the first in history to be described and pictured, Ramses III destroyed their fleet.

"No land could stand before their arms," Ramses has his scribe write. "A camp [was set up by them] in one place in Amor [perhaps in northern Syria]. They desolated its people. . . . They were coming forward toward Egypt, while the flame was prepared before them. Their confederation was the Peleset, Tjeker, Denyen and Weshesh." Of these names and others, disguised in the orthography of the Egyptian scribes, one can be identified with certainty: the Peleset are none other than the Philistines. Further Egyptian accounts record still others which suggest tantalizing identifications. Are the *Tursha* Tyrrhenians or Etruscans, in this age still an Asia Minor people not yet having migrated to their historical abode in central Italy? Are the *Akaiwasha* Achaeans, Homer's name for the Greeks?

What faced Ramses was no mere hit-and-run raid such as Egypt had been putting up with since the days of Akhenaten. These attackers from "the northern countries which were in their islands" had consolidated their forces in northern Syria, had sacked the seaports of the Phoenician coast, and were sweeping down like a flood upon Egypt. It was a veritable migration. And, as the main body moved forward by land, the fleet kept pace along the coast.

Ramses' victory was total. To celebrate it he erected a great temple near Thebes, and it was on its walls that his scribes wrote the story of his conquest and his artists portrayed, in carefully carved reliefs, its highlights. The encounter on land took place first, and the sculptures depict the pharaoh's troops smiting the invaders hip and thigh and breaking through the ranks of soldiers to get to the heavy two-wheeled oxcarts which carried the wives, children, and supplies. Once the land was secured Ramses turned to the enemy fleet. Somehow or other he managed to catch it unawares. As he puts it: "Those who entered the river-mouths were like birds ensnared in the net." The picture illustrating this part of the action is unique (Fig. 4). It is the first and only complete representation of a historical sea battle that has come to us from the ancient world. The Egyptian galleys sweep down on the ships manned by the invaders, easily distinguished by their feathered headdresses. Egyptian archers from ships and shore spray them with a withering fire, crippling them severely before they can get close enough to strike a blow with their swords and thrusting spears; the very lookout in one of the crow's nests has been picked off and hangs

FIG. 4. Ramses III's fleet defeats invaders from the north.

dead over the rail. The pharaoh's men then move in with shield and
spear to deliver the coup de grace: in the fight one of the northerners'
ships has capsized; some of the crew are bound captives in an Egyptian
vessel, while others swim to shore only to be pinioned by the waiting
Egyptian soldiers.

But not all the northerners were destroyed in this battle. Battered
remnants made their way northward. The Tjeker planted themselves
about Mount Carmel, and the Peleset settled to the south along the
coast of Palestine. There they remained, not strong enough to try another attack on Egypt but soon sufficiently recovered to resume their
old game of sea raiding and to play a leading role in certain pages of
the Old Testament.

Just about this time, in a different quarter of the Mediterranean, another great attack by sea raiders took place. It was, in all probability,
much smaller in scope than that which Ramses had thrown back, involving fewer men and ships. Yet its story is one of the best known
there is, for it was told not by a scribe or even a historian but by an
immortal poet.

On a hill in northwest Asia Minor overlooking the Dardanelles, early in the third millennium B.C. the city we know as Troy had been founded. It grew steadily more powerful through the centuries. It built massive walls to protect itself, engaged in wide trade, especially in silver, which was mined in the area, extended its rule over its neighbors, and exacted tribute from them. By the thirteenth century B.C. it had become enormously wealthy. Though it had no fleet of its own, its impregnable location and its frowning walls were enough to discourage the ambitions of the ordinary sea raider whose hit-and-run tactics were designed for lightly defended villages. A fortress such as Troy could only be taken by extended siege and full-scale attack.

Sometime in the thirteenth century B.C. the Mycenaeans of Greece, who had always gone in for marauding as well as peaceful trade and now more than ever, took up the challenge. Because many centuries later Homer decided to use what they did as the subject matter of an epic, the Western world knows of this struggle and the men who figured in it as it does of no other. He, of course, got his story not from any set of archives but from popular tradition, and he was himself a creative artist, not a war diarist. Yet the tale he tells is so coherent that behind the imaginative poetry can be discerned a skeleton of fact.

For once the major cities of Greece forwent their traditional enthusiastic pastime of preying on one another and joined hands for a combined operation against Troy. Even the romantic cause that Homer assigns to the war may be true: the expedition may very well have been triggered by the abduction of the irresistibly beautiful wife of one of their chieftains, neatly carried out by an amorous Trojan; wars have been started for less. Each leader contributed ships and men to the great undertaking: Achilles led a contingent from northeastern Greece, Nestor from southwestern Greece, Odysseus from a nearby island—the leaders' names have become household words. Agamemnon, king of Mycenae, the most powerful of the cities represented, received the high command. The various contingents made a rendezvous in a barren cove on the east coast of Greece, and after some difficulty with contrary winds—the prevailing summer northeasterlies are foul for a voyage from Greece to Troy—set sail.

The problem that faced Agamemnon and his staff was basically the same as the one confronted by American forces in the Pacific half a dozen times in World War II: he had to ferry his forces safely to the point of attack, secure a beachhead, and then break through the enemy defenses. It was not the first such action that had taken place in the Mediterranean: obviously, it was by some form of amphibious operation that the Mycenaeans had landed on Crete some two hundred or more years earlier. On that occasion the key to victory was the eliminating at the outset of the fleet on which the Minoans relied for their defense; once that was done, the island's unwalled towns couldn't have been much of a problem. The sail to Troy and the landing were the easiest phases of Agamemnon's operation, for Troy had no fleet. His troubles began once he had drawn his men up on the shore. To lay siege to a strong point in those days was a protracted and costly business, and commanders thought long and hard before undertaking one. Archaeologists have uncovered the walls of Troy, and the visitor even today can get some idea of the magnitude of the task that faced Agamemnon and his forces.

His chief ally was time. He had to keep the garrison bottled up and starve the city out. This meant that he had to secure his own lines of supply, cut off the enemy's, and maintain his forces under rigid discipline in a more or less static position until blockade could ultimately take its grim effect. His fleet gave him uncontested control of the coast, and he sent out constant raiding parties to secure provisions for his men and deny them to the enemy. But his siege was never really complete. The hinterland to the east of the city was always more or less open, and Troy was always able to attract or, with its wealth, buy new allies who refilled the ranks and restored the reserves of food and weapons.

Agamemnon had a problem more troublesome even than the leaks in his blockade. He had to keep an undisciplined highly temperamental gang of sea raiders at the wearing, monotonous task of maintaining a siege. It was like trying to run a music school with a faculty of prima donnas. He didn't even have what we would consider fundamental for his job: absolute power of command. He was merely the chief in a group of leaders who had banded together in a loose confederation for this single expedition; there wasn't to be another like it for some eight hundred years. The Greeks throughout their history have built up an impressive reputation for being resistant to discipline, and the men to whom Agamemnon had to issue orders had a susceptibility to fancied insult of Homeric proportions. It hardly helped matters that, at the very outset, over some ridiculously minor issue a mighty squabble arose, and one of them, in an immortal fit of the sulks, withdrew his forces from the battle line and spent practically the whole of the war in his tent. It was inevitable too that, when large groups of men had to live together under primitive conditions with no knowledge of hygiene, disease would break out. Homer said it came from Apollo; more likely it came from the latrines or the lack of them.

The poet claims that the war lasted ten years. Two probably would be nearer the mark, and that itself is no mean period for a group of sea raiders to have stuck to one project. Even at the end when Hector's death deprived the Trojans of the general who had so brilliantly and doggedly conducted the defense, the city's walls were enough to keep the attackers, weakened by plague, dissension, and casualties, from victory. They had only one move left: to try a ruse. If the stratagem of the wooden horse had not worked, Agamemnon would have had to retire, and the first amphibious operation recorded in detail would have ended in an ignominious admission of defeat.

It was their incomparable fleet that had led the Mycenaeans to try an attack on Troy in the first place. Their fighting ships had no peer in the Mediterranean in that age. Homer is proud of these vessels and describes them with loving detail.

An ancient freighter could be, and most often was, a roomy slow-moving craft propelled by sail alone. A man-of-war had to be a galley, and a fast one at that. It was equipped with sail to use when it was cruising and there was a favorable wind; when there was not, or when it was heading into battle, the sail was stowed away and the vessel driven by its crew of oarsmen. Homer was most struck by the sleek racing lines of the Mycenaean galleys, for he cannot mention them without remarking on their slender, graceful appearance and their swiftness. This is, of course, what we should expect in a sea rover's vessel built first and foremost for speed. He often calls them "black"; they must have been kept liberally smeared with pitch. They were "blue-prowed" or "red-prowed" or "purple-prowed"; that is, they were decorated, as ships have often been ever since, with colored bow patches. He was impressed, too, by the cunning joints and other careful craftsmanship of the shipwrights; the vessels, in his words, are "well-planked," "well-wrought," and "well-balanced."

The smallest, used for ordinary dispatch work and light transport, had twenty oars, the largest as many as one hundred, and the fifty-oared galley was a common size. Even the smallest must have been a full forty feet long: an oarsman needs at least three feet; ten of them on a side totals thirty feet, and we must allow another ten, as we shall see, for decks fore and aft. The hulls were so low that on one occasion when the Greeks, under savage Trojan attack, were driven back upon their beached ships, Hector could reach up and grab the ornament atop a sternpost and Ajax could leap from a gunwale to the ground with ease. Homer happens to mention that the ships were seven feet wide where the steersman sat in the stern sheets, so they could not have been much more than nine to ten amidships. They were so light that, when Odysseus was making a fast getaway from the island of the Cyclops, he was able to get his vessel free of the shore with one good shove on the boat pole. The crews ran them up on the beach every

night. The fifty-oared craft was perhaps ninety feet long and correspondingly beamier. Either size was ideal for sea raiding, low enough
to lie hidden behind some promontory while stalking a prey, swift
enough to dash out and overtake a clumsy merchantman handily, and
light enough in draught to run, if chased, to the protection of the
shore no matter how shallow the water.

Homer calls them "hollow ships"; that is, they were undecked almost throughout, like a dory. There was a scant deck forward for the
lookout and for a few marines when the vessel was engaged in combat,
and there was a slightly larger one aft for the helmsman and captain.
Since these ships offered no more in the way of comfort than a racing
shell, a skipper did all he could to spend nights ashore; if he had to sail
through the night he himself could flake out on the afterdeck under
a scrap of sailcloth, but the crew spent the hours dozing on the
benches. Gear and provisions were stowed under the decks and the
rowing thwarts. When the King of the Winds, to help Odysseus get
home, packed all the winds except the south wind in a bag and gave it
to Odysseus, the only place it could be stowed was under the rowers'
seats. The men, seeing the mysterious bundle under their feet night
and day, could not restrain their curiosity, undid the knot one night
when their captain had fallen asleep from exhaustion, and the pent-
up winds came roaring out; thus was inaugurated the much-suffering
man's long series of mishaps.

Whenever a Homeric skipper could, he sailed rather than rowed.
Like a Viking chief, he and his rowers were companions, and using the
oars was only part of their job; they were his fighting men as well. He
could neither afford nor was in any position to use them up like the
commanders of slave-driven galleys of the fifteenth century and later.
His rowing officer beat only time, never the rowers. When the vessel
was under oars, the mast was unstepped and lowered into a crutch aft
and the sailing gear was stowed under the benches. As soon as a favorable wind came along, the crew leaped to make sail. First the mast was
hauled up by two forestays, its lower part set in place in the mast box,
and secured by a backstay. The single sail with its yard was hoisted and
angled by braces to catch the wind. The weather sheet was made fast,
and the helmsman took his position with the leeward sheet in one
hand and the tiller, a bar socketed at right angles into the loom of the
steering oar, in the other. To shorten sail, Homer's sailors used a system that continued to be standard on all subsequent Greek and
Roman craft, one that has many advantages over the bonnets and reef
points of later ages. To begin with, they abandoned the Egyptian and
Minoan practice of stiffening the bottom of the sail with a boom (pp.
14, 29) and left it loose-footed, as Mediterranean sails were to be for-

ever after. This permitted them to rig brails, in this case a series of lines made fast at fixed intervals along the foot, then carried straight up over the forward surface of the sail to the yard, then brought over the yard down to the deck aft (Pls. 24, 27, 41, 42). These, when pulled, bunched the sail up toward the yard (Pls. 24, 42) just the way a venetian blind is raised; nobody had to go aloft or wrestle with knots in stiff water-soaked lines, and, since the loose ends of the brails could be gathered together (Pl. 41), shortening or loosing sail required a minimum of deckhands. Sails were made of linen, not one piece but patches sewn together for added strength. Lines were of leather strips or twisted papyrus fibers.

When there was no wind the crew had to run out the oars. These were taken from below the benches where they had been stowed and placed against tholes, wooden pins which were used instead of oarlocks as the fulcrum against which the loom of the oar worked. Each oar had a leather strap that was looped about the tholepin; such a strap is essential in rowing with tholepins and, besides, saves an oar from going overboard if a rower happens to lose his grip.

Whether under sail or oars, working these ships was strenuous, uncomfortable, and dangerous. They were much less sturdy than the robust craft of the Vikings, and Homer's sailors were correspondingly far less bold than those reckless sea raiders. When Nestor, for example, sailed home from Troy, his first leg was fifteen miles to the island of Tenedos, his second an all-day run of fifty to Lesbos. Here he held a full-scale conference of his captains to plot the next course. With much trepidation he elected to strike out straight across the open sea instead of island hopping, made it safely to the southern tip of Euboea, and, on landing, set up a great sacrifice to Zeus, "thanking him for crossing that vast stretch of sea"—all of one hundred and ten miles. Usually skippers of galleys stuck to the shore, sailing from one landfall to the next. When they had to travel at night they steered by the stars, but such travel was strictly exceptional. Normally they landed at evening, running the vessel smartly up a beach or, if there was none handy, throwing over the stone anchor in some shallow protected cove; this gave an opportunity to refill the water jars as well as to provide a night's sleep for all hands. On top of these precautions, they limited their sailing to the time of year when the weather was most dependable, putting their galleys into the water at the beginning of spring, around April, and hauling them out in October or so, when the fall set in. Practically all maritime activity, peaceful as well as warlike, was squeezed into the period between these months, and this remained more or less the case throughout the whole of ancient times.

In a famous passage Homer tells how Odysseus made a boat and provides us thereby with the earliest description of shipbuilding on record. The method he has his hero use was no doubt the method practiced in his own day, the eighth century B.C., but, thanks to the discovery of the Ulu Burun wreck (Chapter 3), we now know that ship-wrights had been using this same method well over a century before the Trojan War. Odysseus, in the course of his wanderings, was ship-wrecked and wound up with little more than his own skin on an island inhabited by a goddess. Delighted by the unexpected arrival of this most welcome guest, she kept him by her side for seven years until she was ordered by the higher powers to send the much-suffering hero on his way. The first step was to enable him to build some sort of craft. The goddess gave him a double-edged bronze ax, an adze, and a drill and led him to a spot where there was a fine stand of aspen, alder, and pine. Odysseus got busy:

> He felled twenty trees in all, lopped them clean, smoothed them care-fully, and adzed them straight and square. . . . Then he bored them all and fitted them to each other. Then he hammered it [i.e., the craft] with pegs and joints. He laid out the bottom as wide as a good shipwright would for a beamy freighter. Then he worked away setting up decks by fastening them to close-set frames. He finished by adding the long gun-wales. He stepped a mast and yard and added a broad oar to steer with. He fenced the hull about with plenty of brush [sc., on the floor]. The goddess brought him cloth for a sail; he fashioned that too, a fine one. He rigged braces, brails, and sheets, and, putting the craft on rollers, hauled it down to the sea.

For a long time this passage was obscure; it seemed hard to follow what Homer was saying. Now that marine archaeologists have uncov-ered the remains of ancient wrecks and we can see how these were made, his words have become perfectly clear. We had been misled by the later way of putting together a wooden boat, which, as noted ear-lier, starts by setting up a skeleton of keel and frames and then fastens to this a skin of planks. The poet, however, as we would expect, is describing the technique that was standard in the ancient world, the building up of a shell of planks, each fastened to its neighbors by mor-tise and tenon joints. Odysseus, after adzing his logs into planks, "bored them all," that is, drilled first into the upper and lower edges of each plank to make the mortises, the slots that will receive the tenons (carpenters traditionally rough out such slots with the drill and finish off with the chisel); then he "fitted them to each other," that is, knocked the planks together, thereby driving the tenons into the mor-tises (cf. Pl. 9); he kept building the shell up, plank upon plank, until it had the ample lines a good shipwright will lay out for "the bottom of a beamy merchantman"; then "he worked away setting up decks by fastening them to close-set frames," that is, inserted a strong set of frames into his shell and fastened the decking (no doubt just at prow and stern) to them.

What precisely did these seagoing greyhounds that carried the Greeks to Troy look like? Homer's heroes lived in Greece probably between 1300 and 1200 B.C., and the general age that his tale is set in came to a close not long after that. In the ruins of the Greek cities of this period archaeologists have found very few representations of ships. One, drawn on a pottery container that was made about 1150 B.C., shows a vessel that suits fairly well what we have gleaned from the poet (Pl. 11). The hull is long and low, and the prow, unlike those, for example, on Egyptian craft, rises abruptly without curve from the keel. Homer often compares the shape of his ships to the "straight horns" of cattle as against, say, the curly horns of a ram. This prow is straight but hardly "horned"; its blunt top is finished off with a fish-shaped or bird-shaped ensign. But another picture drawn on a vase of about the same date shows a bow profile that neatly fits Homer's simile (Pl. 12).

The Mycenaeans were a people whose history, as we have seen, was intimately connected with the sea. Yet they need not have been the inventors of the ships we find them using. From the Aegean area, particularly the island of Syros, come representations dating to the third millennium B.C. of galleys that are long and low and whose prows rise straight from the keel and are often topped by a fish-shaped ensign (Pl. 13). It is quite possible that these served as prototype for the ship-builders of the Mycenaeans.

The most careful pictures we have of Mediterranean warships of this age are those, carved on the walls of Ramses' temple, which portray the vessels of the peoples whom he defeated in 1190 B.C. (Fig. 4). Like any sea raider's ship, these are light and lie low in the water. They appear without oars, but this does not mean that they were driven by sail alone, as some writers have hastily concluded; a sea raider could no more depend upon a pure sailing vessel than a jockey could on a cart horse. The Egyptian artist has shown them this way to prove how sagaciously Ramses had seen to it that "those who entered the river-mouths were like birds ensnared in the net." They were taken so completely by surprise that their oars were still stowed beneath the thwarts; probably they were caught while at anchor. There are differences in detail between these ships and those of the Mycenaeans as pictured on vases, notably that these are double-ended, that is, identical at prow and stern, whereas the others are never so: their prows are straight and their sterns are curved. The Egyptian galleys in the pictures show many important changes from their predecessors. The heavy hawsers that used to be necessary to hold the hull together are gone. These ships must have had some sort of inner structure, and, indeed, their whole appearance gives the impression of a sturdier hull than any attested from Egypt hitherto. The rig, too, has novelties: the boom along the foot of the sail is gone and vertical brails have made their appearance. It looks as if the naval architects finally had the good sense, in designing ships for the open sea, to copy the sturdy hull and handy rig that their Mediterranean neighbors were using.

To the merchant skipper, anxiously slogging his way to port, it made little difference whether the ominous black shape he spotted on the horizon had the curved stern of a Mycenaean ship or the straight one of a ship of the northerners who spread such terror in Ramses' day. Both spelled trouble for him. Centuries were to pass before this condition improved.

Chapter 5

RAIDERS AND TRADERS

WHEN ODYSSEUS landed at Ithaca after twenty years of war and wandering, alone and helpless, disguised in beggar's rags, an aged swineherd gave him shelter and, in the course of the evening, not knowing his guest's true identity, asked him for the story of his life. (In addition to being conventional courtesy, this would of course give the old fellow a chance of telling *his* in return.) Odysseus naturally had a tale ready. He was a sea raider from Crete, he announced, had served in the Trojan War and had had the luck to come back alive. Then he proceeded to tell the following:

> I spent only one month enjoying my wife and children and home. Then I got the urge to ready some good ships and crews and lead a raid against Egypt. I readied nine ships and it didn't take me long to get them manned.
>
> My trusty men feasted for six days; I had plenty of animals on hand to sacrifice and to eat. On the seventh we slipped our mooring and set sail from Crete. The wind was fair, a fresh northerly, and we sped along as if we were running downstream in a river. No ship ran into trouble, no one got hurt, no one got sick, and the wind and the helmsman kept the course. In five days we arrived at well-watered Egypt and anchored our ships in its river.
>
> I assigned trusty men to guard the ships and sent a scouting party inland to find lookout spots. But they, getting too cocky and driven by their greed, immediately began to plunder the smiling countryside, killing men and carrying off women and children. The word soon reached a city: the people heard the shouting and at dawn sallied forth. Soon the whole plain was full of men and horses and the flash of bronze armor. My men couldn't fight back: Zeus the god of thunder had sent panic upon them and destruction threatened on all sides. Many of us were killed, the rest carried off as slaves.

The incident (as well as the rest of the story, which is irrelevant here) is made up, to be sure, and by a famed liar at that. But Odysseus deliberately chose to tell something the listener would nod knowingly at, something so everyday that his suspicions would never be aroused. This makes it even more valuable than a fragment of history, the factual record of a specific instance. It is the sort of thing that happened in the twelfth and eleventh centuries B.C. when, in the wake of the large-scale destruction caused by the hordes who had swept down upon Egypt and others like them, lawlessness prevailed on the seas and trade dwindled away. The situation was ideal for this sort of piracy.

Our stereotyped conception of a pirate is a swarthy mustachioed ruffian, heading a cutthroat crew, who pounces upon a helpless merchant ship, collects the valuables, singles out the desirable captives for the slave block, and offers the rest a walk on the plank. The ancient world, as we shall see, came to know this type all too well in later centuries, complete (except perhaps for the mustaches) even to a version of walking the plank. But Odysseus' story and others like it show that pirates at this remote age were raiders of coastal towns, more like tenth-century Vikings than like eighteenth-century Barbary corsairs. They worked in groups because a single boatload of men would not be enough against even a small village. They plundered on land rather than the sea because the pickings were far more profitable. A town could yield a rich harvest of cattle, furnishings, adornments, perhaps some objects of gold and silver, but above all women and children who would bring good prices on the slave market. And a raid, if pulled off properly—as Odysseus' was not—was not too dangerous, for all its adventurousness and bountiful return. A stealthy entry into a harbor at night with muffled oars, some careful professional scouting, a sudden attack at dawn, a rush back aboard, a few hours of grueling work at the oars—and every surviving member of the crew found himself considerably richer than he had been twenty-four hours earlier. This was much simpler, surer, and more rewarding than taking on a merchantman which might, on capture, turn out to have little of real value on board—a load of building stone, perhaps, or wood, or cheap pottery— or even to be sailing in ballast. Moreover, slave dealers were much more interested in young girls and boys who could be trained for household work than they were in weather-beaten merchant seamen. Nor was there any need to raid shipping to fill up the rowers' benches, for, again like Vikings and unlike Turkish corsairs, each sea raider fought and pulled an oar. The slave trade in that era was the chief support of piracy and it was to remain so for many centuries thereafter, even, as we shall see, in times when rich cargoes of merchandise were available for highjacking.

Any town was fair game for the sea raiders, but naturally the richer spots were preferred. Odysseus shrewdly locates his incident in Egypt. The land of the pharaohs was no longer the political power it had been in the past, but the Nile which watered and renewed the fields each year guaranteed the country's economic health, and Egypt's prosper-

ous villages were inviting targets. Even in its palmy days Egypt had
had troubles: one of the Tell el-Amarna letters, from the files of one
of Egypt's most powerful rulers, concerns attacks the country had suffered at the hands of raiders from Asia Minor (Chapter 4). Homer at
one point provides what amounts almost to a directory of the places
the raiders operated in. He has a visitor to the court of Menelaus remark on the richness of the treasures he saw all about the palace. "Ah,
yes," Menelaus replies, "I wandered for seven years and suffered
much to collect these treasures and bring them home in my ships. I've
been to Cyprus, Phoenicia, Egypt; I've seen the people of Ethiopia and
of Sidon, and I've been to Libya." Phoenicia, with its cities of Sidon,
Tyre, and Byblos that had grown rich as seaports, was bound to catch
the raiders' eye. Homer makes one of the nurses in the Odyssey—
nurses were invariably slaves in this period—the daughter of a wealthy
citizen of Sidon from whom she had been kidnaped by pirates. But no
place near the sea was really safe. On the very first leg of their voyage
home from Troy, apparently just to get back into practice, since
heaven knows they had loaded enough booty when they left, Odysseus
and his men on coming to a town in Thrace "sacked the city and killed
the men and, taking the women and plenty of cattle and goods, divided them up." It was an age that men did not easily forget. Over half
a millennium later the great Greek historian Thucydides wrote:

> In ancient times both Greeks and non-Greeks who lived along the coasts
> or on islands, once they began to cross in ships to each other's shores,
> turned to piracy. . . . They would fall upon and plunder the towns, which
> were either unwalled or mere clusters of villages. Most of their livelihood
> came this way; it was a pursuit that hadn't as yet received any stigma but
> was even considered an honorable profession in its way. . . . So, because
> of the chronic piracy, cities long ago, both on islands and along the coasts
> of the mainland, were built away from the sea.

All that we have been saying of life on the sea in this period—the
ubiquitous raiders, the difficulties the legitimate trader had, the feeble
position of Egypt—comes graphically into focus in one of those
unique documents that every now and then time is kind enough to
spare for later ages. A reed called the papyrus once grew in abundance along the Nile, and from strips cut from its stalk the ancients
made a very efficient form of writing paper. Of the vast number of
documents that must have been inscribed on papyrus paper, only
some thousands have survived. The substance disintegrates in any
sort of dampness; almost all of those that we have owe their preservation to the supremely dry climate of Egypt. They lay undisturbed in its
arid sands for centuries, until some peasant stumbled across them or
some archaeologist dug them up.

One day a group of Egyptian fellahin, rooting around for fuel, unearthed a mutilated papyrus roll. In due course it found its way into the hands of dealers and, eventually, of scholars. Often, papyrus documents turn out to be discouragingly repetitive: many an archaeologist has had high hopes dashed by finding that the well-preserved roll he has just uncovered is only one more copy of the Iliad or of the Book of the Dead, the Egyptian bible. But this piece was unique. It was the carefully drawn-up report of an Egyptian priest named Wenamon who had been sent by his superiors around 1100 B.C. on a business trip to Byblos. Reading Wenamon's account we can for a moment relive a fragment of a trader's life in the twelfth century before Christ.

Wenamon came from Thebes far up the Nile. His official title was "Eldest of the Hall of the House of Amon" (Amon was the supreme Egyptian deity). Whatever his exact clerical position was, it is clear that he stood fairly high in the church hierarchy or he never would have been chosen for the assignment.

Every year during a sacred festival at Thebes, an image of Amon was carried on the Nile in a ceremonial barge. This particular year, apparently, a new one had to be built and, since Egypt is practically treeless, the lumber had to be imported. The best and most convenient source was still, as thousands of years before, the famous stand of cedars in Lebanon (Chapter 2). Someone had to go to Byblos to arrange the shipment. Herihor, the high priest of Egypt, selected Wenamon. For his expenses and the cost of the purchase he was to make, Wenamon was entrusted with five pounds of gold and seven and one half of silver (since the invention of coinage lay more than five hundred years in the future, the money was necessarily in bullion). And he took along something that was equally important, a statuette of Amon-of-the-Road, that is, of Amon in his role as protector of travelers. On the fifth of April, Wenamon set off.

It was a time when Egypt was at one of the numerous low points of its long history. The country was not even united under one ruler. From the capital at Thebes, where Wenamon as a member of the priestly college lived, Ramses XI ruled only upper Egypt; from Tanis, a relatively minor town in the delta area, Nesubanebdded, a local prince, controlled lower Egypt. So Wenamon's first move was to make his way down the Nile to the court at Tanis to present himself to this ruler and his queen, Tanetamon. He submitted a letter of introduction from Herihor, his credentials—or passport, as it were—and their majesties received him graciously. They did not go so far as to order a special ship for him, but they arranged passage on a vessel bound for the Levant under the command of a captain named Mengebet whom they presumably instructed to take special care of this particular passenger. On April 20, Mengebet's ship cast off and set sail.

The first port of call was Dor, just south of Mount Carmel, where the Tjekers, one of the warlike peoples who had attacked Egypt a half-century earlier and been repulsed (Chapter 4), had established themselves. Here Wenamon was received so handsomely that even he, who held no inconsiderable notion of his own importance, was content. But then disaster struck, the disaster that so often befalls travelers, modern as well as ancient: he was robbed of all his money. The only valuable that escaped was the sacred image of Amon-of-the-Road.

Attempts to track down the thieves and recover what had been stolen proved useless. But Wenamon gave no thought to turning back; he stoutly continued on his way. The ship sailed past Tyre and then, before arriving at Byblos, perhaps at Sidon, he found the chance to recoup at least part of his loss. It took a desperate expedient: he had to resort to robbery himself. He held up some Tjekers and took thirty *deben* of silver—about seven and a quarter pounds—from them. How was an unarmed peaceable Egyptian priest able to do this, particularly to a group of Tjekers, fighting men par excellence? We have no idea; the papyrus is mutilated and many lines are lost at this critical point.

Finally, he reached his destination at Byblos—only to be greeted by the harbormaster with a disconcerting message from Zakar-Baal, the ruling prince: "Get out of my harbor!" The Tjekers must have sent word ahead to Zakar-Baal about Wenamon's crime, and the prince, responsible for the well-being of a busy seaport and aware of their reputation as sea raiders, would hardly want to show favor to anyone in their bad graces.

Wenamon, however, as we have already seen, was not a man to be easily discouraged. For no less than twenty-nine days he hung around the harbor. Daily the harbormaster paid him a visit with the same peremptory order—but took no action to put it into effect. It looks as if Zakar-Baal was carefully straddling the fence, making public announcements to placate his dangerous neighbors but doing nothing to jeopardize what he knew would be a profitable business transaction.

Finally even Wenamon gave up hope. Mengebet's ship had left by this time, but he found another scheduled to depart shortly for Egypt. He booked passage on it, and put his secretary and all his luggage aboard. He himself hung back, planning to delay until after dark when he could get his precious image on the ship without being observed. "I waited for the darkness," he notes, "thinking that when it descended I would get the god on board so that no other eye may see him."

But at this moment the unexpected happened. The harbormaster approached with the announcement that Zakar-Baal had scheduled an interview for the following morning. Wenamon, understandably enough, was suspicious. "I said to him," he writes, "'Aren't you the one who came to me daily to tell me to get out of the harbor? And aren't you telling me to stay now just to make me lose my ship so that you can come back and start ordering me to go away again?'" Zakar-Baal met this cogent objection by issuing an order to hold the ship.

Wenamon has a ready explanation for the sudden change of attitude. The previous evening, while Zakar-Baal was conducting sacrifice, one of the young nobles at court suddenly fell into a frenzied fit and began to scream, "Bring the god here! Bring the messenger who is carrying him! Amon is the one who sent him from Egypt and made him come here." Wenamon is clearly out to convince the reader that the influence of his wonderful image had reached the court. Perhaps so. But we are entitled to the conjecture at least that what reached there may have been something more tangible, some of the stolen silver that Wenamon was now able to jingle, for example. He could hardly have spent his twenty-nine days just taking in the sea air, and bribery ought to have come easily to a man who had stooped to robbery. On the other hand, the fit may have been a device engineered by Zakar-Baal to end a little comedy that he had been directing for a considerable time by now. The prince, as the continuation of the story reveals, was a most engaging character with a sharp eye for business and a well-developed sense of humor, a fact that Wenamon never tumbled to. He particularly liked to take his self-important visitor down a peg or two and there is no question that he thoroughly enjoyed keeping the Eldest of the Hall of the House of Amon on tenterhooks and making him cool his heels around the harbor. Besides, it satisfied the requirements of protocol toward his Tjeker neighbors. But it was no time for jokes when a potential customer was on the point of decamping without leaving an order. So Wenamon was suddenly summoned to the palace.

"I found him," he reports, "sitting in his upper chamber, leaning his back against a window, while the waves of the great Syrian sea beat against the wall behind him." It isn't usual for Wenamon to include circumstantial details like this; the interview and its setting must have burned itself into his memory. "I said to him, 'The blessing of Amon upon you.'" The Egyptian must have been all wound up for an extended exchange of amenities, as at home. If so, he was disappointed. Zakar-Baal, all business, came right to the point: "How long ago did you leave Egypt?" he asked. "Five months and one day," the envoy replied, probably with feeling—the voyage could have been done in a couple of weeks at most. Then came the question that Wenamon must have been hoping against hope he would be spared. But he must have seen at the very first moment of the interview that a man like Zakar-Baal, who kept one waiting for a month and brusquely dispensed with all one's carefully thought-out phrases, would inevitably ask it.

"Where," the prince said next, "is the letter of the priest of Amon which you should have with you?" Wenamon had set out with credentials, of course, but at that moment they were lying in some pigeonhole in Tanis: he had presented them there and forgotten to ask for them back. There was nothing to do except play the hand out: "I gave it to Nesubanebded and Tanetamon," he replied, probably with the sort of expression a motorist tells a traffic cop that he has left his driver's license at home. Zakar-Baal saw a fine opportunity for a scene. "He became very angry," Wenamon writes, and we can readily picture the prince working himself into a rage with histrionic art, "and said to me, 'What! you don't have the letter! And where is the ship with its Syrian crew that Nesubanebded gave you? Didn't he turn you over to this foreign ship captain just to have him kill you and throw you overboard? If that had happened where would people have looked for the god [i.e., the statue of Amon]? And where would they have looked for you?'" Wenamon continues: "I said to him, 'What makes you think it wasn't an Egyptian ship? Nesubanebded has only Egyptian ships. He has no Syrian crews.' He said to me: 'There are twenty ships belonging to this harbor which do business with Nesubanebded. And isn't it a known fact that at Sidon, where you have been, there are fifty which do business with Werket-El and are anchored near his office?'" It was a snide remark that hit home: foreign bottoms now carried most of Egypt's trade items; there was little left of the native merchant marine, and Wenamon knew it. He knew it so well that, though rarely at a loss for words and usually ready with quite a flow of them, he had to admit that he "was silent at this critical moment."

Zakar-Baal had had his fun and it was now time to get down to business. "What have you come for?" he asked. "I have come," was the reply, "for timber for the sacred barge of Amon-Re, King of Gods. Your father supplied it, your grandfather supplied it, and so will you."

Since the prince held all the cards, he could afford to overlook bluster of that sort. "They certainly did," he answered in the best of spirits, "and if you'll pay me I'll do it too. Why, when my family carried out the commission, the Pharaoh—blessed be his name—sent six shiploads of Egyptian merchandise which were unloaded into our warehouses. What are you bringing me?" At this point Zakar-Baal could not resist another chance to torture the poor Egyptian: he called for his secretary and ordered him to bring out the old ledgers. Entry by entry he went over them for Wenamon's benefit. And there must have been plenty of entries, for the grand total of receipts was 1,000 *deben*.

There had been long periods when Lebanon was an Egyptian possession (Chapter 4) and the pharaohs did not have to buy the cedar they needed but just took it. Even less than a century before Wenamon's journey, Egypt had held all the lands south of Zakar-Baal's principality, and his predecessors had been careful to treat this powerful neighbor with courtesy and respect. Things were very different now, however, and Zakar-Baal, who must have hugely enjoyed the whole interview, gleefully reminds Wenamon of this fact. "If the ruler of Egypt were the owner of my property," he tells him, "and if I were his servant, he wouldn't have had to send money. . . . But *I* am not your servant nor your master's. All I have to do is say the word and the logs will be ready on the shore. But where are the ships you should have brought to transport them? Where are the lines to lash them?. . . What are these silly trips which they have had you make!" At this crack Wenamon finally lost his temper. "I told him," he writes, "'Not true! What I am on are no 'silly trips' at all! Every ship on the river belongs to Amon and so does the sea and Lebanon which you call your own. The cedars grow only for his sacred bark, for he owns every ship. It was he, Amon-Re, who ordered Herihor my master to send me bearing the god with me. But you have made this great god spend these twenty-nine days moored in your harbor!'" After going on in this way for a considerable time, he wound up with, "Have your secretary brought to me, so that I may send him to Nesubanebded and Tanetamon, the rulers whom Amon put in the north of his land, and they will have all kinds of things sent. I will send your man to say to them, 'Make an advance until I get back again to the south, and I shall then have every bit of the debt due you brought to you.' That," he added, "is what I told him."

This is precisely what Zakar-Baal wanted to hear. He must have known through his agents that the envoy had only a niggardly thirty *deben* of silver with him. Now he was being offered whatever price he wanted to set on his product. The secretary was forthwith dispatched to Egypt, and Zakar-Baal, no doubt with most of Wenamon's stolen money in his cashbox as a down payment, let him take along several important timbers: the keel, sternpost, stempost, and four others. Nesubanebded and Tanetamon did just as the envoy had promised: in forty-eight days the secretary returned with a shipment that contained the following impressive inventory:

    4 jars and 1 bowl of gold
    5 jars of silver
    10 garments of royal linen
    10 bolts of good South Egyptian linen
    500 rolls of finished papyrus paper
    500 cowhides
    500 coils of rope
    20 sacks of lentils
    30 baskets of fish

There were some items for Wenamon personally too: five garments of good south Egyptian linen (he probably needed these badly; he had had no idea he was going to be away for better than a half-year), five bolts of good south Egyptian linen, one sack of lentils, and five baskets of fish. "The prince was glad," notes Wenamon, "and detailed three hundred men and three hundred cattle, and he put supervisors at their head, to . . . cut down the timber." Eight months after the envoy had left his native land, the timber lay on the beach cut and stacked, ready for loading.

But even then Zakar-Baal had to have a last bit of fun. "You know," he told Wenamon, "I have not done to you what was done to the messengers from Khaemwaset: they spent seventeen years in this land—and died here." Then, turning to an attendant, he said, "Take him and show him their tomb." This was a little too much. "Don't show it to me!" was Wenamon's agonized reply. At this point, perhaps to recover his own spirits, the Egyptian launched into a long disquisition to the effect that Zakar-Baal will be so proud of having done business with Amon and his divine and human associates (these being, of course, the sacred image and Wenamon) that he will not stop until he has rendered the transaction immortal by erecting a permanent stone monument with the whole story inscribed thereon. "That will be just fine," is, in effect, Zakar-Baal's reply.

But nothing was destined to go right for the poor envoy. Just when things looked brightest—the timber was ready on the beach, several payments on account were already in the prince's hands, both sides had agreed amicably that the balance would be remitted later—and Wenamon was on the point of giving orders to load the cargo, suddenly eleven ships sailed into the harbor to deliver a pregnant message to the palace: "Arrest him! Don't let a ship of his leave for Egypt!" If the story didn't date centuries before Greek drama was born, we might think we were reading a typical Greek tragedy with Fate inevitably swooping down on a man at his best moment to exact retribution for wrongs done long before. For the ships were manned by Tjeker sea raiders, there to demand justice for the thirty *deben* of silver that had been stolen from them almost a year ago. Wenamon, who a little while earlier had been chattering about seeing his name inscribed on an eternal monument, at this point just gave up: "I sat down," he reports, "and cried." Apparently he carried on so that even the prince became aware of it and sent his secretary down to find out what happened. "How long shall I be left here?" wailed Wenamon, pointing to the ships. "Don't you see those there who are coming to arrest me?" He worked himself up into such a state that Zakar-Baal himself got a little worried; after all, a customer deserved some consideration. His solution has an incredibly modern cast to it: he sent Wenamon a ram, two jars of wine, and an Egyptian dancing girl. (The envoy, scrupulous reporter that he is, has saved her name for posterity: Tanetnot.)

Let us hope that Wenamon relished his mutton and wine and had a distracting evening with Tanetnot, because there wasn't much enjoyment for him in what he was to go through the next morning. Zakar-Baal was on the spot: he didn't want to lose a customer, especially one with a balance still due, and at the same time he was loath to offend dangerous neighbors. He solved the problem with yet another of his wily compromises. He could not, he explained to the Tjekers, put a messenger of Amon under arrest, he was dutybound to let him set sail. "Let me send him off," he added, "and then you go after him to arrest him." In other words, let him clear my harbor and you grab him as soon as he enters the open water.

So Wenamon was allowed to depart—and, for once, fate came to his aid. "The wind cast me," he tells us, "on the land of Alashiya." From these few words we can make a good guess as to what happened. Alashiya was the Egyptians' name for Cyprus or the coast of Asia Minor to the north of it—just the reverse of the direction Wenamon presumably wanted. The wind that forced him to go there must have been a storm wind, and a storm wind would have discouraged the Tjekers from attempting pursuit; after all, they were aboard light galleys, whereas Wenamon, with his ponderous cargo, was on a sturdy merchantman.

There were other vicissitudes in store for the much-suffering Egyptian. Most of these, however, will forever remain a mystery, for the papyrus is incomplete, breaking off in the middle of a sentence. Did the shipment arrive? Did Zakar-Baal get the balance due him? We will never know. All we can be sure of is that Wenamon got back, or else the report would never have been written.

Years after Wenamon had returned to Thebes, vessels continued to make the run between Syria and Egypt, hauling timber and wine from the one in exchange for textiles, papyrus, and hides from the other. In Byblos, Zakar-Baal's children must have kept adding entries to the ledger their father had so mischievously shown the Egyptian envoy. But wherever the legitimate trader was to be found, so was the pirate. To the south of Byblos the Tjekers went on matter-of-factly pursuing their profession of raiding. The shores of Greece, which sent forth the merchantmen that carried among other things the distinctive pottery archaeologists constantly come upon in excavation after excavation on the Aegean islands and the littoral of western Asia, also launched the plunderers who made life miserable for coastal villages the length and breadth of the eastern Mediterranean. People moved away from the coasts in terror and took up a new way of life inland. But finally, a century or so after the opening of the first millennium B.C., lawlessness on the seas tapered off and commerce reappeared. It was now in the hands of the two maritime peoples par excellence of the ancient world, the Greeks and the Phoenicians. Let us turn to their achievements.

Chapter 6

THE DAWN OF MARITIME EXPLORATION

ONE DAY, some three thousand years ago, a vessel left the harbor of Iolcus, on the northeast coast of Greece, where Volo stands today, swung its head to the east, and got under way. The world's first recorded voyage of overseas exploration had begun.

The account of this trip is unfortunately not set forth in a matter-of-fact ship's log or a diary, something that would leave scant room for ambiguity, but in a tradition, half sailor's yarn, half poetic fancy, that had a leisurely thousand years or more in which to work itself up. The very names involved have an uncomfortable vagueness about them. The skipper's name was Jason, "the healer," and his ship's was *Argo*, "the swift." These offer no difficulty. But the far-off country that Jason made his way to was called Aea, which means in Greek nothing more than "land," and its ruler Aeetes, "man of the land." The native woman he brought home from there was Medea, "the cunning one." His son is named Euneus, "good man aboard ship," which is almost too apropos. And what can we say of woman-headed birds and movable cliffs and a dragon, all of which he and his crew, the Argonauts, met en route, or of the prize itself that they brought home, a fleece of gold? The task is to distill, from a mass of mythological fancy found in Greek poetry that spans almost a millennium, the sober details that Jason would have entered in his log. It's somewhat like having to reconstruct a naval diary from the stories of Sinbad the Sailor.

The legend of the voyage of the *Argo* goes something like this:

Jason was a young prince who, like Hamlet, was the victim of an unscrupulous uncle: his aged father had been pushed off the throne by a brother, Pelias. Since outright murder of the son (the father was old enough to be left out of the reckoning) would entail unfortunate political repercussions, Pelias availed himself of a time-honored method of getting rid of a popular rival. He set Jason the job of finding and bringing home the fabulous golden fleece. It's as if Ferdinand and Isabella had dispatched Columbus to bring back, on pain of death, the latitude and longitude of Eldorado.

Jason collected a crew to man the fifty-oared galley *Argo* that had been specially built for the voyage, and set a course for the east. The vessel sailed swiftly across the Aegean, through the Dardanelles and

Bosporus and into the Black Sea, encountering numerous difficulties, including a brush with the Harpies, creatures with bodies of birds and heads of women. Once in the Black Sea, Jason was in completely unknown waters; like Columbus he could only cry "Adelante!" and press unremittingly eastward. At last, after a not overly trying voyage, the Argonauts dropped anchor at their destination, a country they called simply Aea, "land," but which later Greeks identified with Colchis in the far eastern corner of the Black Sea.

Here they ran into troubles of a different sort. Aeetes, the ruler, for obvious reasons showed considerable reluctance to surrender the fleece and was able to back his reluctance with armed force. Moreover, the prize was guarded by a dragon, formidably equipped for dealing with intruders, and discouragingly vigilant. In the nick of time all problems were solved by a stroke of pure luck: Medea, the king's daughter, a handsome young woman and skilled sorceress, fell in love with Jason and in short order accomplished what no amount of Greek muscle and bravery could have. Some time later, just before dawn the *Argo* crept out of the harbor with the fleece—and Medea—safely aboard. In a few hours Aeetes launched his navy in pursuit.

The trip back was a nightmare. To elude Aeetes, Jason laid out a different course home. He lost his way and wandered to the ends of the earth. The ship had to undergo the horror of running the gantlet of the "wandering rocks," two huge cliffs that, when anything tried to pass between, drove together swiftly enough to crush a bird, to say nothing of an object as slow as a ship. At one point the crew had to make a backbreaking portage, pulling the vessel overland on rollers for twelve long days. Much time elapsed before the *Argo* finally was run up on the beach in the harbor of Iolcus.

The aftermath of the voyage tells more of human emotion than of maritime history. Medea again proved invaluable to her lover. Her magical recipes were able to restore his aged father to youth and to do away with Pelias (she gave the youth recipe to his daughters, simply omitting to tell them of one key ingredient). But success and fame made Jason ambitious. An opportunity came his way to marry the daughter of the ruler of Corinth and ultimately to inherit that rich kingdom. Medea rejected his cold-blooded arrangements for putting her aside and, in a burst of immortal rage, took her revenge by slaying not only his fiancée but the two children Medea herself had borne him. Of his great days there was but one thing left to Jason and that a mere symbol: the hulk of the *Argo*, which now lay rotting on the beach at Iolcus. He returned there to spend his days prowling dreamily about it. Even this inanimate object turned against him: one day as he lay asleep by it a decayed timber fell and killed him.

So much for what the storytellers and poets made of the voyage of Jason and the *Argo*. What can we make of it?

We must first guess at the date; poets and spinners of yarns are not much interested in strict chronology. When the naval power of Crete had been destroyed and that of Mycenae had degenerated (Chapter 4), raiders and rovers swarmed over the eastern Mediterranean. To this age, the period between 1200 and 1000 B.C., when Wenamon was sailing to Lebanon and Homer's pirates were raiding Egypt, after the time when Crete had yielded the initiative on the seas to the Mycenaeans and before the time soon to come when the Black Sea would be nearly as familiar to Greek skippers as their own Aegean, the tale of Jason and his voyage very likely belongs. There is a significant twist in his story that sets him apart from his contemporary sea heroes. Jason was no raider who sallied forth to pounce on the first or best available town for plunder. He was the leader of a carefully equipped expedition whose express purpose was to cross uncharted waters to gain something known only through vague hearsay.

He headed eastward. Why not westward? The golden apples in the garden of the Hesperides, which later Greeks located near the Strait of Gibraltar, would seem just as fair and tangible a prize as a golden fleece. But perhaps not. Subsequent ages knew that the people who lived at the farther end of the Black Sea where Jason's Aea was located had a way of washing gold from a river by tying fleeces in the stream so that particles of the dust would adhere to them. It was the earliest known form of placer mining. If we assume that rumors of this had reached Jason's part of the world, the "search for the golden fleece" suddenly comes into focus; it becomes a search for treasure, a completely understandable reason for daring exploration.

There was, too, perhaps another reason for heading eastward: adventure was more quickly come upon. It was a short sail from Iolcus to the Bosporus, probably little more than a week if that, and once that strait had been navigated and his prow was cutting the surface of the Black Sea, Jason was where he wanted to be, passing, along the north shore of Asia Minor, settlements that belonged to strange races. Had he gone west, he would have had to slog it out to the seas beyond Sicily before striking unknown territory. For, centuries earlier, Minoan and Mycenaean ships had sailed this far and all the waters up to the straits between Sicily and Tunisia were well known (Chapter 2).

Jason, then, elected to go east. He could not have had much trouble rounding up a capable crew. There must have been an ample supply of hardfisted seamen lounging about the wharves of Iolcus and nearby ports eager to sign on a voyage that promised to be interesting and profitable—no more trouble probably than Leif Eriksson and other Viking leaders were to have millennia later in gathering crews for their epoch-making ventures westward. Later Greek tradition has it that the Argonauts were an all-star team, that Heracles and Theseus and Orpheus and others from the galaxy of Greek heroes went along, but this is poetic emnbroidery. Jason's expedition was successful, which meant it had a complement of obedient able-bodied seamen and not a collection of prima donnas. Rowing a galley was a complicated technique that demanded training and coordination; none of the twelve famous labors of Heracles involved pulling an oar. The oldest versions of the legend imply that Jason used only the leaders from his own neighborhood, and this must surely be right.

The *Argo* coasted along the northern shore of Asia Minor and met the usual problem that confronted a strange ship in those days: attacks by natives wherever it tried to put in for the night or for provisions. For the vessel could not stay at sea any length of time. Roomy merchantmen that could were being built in this age, but the *Argo* was not one of these. Jason wisely chose a fighting craft for his expedition, one that would not be so completely dependent upon the winds as would a sailing freighter, and which could either withstand or run away from attack. It could not have been very different from those used in the war against Troy: a slender galley mounting twenty-five rowers on a side, with a sail and mast that could be easily and quickly unstepped (Chapter 4). When traveling without a break night and day, the crew slept at the oars, and there was little room for provisions. Frequent stopovers had to be included in the itinerary.

One of the more unusual encounters on the outward leg of the voyage, according to later legend, was a set-to with the Harpies, creatures who, as represented in Greek art, have the bodies of birds and the heads of women. They somewhat resemble winged sphinxes, a fact that may account for their presence in Jason's story. Archaeologists have discovered that the winged sphinx is a form that originated, and is commonly found, in Asia Minor. It occurs in Hittite sculpture, for example. Can the Harpy be the poetic end result of what started as a description by one of Jason's sailors of a picture or bas-relief he had seen somewhere during this trip along the northern coast of Asia Minor?

The voyage out was nothing compared with the return, both from Jason's point of view and from that of the historian who tries to track down the nuggets of fact behind the vagaries of tradition. One thing is clear: the *Argo* did not return the way it came. To avoid pursuit Jason charted a different course—and this is where the trouble begins. The various versions of the legend bring him home by different routes, each more fanciful than the next. One actually has it that the crew carried the ship all across Europe, launched it in the North Sea, and sailed it back around Spain and through the Strait of Gibraltar. The poet Pindar, who, writing in the fifth century B.C., is, except for Homer, the earliest to describe the journey, takes the ship to the western Mediterranean and the shores of Libya before taking it back safely to Greece—but Pindar's virtuosity lies in his glorious imagination, not his historical accuracy. Sophocles, that most level-headed of dramatists, happens in a certain passage to drop the remark that the Argonauts sailed out along the southern shore of the Black Sea and back along the north. This makes complete sense—just how complete we shall see in a moment.

If Jason was to return by a different route he had but two alternatives: either to strike boldly across the open sea and follow a straight line from Colchis to the Bosporus, or else to coast along the northern shore. He could hardly have hesitated in making up his mind: if he had left Iolcus at the very beginning of the sailing season, the first days of spring, the time spent in the voyage out and at Aea would have used up the rest of spring and most of the summer; he would have faced an extended sail through open waters with winter coming on, and that was out of the question. Even if his course had lain across familiar instead of totally unknown waters, a cramped open galley wasn't the ship for this sort of routing. The Argonauts must have done it the slow way, groping timidly along the strange coast of southern Russia. And as they worked farther and farther north, and winter overtook them, they must inevitably have run into a phenomenon completely out of their ken—ice.

It was during this leg of the voyage, the legend has it, that the *Argo* encountered its most nerve-racking adventure, the passage through the "wandering rocks." These became famous in Greek mythology. Homer has Circe carefully brief Odysseus about them when he was taking off on a course that brought him into waters the *Argo* had passed through. And well she might. Storms and high winds and shoals and the like were nothing new to Mediterranean sailors. But what must have amazed the Argonauts, or Odysseus, or any other son of Greece who knew only its mild equable climate, were the ice floes off the wintry Russian shores. A blow from one could easily leave a ship like the *Argo* a mass of splintered wreckage. The climax of Jason's report must surely have been his description of these monstrous formations which floated about so dangerously that only a master hand at the helm could bring a ship safely through them. The details would become more lurid with each telling, and it should not have taken many generations for the floes to become Homer's "precipitous cliffs against which the giant swell of Amphitrite breaks with a shattering roar."

What of the grueling portage of twelve days' duration? On the northern shores of the Black Sea, the peninsula of the Crimea thrusts downward for some one hundred miles, marking off the Sea of Azov on the east. The Argonauts, following the coastline, would automatically wander into this body of water and find themselves in an icy cul-de-sac. We can easily imagine that a portage across the neck of the peninsula to the open water on the west, despite its obvious hardship, would look to them preferable to fighting their way back through the floes of the Sea of Azov to its mouth, running once again the gantlet of the "wandering rocks."

Mankind likes to treasure the names of the men who do things first, who invent or discover. Whatever the reason for which the *Argo* made its journey—whether for gold as I have suggested, whether for commerce, with the fleece symbolizing the golden grain of the Crimea that was to become so important later in the Greek economy; whether, as the mythologists suggest, Jason "the healer" traveled east toward the dawn in search of the golden clouds that would "heal" the parchedness of his arid homeland—Jason's name must be added to the list. The expedition he headed was the first we know of that sailed forth to explore new lands. There were, to be sure, maritime explorers of earlier date than he. Cretan skippers, as we have seen, made their way westward and traveled the waters up to Sicily centuries before the *Argo* set sail. But their names have been lost; we know of their accomplishment only through a dim spoor of potsherds. History in its wayward fashion has preserved the name of Jason. We don't know who next duplicated his feat, since the second person to do or find something is rarely remembered; but a second there surely was, and a third and so on until—it was a long process and took a number of centuries—a once mysterious body of water became totally familiar. The earlier navigators called the Black Sea the *Pontos Axeinos*, the "unfriendly sea." They soon changed it to *Pontos Euxeinos*, "friendly sea."

Chapter 7

WESTWARD HO!

THERE WAS A TIME when sailors, leaving behind the seas they knew, turned their prows toward the west, into uncharted waters, and stumbled upon a new world. The effect was electrifying. Nations rushed men to explore and colonize the new territories, freighters to trade with them, and warships to settle disputes. History in a way was only repeating itself when the Portuguese opened up Africa, and the Spanish, America. The first great age of western discovery and colonization took place almost two and a half millennia earlier, and the principal roles were played by the Greeks and the Phoenicians.

The years around 1200 B.C. mark a critical period in the history of the eastern Mediterranean. This was when huge migrations of aggressive peoples, such as those thrown back by Ramses III at the doors of Egypt (Chapter 4), descended upon the area and snuffed out much of the thriving civilization that was there. On the seas, lawlessness prevailed: rovers such as the Tjekers who so troubled Wenamon or pirate bands such as the ones Odysseus described (Chapter 5) prowled unchecked and all but banished trade from the water. Over the Greek world a dark age descended that lasted until 900 B.C. or so. The evidence for it is provided almost wholly by archaeology but it is nonetheless clear. The finds reveal that during these centuries communities of the Mycenaean Age had become far smaller and meaner, had lost all signs of wealth, and had hardly any objects from other places, indicating that trade was minimal. From 900 B.C. on things slowly got better, and ultimately a new civilization began to emerge—that of the Greeks familiar to us from written history.

Conditions on the sea started to improve even earlier, about 1000 B.C., and merchants once again were willing to send goods to destinations overseas. Here was an opening for some enterprising maritime people, and there happened to be one such available to seize it—the inhabitants of that part of the coast of the Levant where the great ports of Byblos, Tyre, and Sidon lay. They had been keen and active traders as far back as the days when they sold boatloads of Lebanese cedar to Snefru of Egypt (Chapter 2). Now their descendants, the Phoenicians—to give them the name they bear in history from this point on—become major figures in the burgeoning trade of the eastern Mediterranean. Their geographical location was ideal. From Tyre and Sidon routes led into the hinterland and beyond, connecting eventually with India, and over them caravans brought to Phoenician warehouses the luxury products of the east. Just to the south lay Egypt, which had connections with Arabia and Somalia (Chapter 2), the prime sources of frankincense and myrrh. No other nation was as well located to serve as middleman in the distribution of wares from all these quarters.

It is hard to tell much in detail about the Phoenicians. Even their name is a puzzle. They called themselves Sidonians, from the city that was their chief center until Tyre outstripped it about the beginning of the first millennium B.C., and their land Canaan. It was the Greeks who named them *Phoinikes*, which some linguists think comes from a root meaning "sea" but which most connect with the Greek adjective *phoinos*, "dark red." The Phoenicians made a specialty of dyeing textiles, using certain species of a sea snail, Murex, which has a glandular secretion that produces various shades of red and purple. (There are actual hills outside of Tyre and Sidon today, made up from bottom to top of the shells of these creatures discarded by the ancient dye factories.) To their Greek customers the Phoenicians may have seemed principally textile traders, "red(-garment)" men. They were businessmen first and foremost, they produced no poets or historians to chronicle their accomplishments for posterity—and their business ledgers have gone the way of all such objects. Moreover, being more interested in profit than publicity, they kept their trade secrets to themselves. The story is told that once, when a Phoenician merchant was being tailed by a foreign skipper out to discover the source of certain trade items, he deliberately ran his ship on the rocks to thwart such snooping. To honor this heroic sacrifice on behalf of the national income, the government rewarded him not with anything trivial like a statue or monument but with reimbursement in toto for all loss sustained.

They were sharp traders. Vergil portrays Dido, the first queen of the Phoenician colony of Carthage, as a romantic figure who commits suicide after an unhappy love affair with Aeneas, but even she was a canny hand at driving a bargain. Legend has it that, when she was founding Carthage, she made a deal with the natives on the site to pay them an annual rent for as much land as a bull's hide could cover. She then skived a hide and managed to encircle with the pieces enough ground for an imposing city. The Dutch—another people that needed no lessons in trading—hardly did better when they bought Manhattan Island for twenty-four dollars' worth of trinkets. The Phoenicians even had ways of handling barter with natives whose language they couldn't understand. Herodotus, the inquisitive Greek of the fifth century B.C. who is called the Father of History but could just as appropriately be called the Father of the Travelogue, had a keen eye for a good story, and he reports that the Phoenician colonists of Carthage would arrive at a native village and

> unload their wares and lay them out in a row along the beach. Then they would go back aboard their ships and raise a smoke signal. The natives, seeing the smoke, would come down to the shore, lay out an amount of gold in exchange for the goods, and draw back some paces from them. Then the Carthaginians would come ashore and take a look. If the gold seemed up to the value of the goods, they picked it up and left; if not, they went back aboard ship and sat there. Then the natives would approach and keep adding to the gold until the sellers were satisfied.

The reputation for honesty that, judging by this story, they had among savages was not always maintained among other customers. Their merchants were often ready to pick up extra money in shady transactions, especially in the slave traffic. Odysseus' swineherd, for example, born a free Greek, had been kidnaped and sold on the block by a crew that originally dropped in at his island for legitimate barter.

The Phoenicians were involved in some celebrated business deals. When King Solomon was about to proceed with the building of his famous temple about 970 B.C. and needed timber, he naturally turned to Phoenicia with its well-known Lebanese cedar and negotiated a contract. He wrote to Hiram, who was king of the great export center of Tyre at the time:

> Now therefore command thou that they hew me cedar trees out of Lebanon; and my servants shall be with thy servants: and unto thee will I give hire for thy servants according to all that thou shalt appoint: for thou knowest that there is not among us any that can skill to hew timber like unto the Sidonians. . . .
>
> And Hiram sent to Solomon, saying, I have considered the things which thou sentest to me for: and I will do all thy desire concerning timber of cedar, and concerning timber of fir.
>
> My servants shall bring them down from Lebanon unto the sea: and I will convey them by sea in floats unto the place that thou shalt appoint me, and will cause them to be discharged there, and thou shalt receive them: and thou shalt accomplish my desire, in giving food for my household.
>
> So Hiram gave Solomon cedar trees and fir trees according to all his desire.
>
> And Solomon gave Hiram twenty thousand measures of wheat for food to his household, and twenty measures of pure oil: thus gave Solomon to Hiram year by year.

In the days before money was invented, a buyer had the choice of paying in uncoined precious metal, or of bartering. It was because Solomon had no access to gold—he had to exchange Palestinian wheat and oil for his timber—that he entered into his next business operation with the Phoenicians.

For centuries the inhabitants of the northern end of the Persian Gulf had been trading with India and Arabia and Africa (Chapter 2). The products involved were for the most part luxuries: ivory, silks, and spices from India; ivory and incense from Africa; incense and perfumes from Arabia. The profits were correspondingly large. Solomon, though he controlled a port on the appropriate waters in Ezion Geber at the southern end of the Negev, ruled a nation that had no merchant marine or, for that matter, no experience with the sea at all, and was consequently in the exasperating position of seeing all this lucrative trade bypass him. What arrived at the Persian Gulf was transported for Mediterranean distribution by caravan to the Phoenician ports, especially Tyre; what came to Egypt was floated downriver to the mouth of the Nile and carried from there in Phoenician bottoms. Even the Phoenicians, though so much of the trade passed through their hands, were not satisfied: they had to share the profits with caravaneers in the one case or Egyptian middlemen in the other. So when Solomon conceived the idea of building a fleet of his own which, working out of Ezion Geber, could trade with India—for that is most probably what Ophir, the place-name he uses, refers to—and of manning it with Phoenician sailors, Hiram didn't have to be asked twice:

> And king Solomon made a navy of ships in Ezion-geber, which is beside Eloth, on the shore of the Red sea, in the land of Edom.
> And Hiram sent in the navy his servants, shipmen that had knowledge of the sea, with the servants of Solomon.
> And they came to Ophir, and fetched from thence gold, four hundred and twenty talents, and brought it to king Solomon.

From Egypt in the south to Asia Minor in the north and westward to Cyprus, Rhodes, and Crete, Phoenicians had the trade routes more or less to themselves for the centuries between ca. 1000 and 800 B.C. It must have been some time during this period—the date cannot be fixed exactly—that they passed along to the Greeks one of the greatest gifts that the East was to give to the West. The Phoenicians, unlike their neighbors who wrote in complicated hieroglyphs or cuneiform, used an alphabetic system of writing that a Semitic people had invented, probably centuries earlier. In the course of trading operations, most likely in the lower Aegean area, some of their merchants brought it to the attention of Greeks, who immediately recognized its superlative convenience and swiftly adapted it for writing their language. Subsequently they in turn gave it to the Romans, who passed it on to the Western world. In this transfer the Phoenicians were not creators but middlemen. Their next great contribution was one that they conceived and carried out completely by themselves.

Even in the great days of Minoan and Mycenaean expansion (Chapter 2), the western limit of the ancient world had been Sicily and Sardinia. Beyond this lay uncharted seas and terra incognita. Not long after the turbulent conditions that prevailed in the Mediterranean between 1200 and 1000 B.C. had calmed down, daring Phoenician sailors headed their prows into the waters beyond. Within a short time they had put the stamp of success on their venture by planting the outposts of Utica and Carthage in North Africa, not far from where Tunis is today. Phoenicians rarely did anything for mere curiosity or adventure; it must have been maritime commerce that was the attraction. Their merchants are next reported sailing even beyond Gibraltar into the Atlantic to trade with Tartessus, as the coast of Spain beyond the strait was called. Here the natives mined silver locally, but, even more important, here tin was to be had, a metal that was much in demand for two reasons: there were no deposits easily available in the Mediterranean area, and it was of vital importance because, fused with copper, it forms bronze. The tin to be bought at Tartessus came from regions farther north, so far out of the ken of the ancient mariner that he long knew them only vaguely as the "Tin Isles"; the best guess is that the source was Cornwall in England. Around 800 B.C. or so the Phoenicians set themselves up permanently in the far west by establishing on a fine harbor beyond the strait the key center of Gadir, or Cadiz, as we call it now.

The first great line of travel the Phoenicians laid down was from Tyre to Utica and Carthage. Climate and current dictated the next step. The western Mediterranean is swept by northwest winds during the summer months, which made up the ancient mariner's chief period of activity. To sail westward along the North African coast from Utica or Carthage was to risk a lee shore and buck a hostile current in the bargain. By working to the north at the outset, and following a general southwesterly slant from there to the strait and using the African shore only for the homeward leg, Phoenician skippers were assured of favorable wind and current for the round-trip. And so the Phoenicians planted way stations at strategic points: on Sardinia for that first leg northward, on Ibiza and the Spanish Mediterranean coast for the long slant to the strait, and in the neighborhood of Algiers or Oran for the homeward lap. No details about any part of this striking achievement are known. The Phoenicians wanted no competitors, and they not only were tight-lipped about what they were doing but even surrounded their activities with an effective smoke screen of sailors' yarns no doubt filled with hair-raising details of shipwrecks and sea monsters.

It was the colony of Carthage that was destined to become the greatest Phoenician center in the western Mediterranean. According to legend, its founding took place under the leadership of Queen Dido. It carried out a program of colonization of its own, sending out expeditions to explore and occupy new sites and to convert former way stations into full-sized communities. By 700 B.C., Carthagians had moved into Sardinia, had founded several colonies in Sicily, including Palermo with its fine natural harbor, and had planted Malaga plus a few other towns on the Mediterranean coast of Spain. Their ships even traversed the Strait of Gibraltar to sail down the African coast and establish there a pair of colonies, one as far south as Mogador due west of Marrakesh. This took care of the new territory to the west, but there was still the link to the homeland far to the east to think about. So Carthage occupied Pantelleria and Malta, which, combined with Phoenician settlements that had long been established on Crete and Rhodes and Cyprus, gave it a set of convenient stepping-stones back to the home port of Tyre.

Carthage's work was now complete. The west was fully open—but to Phoenicians alone. Through a wide-flung network of stations, the trade in tin from the Atlantic coast and in silver and lead and iron from Spain was firmly in her hands. She became one of the foremost powers of the ancient world. But over three centuries had now passed since the Phoenicians had discovered this new world, and during this time another energetic maritime people had embarked upon a career of colonization.

While Phoenicia was sailing the eastern and western Mediterranean with a completely free hand, the Greek world was emerging from the dark age that had fallen upon it when massive invading migrations destroyed the brilliant civilization of the Mycenaean Age. By 800 B.C. it had by and large taken the shape it was to have in its heyday three centuries later. It was a conglomeration of independent cities that dotted not only the peninsula of Greece but also the islands of the Aegean Sea, Crete, Rhodes, Cyprus, and, above all, the western coast of Asia Minor. Their vessels, merchantmen and warships, once again plied the sea in numbers. The time was ripe for Greece to embark on its own program of colonization.

The Phoenicians had picked out a limited number of commercially advantageous sites and exploited them for trade; their impress was only skin-deep. The Greeks, between 750 and 550 B.C., in a series of concerted bursts of activity, settled themselves the length and breadth of the Mediterranean and the Black Sea, "like frogs round a pond," as Plato put it. They founded in the neighborhood of 250 colonies, a number of which have had a continuous existence ever since. In a way it was like administering injections of Greek culture into the body of barbarism at 250 different points. Most of them took, whether the recipients were Scyths on the shores of southern Russia, Italians in southern Italy, or Gauls at the mouth of the Rhone. In a very real sense, the boatloads of Greeks that crossed the sea in those two centuries were the advance guard of Western civilization.

Like the Phoenicians, Greek colonists usually picked sites for hard-fisted commercial reasons. When they settled Syracuse in 733 B.C. or the site of Istanbul in 658, they took over two harbors that were among the very best in the Mediterranean and that were ideally located for trade. But the people who joined in the founding expeditions were not all merchants and sailors. Often they were poverty-stricken peasants (the soil of Greece is so poor that the threat of overpopulation has dogged the country during almost the whole of its existence) who went out to the colonies in much the same spirit as the southern Italians and Sicilians who flocked to America at the beginning of this century. Sometimes they were political exiles from their home; there were even cases when out-of-power parties would quit en masse and join a group leaving to found some new city overseas. Rhegium is a good example of the mixed motives that lay behind a Greek colony. It was planted in a perfect position to command the trade that passed through the Strait of Messina between Sicily and the mainland; yet its founders included one-tenth of the population of the Greek city of Chalcis who were bidden to leave because of famine, as well as a band of political exiles from southern Greece. Many men must have gone along on colonizing expeditions simply for the ride, for the sheer adventure of it. The Greeks were wanderers at heart—it was no accident that the story of Odysseus was one of their national epics—and they were to be found knocking about odd corners of the ancient world at all times. For such roving spirits the age of colonization must have offered unparalleled opportunities.

In some foundations commerce played no part whatsoever. Many of the little colonies that lined the sole and instep of the boot of Italy were agricultural communities purely and simply; the founders had left the old country because of hard times, to build homes in a new territory that was a land of milk and honey by comparison. Occasionally a city literally transplanted itself because life had become unbearable, generally for political reasons, in the old site. The people of the

little town of Teos, for example, on the Asia Minor coast could not
stand the thought of living under the rule,of Persia, a mighty empire
that was aggressively extending its way westward; and when that
threat appeared the whole populace moved and established itself on
the coast of Thrace. Tarentum—Taranto today—was founded as a
refuge for a group of political exiles from Sparta. It was the only permanent colony that that ultraconservative city planted, and one of the
stories about the Spartans that made the rounds in ancient days offered an interesting reason. Toward the end of the eighth century
B.C. the Spartans left for a war that took them twenty years to win.
When they returned they found—and viewed with considerable disfa-
vor—a group of almost full-grown children, obviously born during
these two decades. After some complications these "sons of virgins," as
they were called, since they were rather too public proof of the dilu-
tion of the pure blood the Spartans were so proud of, were packed off
in a group to continue their lives elsewhere, and the founding of Tarentum was the result.

There is a good deal known about the way in which the Greeks went
about founding a colony. The initiative always came from a particular
city, although outsiders, as long as they were Greek, could and very
often were encouraged to participate. A smallish town like Megara,
for example, which was responsible for an incredible number of settlements, would have completely drained off its population without help
from outside. The first step was to appoint an "oecist," or founder, to
lead the expedition. Since he played the major role, the colony he succeeded in planting often worshiped him after his death. Even when all
details about the founding of a given place were lost, the oecist's name
lived on; they were the William Penns and Roger Williamses of their
age. The oecist's first step was to consult the famous oracle of Apollo
at Delphi about a site to colonize. Usually the priests of the shrine had
got intelligence of the desired location or locations and simply went
ahead and confirmed one or the other, provided no conflicts were involved. The Delphic Oracle performed a vital function in this period:
it was the priests' responsibility to see that clashes were avoided by,
among other things, diverting colonies that looked as if they would
encroach on previously established foundations, and on the whole
they did their work well. Their role was rather like that played by the
Vatican when, at the end of the fifteenth century, it headed off a po-
tentially ugly situation by setting up a dividing line in the new world
between Portugal and Spain.

All the next steps are lost. No ancient writer ever bothered to tell
how the ships were collected, what they were like, how they were
loaded, or how the oecist managed to keep his sanity during a voyage,

often lasting over a month, in which he had to oversee men, women, and children—and assorted livestock—who were leaving all the certainties of a traditional homeland for the most uncertain of futures. The only hint of detail saved through the centuries is the random mention of a colonist who, en route to found Syracuse, swapped his allotment of land for a homemade cake; whether because he was that hungry or that drunk or that homesick for something from the past is not divulged.

The colonists as a rule were spared the rigors and dangers of landing on an unknown shore. Sailors and traders had long before scouted the site, determined the number and state of mind of the natives, and forwarded reports to the founding city (some of which no doubt found their way to the priests at Delphi), and the area had even been apportioned into lots for distribution. Sometimes the natives welcomed the newcomers. When the group that founded Marseilles landed, so the story goes, they were invited to a native bridal ceremony where the chief's daughter, in accordance with immemorial custom, was to hand a cup of water to the one among the young braves she wanted to marry. With an unerring eye, in the best Pocahontas tradition, she picked the newly arrived oecist. Not such charming anecdotes but sober records show that often enough the Greeks drove the natives out, although usually they managed to achieve some sort of accommodation with them. Sometimes, as was to be expected, whole colonies were lost as completely as Sir Walter Raleigh's ill-starred settlement on Roanoke Island. Three tries were needed to found Abdera on the Thracian coast; the natives wiped out the first two expeditions and the third took hold only because the entire population of a Greek city decided to emigrate there to escape Persian bondage.

The only allegiance a colony owed its "metropolis," its "mother city" as the Greeks put it, was sentimental: the fire on the sacred hearth of the new foundation was kindled with flame taken from the hearth at home; familiar place-names were applied to the new environment like the "New England," "New York," or "New London" of American colonial days. If, as often happened, the daughter decided to send out a colonizing party on her own, she would give the metropolis the privilege of supplying an oecist, and if the mother city got involved in a war the daughters usually could be depended upon to support her.

Practically every established Greek city took part in the movement overseas to some extent and boasted one or more colonial offspring. But there were two key figures, particularly from the point of view of commercial expansion. The one, Corinth, concentrated her attention on the west, the other, Miletus, on the east.

Eastward of the Mediterranean lay the Black Sea. It was outside the orbit of the early Greeks, and their ships had not cut its waters since the pioneering voyage of Jason and his Argonauts. A formidable pair of gates barred it: the straits of the Dardanelles and the Bosporus. During the summer months, the prime period of activity for the ancient mariner, a ship going through had to sail almost into the eye of the prevailing northeasterlies and buck a current that spilled out of the sea beyond like a millrace. Yet once through, not only was the sailing clear but the returns were substantial. On the north shore the rich fields of the Crimea produced surpluses of wheat that could be sold at good prices in the grain-poor cities of Greece; the shallow waters teemed with fish; and on the south coast there were gold and silver and iron to be mined.

On the lower part of the western coast of Asia Minor, less than two hundred miles from the Dardanelles, stood the city of Miletus. It is a pile of ruins now; the harbor has silted up and the focus of trade moved elsewhere. But beginning with the eighth century B.C. and long thereafter, it was a great commercial center. Its merchants sent their ships southeast to Phoenicia, south to Egypt, and west to Italy, and enticed to their warehouses caravans bearing products from the Asia Minor hinterland and beyond. Its sheep breeders developed a prized quality of wool that commanded a market everywhere and its cabinet-makers were known for the fine furniture they turned out. The city, by mingling its native Greek culture with the rich foreign influences that rode in on its far-flung trade, acquired a reputation for intellectual distinction as well. Two of its natives haunted the bustling quays, listened to the reports of returning sailors who had scouted sites for colonies or helped found them or gone out on trading voyages, and, collating this material, launched the twin sciences of cartography and geography: Anaximander of Miletus around 550 B.C. drew up the first map of the inhabited portion of the earth; half a century later, Hecataeus of Miletus published an improved version along with the first work of geography, a book (now lost) entitled *Circuit of the Earth*, which described the known world from Spain to India. Thales, the first and one of the greatest of the Greek scientific philosophers, was a native, and along with his fundamental study of the nature of the universe found time, like a good Milesian, to work out a geometrical procedure for determining the position of a ship at sea and even, one year, to make a financial killing by cornering the olive-press market.

By the eighth century B.C. the skilled mariners of Miletus, along with those of Megara and perhaps other Greek cities, found out how to make their way into the Black Sea. They discovered that favorable southwesterlies were to be picked up along the Dardanelles and

Bosporus during the early weeks of spring, that the hostile current created favorable eddies along the shores, and that even in summer a ship could go through on the night breeze that blew up the straits. In the seventh and sixth centuries B.C. Miletus dotted the Sea of Marmora and the northern and southern shores of the Black Sea with colonies. The site of Istanbul with its superb harbor, the famous "Golden Horn," ideally located on the European side of the Bosporus, fell to the lot of the little town of Megara, which planted on it the colony of Byzantium; perhaps its ships beat Miletus' to the spot. Even Megara needed two chances, for the first colonists it sent out passed up the site and settled on the Asiatic shore opposite instead; this so exasperated the priests of the Delphic Oracle that, when a second expedition was readied seventeen years later, they waspishly instructed the oecist to settle opposite the city "of the blind." But the Black Sea was almost a Milesian lake: the tons of wheat and fish shipped out annually were financed by the traders and bankers, and hauled by the skippers, of Miletus and its colonies. To make things perfect, its ships did not have to return in ballast. They arrived loaded with Greek pottery and bronze manufactures, which had a ready sale among the natives, as well as with wine and olive oil for the Greek colonists of the northern shore, who never acquired a taste for the local beverages or learned to cook with the local butter and were eager customers for these reminders of life in the old country.

The city of Corinth had a unique location. It commanded the isthmus that connects the northern portion of Greece with the Peloponnese. Its ships could take off from a harbor on the east of the isthmus into the Aegean and, from one on the opposite shore, could proceed straight through the Corinthian Gulf to the west; every other Greek city had to send its freighters the long way around the Peloponnese to get to the west.

Many centuries earlier, Minoan and Mycenaean traders used to come regularly to the shores of Sicily and southern Italy and sell their wares to the peoples living there (Chapter 2). But this contact had long ago become a thing of the past, and now, a half millennium later, uncivilized tribes inhabited the areas, while north of Naples the peninsula of Italy was controlled by a powerful and warlike people called the Etruscans. The first Greek ships that in this age sailed through the strait between Sicily and the mainland and entered the Tyrrhenian Sea quickly discovered two things: that the Etruscans held the waters from this point northward, and that they would buy practically any Greek manufactures offered them. And so it was natural that the first settlement in this new Greek penetration into the west, founded probably about 750 B.C., was on the little island of Ischia off Naples, a strategic location for an entrepôt to serve Greek and Etruscan. Within twenty years Corinth had entered the field: in 733 it planted the colony of Syracuse on the site of one of the finest harbors in the eastern Mediterranean. In the next few decades a dozen towns sprang up along the coasts of Sicily and southern Italy, but Syracuse's position and its harbor, backed up by Corinth's trade, guaranteed it preeminence. In the earliest finds on all these sites, archaeologists have uncovered the products of various Greek states; within a generation, the finds are prevailingly Corinthian. A monopoly had begun that was to last for a century.

Other Greek cities had established colonies on both sides of the Strait of Messina. Corinth negotiated treaties to give it right of way and, with Syracuse recognized as the distribution point for most products from Greece, its trading position was set. But only in the eastern part of the island. When the Carthaginians decided to move into Sicily, finding the eastern half firmly in Greek hands, they laid hold of the western. The Greek colony nearest them, Selinus, as a result of its location was always in a tight spot. It traded with its Carthaginian neighbors as well as with their home base on the African coast opposite, and, when Greeks and Carthaginians eventually came to blows, it could never be trusted to put sentiment before business.

Corinthian ships arrived loaded with fine pottery, oil and perfume; Egyptian work such as faience, amulets, and scarabs; and heavy loads of marble (the local rock was too soft for first-rate building stone). What wasn't distributed from Syracuse to eastern Sicily continued through the strait to the Naples area for sale to the Etruscans. The latter paid for their imports in refined metals, while Sicily paid in the product so all-important to the Greek economy, wheat. Around 600 B.C. Corinth's trade was so prosperous that it found itself faced with a real problem: its superb location on an isthmus, which made commerce in both directions possible, also forced it to maintain duplicate navies, one on the eastern side to guard its interests in Asia Minor and Syria and Egypt, and one on the western for its interests in western Greece and Sicily and southern Italy. Similarly, its merchants who were involved in shipping goods from ports in the east to those in the west either had to portage their cargoes over the isthmus or send their ships on the arduous voyage around the Peloponnese. Periander, who ruled Corinth at the time, toyed with the idea of cutting a canal but gave it up as too big a project (one wasn't actually attempted until the time of Nero, who had the vast resources of the whole Roman Empire at his disposal; see Chapter 17). He did the next best thing: he built an ancient version of a marine railway—a *diolkos*, as it was called—over three miles long. It was a road, carefully paved with limestone slabs and so engineered that all grades were held to a minimum, that spanned the isthmus. A pair of tracks was cut in the stone surface and on them rode a wheeled platform, probably pulled by oxen. The *diolkos* enabled warships, which were light and slender, to be efficiently switched from one side of the isthmus to the other, eliminating the need for duplicate navies. No doubt small merchant craft traveled over it as well, while the larger merchant ships, too heavy to be put on the *diolkos*, would have their cargo do the traveling instead—including even cargoes of massive timbers or of the ponderous blocks of stone for building or sculpture that the Aegean islands shipped westward, materials that would be far beyond the capacity of porters or beasts of burden. Corinth no doubt made this eminently desirable facility available, at an appropriate fee, to all merchants, collecting thereby a tidy income.

About 550 B.C. Corinth began to lose its tight monopoly in Sicily and southern Italy. From this point on, Athenian and not Corinthian pottery prevails in the archaeological excavations. It was just about this time, too, that the Sicilian cities began to coin their own money. Barter was all right for the strict exchange of wheat for Corinth's manufactures, but money gave a town more latitude in its choice of commercial contacts. The versatile Corinthian merchants shrewdly met the changed conditions: they sold the cities the silver needed for coinage and they supplied Athens with bottoms to haul its newly acquired trade in pottery.

Beyond Sicily lay the far west, a vast and vital area that the Phoenicians had turned into their private preserve. If a story that Herodotus tells can be believed, it was a sheer fluke that first brought the Greeks into this quarter and opened their eyes to its value. A certain Colaeus, skipper of a vessel from Samos, an island off the western coast of Asia Minor, on one occasion had particularly bad luck with the winds. Headed for Egypt, sometime around 650 B.C., he was first blown off course and forced to land well west of his destination, at Cyrene on the North African coast, a little west of where Derna now stands. He took on fresh provisions, raised anchor, shaped a course once more for Egypt, and this time was caught in an easterly gale, probably the same sort that seven hundred years later was to carry St. Paul from Crete to shipwreck off Malta. Colaeus scudded before it the whole length of the sea and even through the Strait of Gibraltar, and finally reached land in Tartessus, the Spanish coast just beyond the strait, whose natives had never seen Greek products, much less Greeks. He was able to turn in his cargo, probably chiefly Samian pottery and wine, for a fabulous amount of silver and came back home a millionaire.

It was neither his home port on Samos nor any of the major commercial centers of Greece that capitalized on his discovery, but a relatively small Greek town whose sailors had a reputation for skill and daring even in this age of maritime enterprise. The city of Phocaea stood on the western coast of Asia Minor, in the eastern sphere of Greek civilization. But it was to play in the far west the role that Corinth had played in Sicily and Miletus around the Black Sea.

The Phocaeans had the sagacity to take to the sea not in merchantmen but in warships, swift galleys called penteconters, or "fiftiers," because of the number of oars they carried. Moreover, they probably traveled in packs and not singly. Phoenicians and their colonists, the Carthaginians, firmly established in the western Mediterranean, may have been able to discourage Greek freighters from entering those waters, but a flotilla of Phocaean penteconters, stripped for action, was a different matter. The Phocaeans were friendly with the powers that controlled the Strait of Messina and had even been granted the privilege of toll-free passage. Beyond, they carried out a skillfully organized program of voyaging that brought them past the Strait of Gibraltar into the tin and silver depot of Tartessus. There are even vague rumors that their skippers ventured farther into the Atlantic, one along the Spanish coast toward the source of the tin, and another southward along the Moroccan coast.

But another accomplishment of the Phocaeans was more significant if not as spectacular. They explored the Gulf of Lion to the south of France and, about 600 B.C., planted a colony called Massilia, the Marseilles of today, at the mouth of the Rhône, a door through which the culture first of Greece and then of Rome was to pass to the whole of France. From here they spread east and west. When they had finished, the Spanish and French coasts, from a bit east of Malaga, which the Phoenicians held, to Nice was firmly settled by Greeks.

The Phocaeans had not only carried out their colonizing in an aggressive and orderly manner, but they had picked a perfect time, about 600 B.C., a period when Phoenician hands were tied. Tyre was busy with wars back home and in Carthage with running help to its colonies in Sicily to fend off attacks from the neighboring Greeks. Once the Phoenicians were free of these entanglements, clash was inevitable. The first took place in 535 B.C. Spurred on by troubles with Persia back home, the Phocaeans elected to move out lock, stock, and barrel and establish a new home elsewhere. As always, they picked a spot with care: the expedition landed on the strategically placed island of Corsica. Neither the Carthaginians nor the Etruscans, who held the seas north of the island, could afford to overlook this. The result was the first of a series of great naval battles. Despite heavy odds—the enemy fleet was precisely twice as large—the Phocaeans held their own, but the victory was a Pyrrhic one: by the end of the day they had lost two-thirds of their vessels and the rest were badly damaged. The remnants of the expedition abandoned the attempt to colonize Corsica and transferred to a site in southern Italy, well in Greek territory. The Carthaginians had taken the first step toward closing the Strait of Gibraltar to competitors. Two more naval engagements were fought in the next fifty years, and the Greeks won both. But these were defensive actions: victory meant that they could maintain their hold on the eastern portion of Sicily, southern France, and northeastern Spain; the rest of the western Mediterranean belonged to Carthage, and by 480 B.C. it had bolted the gates of Gibraltar. The situation in the west was now fixed in the form it was to have until the coming of the Romans centuries later. The vital trade in tin from the Atlantic and in silver and lead and iron from Spain was an acknowledged Carthaginian monopoly.

In these days there was no one state that had the naval strength to police the seas. Every city involved in trade had to maintain its own fleet, not only to protect its merchantmen against the ubiquitous pirates (whose calling now as before had the status of a recognized profession) but also to repel attacks delivered by commercial rivals, since such attempts were an acknowledged means of discouraging competition. Carthaginians preyed on Greek shipping, Greeks on Carthaginian, and independents on both. The perfecting of men-of-war and the building up of navies went hand in hand with the planting of colonies and the opening up of trade routes.

When the fleets of Carthage and Phocaea clashed off the shores of Corsica in 535 B.C., it was no mere set-to of a pair of packs of Homeric rovers. The ships that fought that day were the result of centuries of improvement. Ever since the age of colonization had begun, the art of shipbuilding had not only been constantly refined but had become a major industry as shipyards worked to meet an ever-expanding demand. As one would expect, Corinth took the lead and its ship designers during this period achieved a reputation they were to hold for years.

The old undecked sea rover, efficient enough for raiding and piracy, was no vessel to protect the new long trade routes now flung across the Mediterranean. By 800 B.C. Greek shipbuilders were taking the basic steps toward creating the craft that was to serve as the standard ship of the line for the next thousand years. A revolution in design was carried out, every bit as sweeping in its time as the mounting of guns on shipboard in the fourteenth century or the introduction of ironclads in the nineteenth.

As in the case of so many other key changes in the ancient world, there are no written records to tell how this one took place. But the course can be followed, thanks to the Greeks' characteristic of insisting on artistic and interesting decoration for their jewelry and especially for their pottery, whether used to grace a banquet or carry slops. And, fortunately for the student of ancient ships, the painters of pottery in this age of colonization liked to include scenes of vessels in action.

A number of early pictures, dating probably from 850 to 750 B.C. (Pls. 14–18), though crude, reveal that a new type of warship had come into existence. It is one clearly derived from those used in Homer's day and before, for it has their rounded stern and straight prow, and the two give the "horned" effect that Homer had noted (Chapter 4). But a revolutionary new feature has been added. The vessel has been given an offensive weapon: from its prow juts a powerful pointed ram. This must have inaugurated a new era in naval tactics. No longer was a sea battle simply a match in which ships closed and the marines on each side fought it out, a sort of land fight transferred to shipboard, as in Ramses' successful attack on the sea raiders (Chapter 4). The ram changed all that: it shifted the emphasis to the men that manned the oars. Victory would go to the crew so trained that it could respond instantly and accurately to command and drive its ship to that point from which a blow of the ram could be launched at the enemy's vitals. Though war galleys continued to seek to grapple and board their opponents—that was a form of fighting that never disappeared—sea battles became more and more contests in maneuvering, the captains using the oars as, centuries later, men-of-war were to use their sails to attain the proper position for a broadside. The very earliest representation of a ram found so far, dating circa 850 B.C., is part of the decoration engraved on a safety pin excavated at Athens, and so, for the moment at least, the invention must be credited to the Greeks. The Phoenicians may have beat them to it, but we have no way of knowing, since they never adorned their pottery or jewelry with pictures of ships.

Homer's vessels had been open, undecked affairs. The new age required something more efficient and protected. A second radically new feature was added, a fighting platform from which the marines could function (Pls. 14, 18). It took the form of a deck that covered most but not all of the ship; it ran over the centerline from stem to stern but not from board to board. A space along the side was left open, and, when the vessel was merely cruising, the rowers sat at the level of the deck and worked their oars from there (Pls. 15, 16). In action such a position was dangerously exposed. The naval architects met this weakness by an ingenious device: they inserted a complete series of rowers' benches at a lower level. When a ship engaged in combat, the oarsmen took their places down there; with their heads well below the line of the deck they were protected from enemy darts and the only exposed personnel were the marines on it, directing fire against the opponents (Pl. 18). Oarsmen placed deep in the vessel for shelter during combat was a fine idea but hardly helpful if they suffocated; so the architects left the area between the upper and lower thwarts open as a low waist covered only with a kind of lattice (Pl. 15). This not only provided ventilation but also an escape hatch for emergencies. Movable panels probably closed in the open spaces between slats when the water was choppy. As we have seen (p. 40), the ancients worked their oars against tholepins instead of using oarlocks; the Greeks called these "keys," and in the paintings they have just that sort of shape (Pl. 17).

In the sixth century B.C. warships saw still more improvement (Pls. 19–21). The prow was straightened and lost its swept-back curve. The stern was finished off in a plume- or fan-like adornment, which became thereafter the distinguishing mark of the warship and was looked on, along with the ram, as a kind of naval scalp: victors cut them off vanquished vessels and took them home as trophies. The low waist and its lattice were almost completely eliminated and, as a result, the hull took on a sleeker, trimmer look (Pl. 21). Though ships manned by twenty rowers, as in Homer's day, were still in use (Pl. 19), larger types were favored because the more powerfully a ram was driven, the more damaging was its blow. Thirty-oared craft, triacontors, were now built for lighter work, and the ship of the line was the fifty-oared galley, the penteconter (Pl. 20). Twenty-four rowers lined each side, and two steering oarsmen at the stern filled out the complement. A single bank of oars was the only arrangement naval architects had hitherto used. It was not always completely successful. In the case of the penteconter it made for an excessively long and slender vessel, expensive to build, difficult to maneuver, and not particularly seaworthy. Yet to shorten it was out of the question, since this meant giving up some of the essential oar power.

Alternative seating of the oarsmen provided the clue for the next improvement in the penteconter. If a galley could be rowed either from the deck line or from some lower point, why not from both at once? And so the naval architects designed a new type of hull, one in which the twenty-four oarsmen were split into two superimposed banks, twelve along the gunwale, and twelve on thwarts below them

rowing through ports in the hull. To fit everybody in, the oars were
staggered so that each one of the upper bank was placed over the
space between two of the lower (Pls. 22, 23). The new craft were
shorter than the old by at least a third. They were more compact, far
sturdier, far more seaworthy—and offered a third less of a target to an
enemy ram. Yet not a rower had been sacrificed. The stage was now
set for the last step, the introduction of a third bank, but that came
somewhat later.

The earliest picture preserved of the new two-banked galley is in a
relief carved to adorn an Assyrian king's palace that was built between
705 and 681 B.C. (Pl. 22). The vessel must be Phoenician because the
Assyrians, having no navy of their own, used the fleets of the Phoenician cities which they controlled at this time. It is a lofty craft with a
full upper deck girt by a bulwark; clearly the designers were interested in providing space and protection for a good-sized complement
of marines. Shortly thereafter, two-banked galleys, lighter and lower
than the Phoenician type, appear on Greek pottery (Pl. 23). It is anybody's guess which of the two nations deserves credit for the invention. Whichever it was, the other quickly followed suit.

Greeks and Phoenicians were conservative when it came to rigging
their vessels. Almost all the new warships carried the same rig that
Mediterranean craft had for centuries, a single broad squaresail; a
very few were now equipped with two such squaresails. But the sails
were almost exclusively for cruising. In battle a vessel had to be able to
move in any direction in its efforts to get into position for a ram attack,
or to maneuver to avoid one, so it was impossible to depend on wind
alone. A captain, on going into action, generally ordered mast and sail
unstepped and left ashore—when stripped for action he had no space
aboard to store such bulky gear—and, from that moment on, depended solely on the muscles and reflexes of his oarsmen. Pirates, who
had to carry sail at all times in order to chase down merchantmen, to
meet their particular requirements actually worked out a special version of the two-banked galley, the *hemiolia* or "one and a half-er." It
was so constructed that, when the quarry was overtaken and the
boarding of it ready to begin, half the rowers in the upper bank, those
between the mast and the stern, were able to secure their oars and
leave the benches; this made available not only an ample space in the
after part of the ship into which mast and sail could be lowered and
stowed away, but a dozen or so hands to carry out the work (Pls. 24,
25).

Although many Greek cities designed and made their own craft,
others found it easier to turn to places that specialized in shipbuilding.
When, in 704 B.C., the island of Samos decided to create a navy, it

applied to Corinth and the latter sent it a topflight architect who superintended the construction of four vessels of the latest design, probably two-banked galleys. There is no telling how many units made up
a fleet at this time. When the Phocaeans fought against Carthage off
Corsica in 535, they managed to put sixty vessels into action and they
had a reputation for having a powerful navy; the Carthaginians, together with the Etruscans who joined them in the fight, had a force of
120.

Let us turn from the warships of the age to the merchantmen, the
sailing ships that were now carrying cargoes almost the length and
breadth of the Mediterranean. The Phoenicians went in for tubby vessels with rounded sterns and bows, and they particularly favored the
horse's head as figurehead for the prow; the Greeks dubbed these
craft *gauloi*, "tubs," because of their shape, or *hippoi*, "horses," because
of the figurehead. The best illustration we have of them appears on a
Hebrew seal of the eighth or seventh century B.C. (Pl. 26); obviously
the type appealed to other peoples of the Levant. The Greeks also
gave their merchantmen capacious well-rounded hulls, but they left
the stempost and sternpost bare of figureheads, preferring arching
curves instead (Pls. 24, 25). One particularly fine illustration shows a
handsome vessel that boasts the same concave bow that lends so much
distinction to our famous American clipper ships (Pls. 24, 25). The
merchant ship's rig is the traditional Mediterranean broad squaresail,
but it is now a great billowing spread that needs a complicated system
of brails. And there is at least one example—the earliest on record—of
a two-master. On the wall of a chamber in an Etruscan tomb that dates
about 500 B.C. is pictured a vessel that is like the other Greek merchantmen of the age in all respects save one: it has a foremast and
foresail (Pl. 27). The foremast has a distinctive forward rake and its
sail is slightly smaller than the main. The Greeks called such a sail an
artemon; it occurs frequently in representations of later date, where it
is much smaller and the mast it is set on has so pronounced a rake that
it slants over the bows (Pls. 42, 43, 45).

These vessels had to work hard. There were few convenient quays
in the ports where they put up; most of the time they simply loaded
onto a beach. And so they carried, lashed on deck, two types of landing
ladder: a short one for beaches that dropped abruptly and steeply,
where they could come in quite close, and a longer one for those occasions when they had to stand farther off on a beach that shelved gradually (Pl. 24).

Around 550 B.C. the vast movement from homeland to colony came to
a halt. The Mediterranean was now a far different place from what it

had been almost a half millennium earlier when the Phoenicians embarked on their pioneering voyages or when the Greeks entered the field two centuries later. Shores that had been uninhabited or populated only by barbarian tribes were now dotted with flourishing colonies. Trade routes crisscrossed the whole of the sea from Cadiz beyond the Strait of Gibraltar to the far eastern shores of the Black Sea, from the mouth of the Po to that of the Nile. Scholars, digesting the mass of information brought back from all these quarters, compiled it and constructed maps from it and inaugurated thereby the science of geography. A half-dozen Greek states had become significant maritime powers, backing their commercial and political interests with strong navies. The fifty-oared galley of Homer's day, redesigned to carry a ram and with its rowers split into two compact banks, had emerged as a first-rate fighting ship. It had seen action in some sharp clashes, especially in the west between Greeks and Carthaginians.

But this was just the dawn of a great age of naval warfare. Within little more than a half-century, battles were to be fought whose names may be found in every history book; and the fine new two-banked galleys were to lie rotting in the yards, rendered obsolete by still another ingenious advance in naval architecture.

Chapter 8

THE WOODEN WALLS

ON THE MORNING of September 23, 480 B.C., Xerxes, ruler of the vast Persian Empire, "king of kings," walked up a hill just west of Athens and sat down on a golden chair set there by his servants. Behind him smoke rose from the city: his soldiers had capped a successful march through northern Greece with the sack of Athens. At his feet glistened the waters of a narrow sound, a mile wide and somewhat over three miles long, which separated the island of Salamis from the mainland. Against the farther shore lay the whole of the Greek fleet, a mélange of contingents from the chief cities. It was tightly corked up in the sound by Persian squadrons stationed at each entrance. The king gave the order to his admirals to move in for the kill and relaxed in his chair for a bird's-eye view of the impending destruction.

Ten years earlier Persia, a nation that covered as much territory as the United States, under Xerxes' father had attempted to conquer Greece, a land smaller than New York State. The attack had been repulsed—much to the surprise of both sides. Now the son was on the point of finishing the job. His land forces had fought their way through northern Greece to Athens; all he had to do was wipe out the enemy's fleet and he could just about write finis to the war. Everything was in his favor: his troops controlled most of the neighboring shores, his ships outnumbered the Greeks at least two to one, and, to top it all, a message received at his headquarters the day before had convinced him that a key Greek commander, Themistocles, was ready to turn traitor. It was Xerxes' great misfortune that this particular figure was one of the wiliest and most gifted admirals in the history of naval warfare.

Themistocles had commanded the Athenian sea forces since the outbreak of the war, some months earlier. He was more than merely a naval tactician; he was a statesman of rare vision. Two years before, when Athens had received an oracle that "the wooden wall would be safe," he convinced the populace that this meant a wall of ships. This wasn't all. The treasury had just received a windfall in the form of a rich strike in the government-owned silver mines, and the voters were on the point of passing the appropriate legislation to divide the money among themselves. Themistocles accomplished the almost miraculous feat of talking them into spending it on the fleet. Thanks to his foresight, when the Persians began their offensive Athens had an imposing navy of two hundred ships. Stiffened by these and guided by Themistocles' generalship, the entire Greek fleet, though terribly outnumbered, had fought the enemy to a draw off Cape Artemisium in northerly waters two months earlier. And it was thanks to his generalship that the fleet was now hemmed in in the narrow waters of Salamis Sound.

This was precisely the way Themistocles wanted it, the only way the Greeks had a chance to win. It came about solely as a result of his subtle and untiring efforts. The whole Greek fleet totaled somewhere between three hundred and four hundred craft. The Persians, strictly speaking, had no ships of their own—Susa, their capital, lay eight hundred miles east of the sea—but, since they controlled the eastern shore of the Mediterranean from the Dardanelles to the Nile, they were able to commandeer squadrons from Phoenicia, Egypt, and the Greek coastal cities of Asia Minor; indeed, they may well have supplied funds for the building, manning, and maintaining of these squadrons. They had at least over seven hundred ships and perhaps many more; some estimates run as high as fourteen hundred. Themistocles recognized that a fight in the open sea where the enemy could deploy all his forces would be disastrous; his only chance lay in waters where the Persians could bring to bear at any one time only a limited portion of their fleet. He chose the cramped Strait of Salamis.

Themistocles' first job was to convince his own allies. Although the heart and brains of the Greek defense, officially he was merely commanding officer of the Athenian contingent—a Spartan held the overall command—and it took all his diplomacy to sell his fellow officers the idea that the only way to win was to crawl into a bottle and allow it to be corked. Next he had to snare Xerxes into the trap. His guile was equal even to this: on September 22 he dispatched one of his slaves to Xerxes' headquarters with the message that the Greek fleet was making ready to slip out of the channel and scatter, thereby depriving the king of the chance to destroy it at one blow. Xerxes rose to the bait: that evening he sent his squadrons off to patrol the waters and block all avenues of escape. His crews spent the night at work on the benches.

So far Themistocles had made all the preparatory moves with superb artistry. He conducted the battle with equal brilliance. Most of the Persian fleet was gathered around the southern entrance to Salamis Sound, their prows pointed toward it. The first step was to suck them in. Themistocles waited patiently until the usual sea breeze, which would tend to move the enemy gradually into the channel, sprang up before he went into action. As soon as he had led out his vessels to face the Persian array, Xerxes' admirals gave the signal to attack—and Themistocles' first command was to back water, as if afraid of contact. Only when he had in this way enticed the enemy well within the channel did he give the order to charge. The Persians' front line, pressing forward into a narrowing space, gradually contracted, and, since the men after a night at the oars were not at their best, ship began to foul ship. Worse was at hand. First its forward motion was checked by the charging Greeks; and then the supporting Persian lines, rowing ahead hard to get into the action and unable to stop in time, broke into its rear. Themistocles' forces, under his rigorous discipline, had maintained their ranks and now they were ready for the kill. In line of battle, driven by fresh crews, they slammed into their opponents, by this time in disorder, ramming with deadly effect. One enemy ship after another, foregoing any attempt to withstand attack, turned to extricate itself and flee. The battle ended in a rout; Greece was not only saved, but a Persian fleet was never to challenge her supremacy on the sea again.

Not one penteconter was to be seen in the two lines as they faced each other across the waters of the sound. A dramatic development had taken place in naval design that had completely changed the complexion of Mediterranean fighting fleets. When Themistocles talked the Athenians into creating a modern navy, he asked for much more than the building of additional units; whatever penteconters there still were in the navy had to be replaced with ships of the new design. The vessels that fought on both sides in the Persian wars were almost all of a type the Greeks called *trieres*, "3-er," more commonly known to us under the Latinized name trireme. With the ships came new ways of fighting; decades before Greeks and Persians clashed in the Battle of Artemisium admirals had learned the handling of the new craft and devised intricate tactics for them.

The trireme was the logical offspring of the two-banked penteconter. When naval architects centuries earlier sought to increase the power and speed of the original long ship with its single line of rowers, they found the solution in dividing the oarsmen into two levels, the lower rowing through ports in the hull, the upper over the gunwale (Chapter 7). How could the power of such vessels be increased still further? One possibility was the addition of a third bank. But there was no longer room for a third bank within the hull itself and, at least in the eyes of Greek navy men, the changes required to make room would result in a deeper, heavier ship, one so much slower that it would cancel out a good many of the advantages of the added line of rowers. Sometime in the seventh century B.C. a Greek naval architect came up with the answer: on either side of the vessel he added an outrigger (*parexeresia*, or "by-rowing apparatus," as the Greeks called it) above the gunwale, projecting laterally out from it. In this way he made room for a third bank of oarsmen without drastic changes in the general lines of the hull and thereby produced a ship with all the speed and maneuverability of its predecessor, but with vastly increased power. Off to the east in the Levant the Phoenicians came up with their own version of a trireme by taking the easier path and fitting all three banks into the hull; it very likely was sturdier, roomier, and easier to build, but it must have been slower and less agile.

The introduction of the trireme did not spell the immediate death of the penteconter. There was an extended period of experimentation. Moreover, the new ship was much more expensive to build, and it took time for navies to assure themselves that what they were getting was worth the increased outlay. It was not until the second half of the sixth century B.C. that the trireme became the warship par excellence of the Mediterranean. It maintained this lordly status during the whole of the fifth and most of the fourth, and in subsequent centuries never ceased serving as a unit in the fleets almost to the very end of the ancient world.

Though no models or complete pictures of Greek triremes have survived, we do have a good deal of information about them, particularly those of the Athenian navy. The official records of the navy yard at Athens, for example, fortunately for posterity were carved on stone and a number of large fragments have been dug up. These list the exact amount of gear of various types issued to the ships, and this reveals not only the number of oarsmen in each bank but the fact that all banks, except for a handful of rowers, used oars of the same length. Parts of the slips where triremes were docked in the navy yard are still visible, and archaeologists have examined and measured them. The length is a little over 121 feet and the width just under 20; these then must be the dimensions of the largest ships. It seems unbelievable, but somehow a massive crew of oarsmen was not only shoehorned into this long slender hull but was able to propel it effectively under the grueling conditions of battle.

So unbelievable does it seem that for centuries a debate raged as to just how a Greek trireme was designed and manned. One school maintained vociferously that three superimposed banks of oarsmen could not possibly row efficiently; they all had to be on one level. Another school argued equally vociferously that, if the men were in three banks, they could not possibly have used oars of the same length. The debate is now ancient history. The questions were answered once and for all in the summer of 1987. At that time there was launched and put through a series of trials a replica of an Athenian trireme, three-banked, fitted with oars the same length, and in all other respects made in accordance with available ancient information and the dictates of the laws of physics, the properties of materials, and so on (Pl.

28). Its performance was spectacular. It was able to sprint at a speed of more than nine knots, travel for hours at four knots with half the crew rowing in turns, execute a 180-degree turn in one minute in an arc no wider than two and one-half ship-lengths. Moreover, the crews needed no endlessly long training; they became adept at the oars within weeks.

Greek triremes lay low in the water: their total height was a little under eight feet and they had a draught of about three, shallow enough to enable them to be drawn up on a beach or portaged on rollers. The lowest bank of rowers—the thalamites, as they are generally called—worked their oars through ports that were not over a foot and a half above the waterline; a leather bag fitted snugly about the oar and its opening to keep out the sea, but in any sort of chop these oars were secured and the ports sealed with coverings. A form of punishment in the fleets was to lash a man to a thalamite thwart with his head sticking out the port; in harbor this was probably not much worse than the pillory, but under way it could be severe. The navy yard records show that there were twenty-seven rowers in this bank on each side. The next higher row, the zygites, had the same number. Each sat above and slightly outboard of the corresponding thalamite and worked his oar over the gunwale. On special benches built on top of the gunwale sat the highest row, the thranites, each only slightly higher than the corresponding zygite but outboard of him; the tholepins for their oars were set in an outrigger that projected about two feet from the side of the ship (Pl. 29). Their stroke was the most wearing, for their oars, pivoting so high up, struck the water at a relatively sharp angle. Since the hull narrowed at each end, it squeezed out the lower banks there but left some room for the highest; consequently there were four more thranites, a total of thirty-one on each side.

Thus a trireme was powered by one hundred and seventy rowers. Their oars were almost all the same length, circa fourteen feet, just about what is standard on some navy cutters today. Slightly shorter ones, a little over thirteen feet, were used at bow and stern where the sides, curving inward, left less room. In this way not only the manufacture of oars but the stocking of spares was simplified. The navy yard records show that each trireme was issued two hundred oars: one hundred and seventy for the three banks and thirty of the two sizes for reserve.

In a trireme the key rowing unit was the group of three consisting of a thranite and the zygite and thalamite below him; it was this triad that gave the vessel its name, a "3-er." There were twenty-seven of these groups on each side with two thranites rowing alone fore and aft. The distance between rowers is a constant, three feet, set by the size of the human body, so that a trireme was not too much longer than an early penteconter with its twenty-four men to a side. But it was infinitely more powerful, more maneuverable, more adaptable. In calm weather it could be rowed from the thalamite bank and in a choppy sea from the thranite. Despite its size and power, it was light and shallow enough for the crew to run it up a beach at night.

The total complement of a trireme, excluding the contingent of marines, amounted to two hundred for, in addition to the one hundred and seventy rowers, there were twenty-five ratings and deckhands and five officers. In the names of some of the latter we can discern the duties on the original long ships that required personnel with authority: *kybernetes*, "helmsman"; *keleustes*, "timebeater"; *proreus*, "bow-man" (i.e., lookout). The names were traditional; they hardly reflected any longer the duties of these officers aboard a trireme. The *kybernetes* did carry over some of his original function, for he was the ship's navigating officer and in battle or storm might even handle the steering oars himself, although at other times he turned them over to quartermasters. This was only a part of his duties. He was the equivalent of the executive officer of today, and if the captain was absent or lost, he took over command. Indeed, as things were managed in the Athenian navy, more often than not he held the actual command at all times. The official commander, the *trierarchos*, "trireme captain" as he was called, was by standard procedure a political appointee: to lighten the burden of supporting their navy, the Athenians had an arrangement whereby a rich man of the community for one year assumed the expense of fitting out and maintaining a galley and also served as its *trierarchos*. If he had any naval experience, it was by sheerest coincidence, and so it usually turned out that he was only the titular commander and the *kybernetes* actually ran the ship. Next in line to the *kybernetes* was the *keleustes*, who was responsible for the training and morale of the oarsmen. Then came the *pentekontarchos*; the name means "captain of fifty" and probably was originally the title of the captain of a penteconter. He had important administrative duties, serving as paymaster, purchasing officer, and recruiting officer. Last came the *proreus* or *prorates*, the bow officer, who was stationed on the foredeck and entrusted with keeping a sharp lookout. These five—*trierarchos*, *kybernetes*, *keleustes*, *pentekontarchos*, *proreus* (*prorates*)—made up, as it were, the commissioned personnel. Then there were various ratings, including a ship's carpenter, deckhands to take care of sail and lines, and a *trieraules*, "trireme flutist," or simply *auletes*, "flutist," whose monotonous tootling gave the time to the rowers. The contingent of marines usually consisted of ten or so spearsmen and three or four archers.

To man the benches of a trireme was almost as difficult and expensive as to build one. The Athenian contingent of two hundred ships at

Salamis, for example, required no less than 34,000 oarsmen. Such a number was much too big to be met by the populace alone, which among other things had to fill the ranks of the land forces at the same time. Moreover, the army, not the navy, was the senior service. Anyone who could afford a soldier's armor and weapons understandably preferred to fight in the field rather than to sweat on a bench in a hot and foul ship's hold; he only submitted to it in emergencies when his city had no other recourse. The core of the rowing crews was the lowest class of citizens, those who couldn't afford to equip themselves as soldiers. The rest simply had to be hired. The chief source of supply was the Aegean islands and the coastal towns of Asia Minor, whose people lived off the sea. Since the service was both arduous and dangerous, it commanded attractive salaries; thranites, who had the hardest stroke, could even receive a premium. A state needed money to maintain a fleet. This was why slaves were never used as regular members of crews: they were far too expensive. Able-bodied slaves sold for a high price, so the initial purchase would require a massive expenditure of funds; the cost of all who died in battle would have to be written off as a total loss; and all survivors would have to be supported for their whole lifetime, whether there was a war going on or not. On rare occasions, when a state was desperate and had no other recourse, it might turn to the temporary use of slaves. Athens, for example, did it once, at a life-and-death moment when it had run out of all other sources of manpower, and it gave the slaves it used their freedom as a reward. Since all the rowers were either citizens or well-paid foreigners, skippers could not be as cavalier with them as the commanders of the slave-driven galleys of later ages; no lashes were carried on Greek triremes.

Fleets of triremes not uncommonly numbered one hundred vessels, at times half that again or more, and so commanders were faced with the task of provisioning twenty thousand to thirty thousand men. Incredible as it may sound, Greek navies of this period never worked out an organized system of supply. Only a few days' rations at most could be carried on board because the sole storage available was some scanty space under the bow and stern decks and this was ordinarily assigned to gear. In an extended fleet movement, supply ships might be taken along. But most of the time the admirals simply put into shore near some town and the men, quitting their galleys, hustled to the local market and bought food. Somehow this haphazard arrangement must have worked, for we never hear of crews going hungry. We do hear of a canny admiral who won a victory cheaply by the simple expedient of lurking out of sight until the enemy commander beached his ships and let the men go off to market; then he rushed in and destroyed or towed off the empty vessels (pp. 95–96).

Greek navies had no admirals as such, just military chiefs who were expected to be competent on land or sea. A man in command of an army one month might expect to find himself at the head of a fleet the next. Moreover, in Athens of the fifth century B.C., where the citizens pushed democratic procedures just as far as they could, they assigned commanders themselves, picking them from a board of ten annually elected by popular vote. Somehow the system worked as well as most: by and large it succeeded in getting the fleet into competent hands, even at times into those of a naval genius like Themistocles; on occasion it turned it over to men of monumental pigheadedness.

The crews had to be rigorously trained. Their job, from the point of view of timing and coordination, was probably as exacting as any aboard a modern warship and incomparably more taxing physically. In 494 B.C. the Greek cities of Asia Minor, in an attempt to throw off the Persian yoke, began to organize a fleet. They turned over the training of the rowers, citizens who had volunteered, to a hard-bitten officer from Phocaea, that city of gifted seamen (Chapter 7). The men were able to take just three days of the punishing régime he put them through; after that they quit. Anyone who has nursed a set of blisters and sore muscles from a few hours in a rowboat can appreciate how they felt.

In general the oarsmen were saved for battle. For cruising, a mast was stepped and braced with wedges, and a large squaresail raised on it. But this rig was useless during battle since a vessel had to be ready to turn in any direction at a moment's notice and simply couldn't depend upon the vagaries of the wind. In addition, since there was scant room to stow such bulky gear, it was generally left ashore when the ship went into action. All that was taken along was a smaller mast and sail, a "boat sail" as the Greeks called it. When a ship turned to flee this was raised; to "hoist the boat sail" was Greek sailor slang for "run away." Warships of the much later Roman navy are depicted with the *artemon* (cf. p. 190). It has been suggested that this is the "boat sail" of the Greek triremes of the fifth and fourth centuries B.C., but it is more likely that the boat sail was a replacement for the regular-sized gear and was used because, being of convenient size, it could always be kept on board.

It was as expensive to maintain a fleet as to man it. A trireme was so lightly built and subject to such severe strain that its life was short. Most had to be scrapped after twenty years of service, many earlier, and one that lasted twenty-five was a veritable Methusaleh. The Athenian navy classified its galleys according to their age and condition. At first they were merely divided into "new" and "old." Then a more discriminating system of four categories was introduced: "selects," "first-class," "second-class," and "third-class." Ships that failed to measure up to even the last category could get a stay of execution by being converted into transports to ferry the cavalry's horses; those that had outlived their usefulness for service of any sort were declared obsolete and struck from the records. Most of the discards were probably cannibalized, although there is at least one case on record of a "war surplus" sale: early in the fourth century B.C., when states were going in on a large scale for the use of mercenary soldiers in their armies (Chapter 9), an enterprising Athenian bought up a discarded trireme, put it into commission, collected a crew, and hired out as a naval mercenary. Though the replacement of obsolete ships accounted for the bulk of the moneys spent on a navy, the purchase and upkeep of the miscellaneous gear each vessel carried involved no inconsiderable expense. The sails came in two grades of linen, heavy and light. Running rigging included two halyards, two sheets, two braces, and eighteen loops of brails. Standing rigging consisted, as in Homer's day (Chapter 4), only of a double forestay and a backstay. Since no shrouds are ever mentioned, the double forestay must have been run to each rail somewhat abaft the prow to provide some lateral bracing; deckhands used it to raise and lower the mast and, from incidental remarks dropped by ancient writers, it is clear that it was considered the key item of rigging. There were four heavy and four lighter cables for mooring lines and for the two anchors that were carried. The latter, made of iron, were very light, under fifty pounds, but additional weight could be added by clamping on stones or pieces of lead. An unusual item that formed part of the regular gear was a set of "undergirdles"; each ship normally carried at least two, often a few more as spares, and, when converted to transport horses with all their extra weight, four. These were massive hawsers that ran from stempost to sternpost and were kept under tension; they gave the long slender hull the longitudinal stiffening that it very much needed.

The trireme had two weapons. The first was its ram, a mighty timber jutting from the forefoot that was sheathed in an envelope of bronze, ending in a blunt, roughly square face with three transverse fins (Pl. 32). This was an improvement over the single-pointed ram of earlier times; such a ram would punch a hole in an enemy hull but ran the risk of remaining wedged in the hole, the consequences of which could be disastrous. The new version was much less likely to get stuck, for, if wielded properly, instead of punching a hole it delivered a pounding blow that would loosen all the seams on either side of where it landed. The marines on its decks were the trireme's second weapon. The Greek vessels that fought at Salamis, like the penteconters, were not fully decked. There was decking at prow and stern and corridors ran lengthwise over the gunwales and probably down the center. In the ensuing half-century more decking was added by extending the corridors laterally to project over the outriggers. Screens, too, were fitted along the sides so that, all in all, the oarsmen received a maximum of protection against missiles. Such ships, covered over on top by a deck and on the sides by screens, the Greeks called cataphract, that is, "fenced in" (cf. Pl. 38); open, deckless craft were aphract, or "unfenced."

Not all triremes were alike; there were differences between those of one state and another just as there are between ships of the same class in modern navies. We have already noted how the version of the trireme used by the Phoenicians varied from the Greek. Though all navies fitted their galleys with rams, some favored the age-old tactic of coming to grips with the enemy to let the marines grapple and board and hence adapted their ships to accommodate a big contingent of them; the navy of the island of Chios, for example, had triremes that could carry as many as forty each. The Athenians preferred the ram attack, an attack in which, disregarding the enemy's personnel, they sought to destroy his vessels by using their own as projectiles, as it were. They made their galleys as light as possible and kept the number of marines to a minimum, relying on speed, maneuverability, and the efficiency of their crews to slam their bronze-shod prows into an enemy's hull.

Ramming was a demanding maneuver. Only a skilled crew and a commander of fine judgment and keen sense of timing could count on consistent success. At the moment of impact the attacking ship had to be traveling at an intermediate speed: if too slow, the enemy could back water out of range; if too fast, the thrust might embed the ram so deeply in the target's hull that it would remain lodged there, leaving the attacker a sitting duck for ram strokes from the other enemy craft. If the first thrust missed or wasn't mortal, the men had to be ready to back water at full speed just enough to get into proper position for a second try and then resume forward motion at the appropriate ramming speed. It was this need to fight a battle in a sort of slow motion, as it were, that made marines an essential part of the complement of all war galleys, even those designed chiefly for the use of the ram. Without such fighters to rake the opponent's deck during the approach to deliver the blow or to stand by to repel boarders after it, the attacked vessel's marines could grapple, board, and stand a fair chance of taking over the attacker.

Those navies which, because of the slowness of their vessels or the poor quality of their crews, could not depend on the ram were forced to rely more on marines. In battle their captains' prime concern was to avoid destruction from a ram stroke, and the standard method of accomplishing this was to keep, at all costs, the prow toward the enemy and give him no chance to get at the flanks or stern. If a captain could do this successfully—it often involved constant and careful backing water—until the enemy crews were weary, he could then bring the fight down to one between marines, in which the advantage lay on his side. If he could destroy enough enemy personnel in this phase, he might even be in a position to attack with the ram himself.

A navy trained in the use of the ram favored two maneuvers in particular, the *diekplus*, the "break through," and the *periplus*, the "sailing around." In battle, opponents generally faced each other in two long lines. In the *diekplus*, a ship or a squadron at a given signal dashed forward so suddenly and swiftly that it was able to row through the enemy's line before the latter was able to take countermeasures, and then wheel when through and ram the unprotected quarters or stern. It was a deadly maneuver but it demanded the utmost in coordination, response to command, and cleanness of execution; only fast ships and finely trained crews, taught to work in unison, could carry it out successfully. The *periplus* was simpler; it was an "end run" around the enemy's flank to take his line in the stern.

An admiral could avoid the *periplus* either by extending his line— though not so much that he would open himself up to a *diekplus*—or, if the locale permitted, by keeping one flank close to shore. There were various ways of countering a *diekplus*. When the Persian fleet tried to carry one out at the battle of Artemisium, two months before Salamis, the Greek commanders, including the astute Themistocles, had a countermeasure ready: they arranged their fleet in a circle with prows pointed outward and sterns inward toward the hub and literally left the attackers no line to break through. Another defense was to draw up a fleet in two lines; the second, held in reserve, could pounce on whatever enemy ships broke through the first. This was only feasible when an admiral had some superiority in numbers; otherwise his lines would be so short that the enemy could turn his flanks with a *periplus*. In a battle near the Arginusae Islands off the western coast of Asia Minor in 406 B.C., the Athenians successfully used this tactic with a fleet of 150 ships against a Spartan fleet of 120; by picking a locale where there were a few islets so conveniently placed that they could be incorporated in the formation, the Athenians were able to draw up a double line wider than their opponent's single one.

When the Athenian navy was in its prime, the only smaller variety of warcraft it had was the triacontor, useful no doubt for scouting and chasing pirates. The penteconter was a thing of the past, completely replaced by the trireme. The latter was far from being only a ship of the line, designed solely for use against enemy units. It was a general workhorse and carried out a multitude of tasks. Stripped of many of its rowers it transported troops; with the oarsmen reduced to sixty it carried horses, thirty to a ship. It was ideal for amphibious operations since it was light enough to be drawn right up on a beach; many a so-called naval engagement was merely a semipiratical attack for plunder by a squadron of triremes on a coastal settlement. Triremes performed convoy duty, escorting freighters to protect them from an enemy or pirates or both. Since there was nothing faster afloat, they served as dispatch boats. The Athenians had a famous pair, the *Paralos* and the *Salaminia*, the swiftest units in the fleet, which they constantly used to carry messages or transport important personages.

The trireme had the two drawbacks of all ancient galleys, lack of space and excessive lightness. It was useless in any sort of heavy weather and, unable to carry provisions in any quantity, had to have bases readily available. Sailing freighters could strike across the open sea, but a fighting squadron had to follow the coast so that each night the men could beach the ships and cook, eat, and sleep ashore. Naval actions always took place in sight of land. Since operating in waters where the enemy held the seaboard was out of the question, commanders were never able to maintain a true naval blockade. They might bottle a fleet in a harbor as Xerxes did to Themistocles' at Salamis, or cut a port from seaborne supplies, but they could not patrol an extended shoreline that was securely in an opponent's hands. This limitation on cruising range made the open sea a sort of no-man's-land and particularly hindered the cleaning up of piracy. The job was never really done properly until the Romans came along with enormous forces at their disposal and the whole Mediterranean coastline more or less under their control (Chapter 15).

The Peloponnesian War, the great conflict between Athens and Sparta and her Peloponnesian allies which began in 431 B.C. and lasted for twenty-seven years, was the heyday of the fleet trained in maneuver and the use of the ram. The Athenians, getting off to a flying start in their battles against Persia, in the ensuing half-century had built up the finest navy the Mediterranean had yet seen. Their ships were the fastest afloat; their crews were trained to a razor's edge, especially in the complexities of the *diekplus* and the *periplus*; and in the early days of the conflict they had a gifted admiral named Phormio who was well able to carry on the tradition started by Themistocles. Their navy was so powerful an instrument that they depended chiefly on it all during the war. Athens deliberately allowed Sparta and its allies to throw a cordon about the city on the landward side. It made no difference: under the besiegers' eyes, freighters convoyed by Athenian triremes brought in all the supplies the populace needed. Like Persia, Sparta was principally a land power and had no ships. Some of its allies, notably Corinth, had sizable navies, but none were particularly enthusiastic about taking on the Athenians except in circumstances where the odds were unquestionably favorable.

During the first years of the war, the Athenian navy carried the art of fighting with the ram to heights never to be reached again, and the zenith was achieved at the battle of Rhion, fought in 429 B.C. in the waters of the western end of the Gulf of Corinth. Here Phormio with twenty triremes signally defeated an enemy fleet of forty-seven, one which, despite the odds, he had to force to come out and fight. When the opposing commanders reluctantly decided to engage, in order to prevent the Athenians from carrying out a *diekplus*, they adopted the countermeasure of the circle. Putting five ships as reserve in the center, they rayed the other forty-two in a ring around them, prows outward; after all, the Greeks had used the same defense at Artemisium and it had worked then.

But the ships and crews of the Peloponnesians were not in a class with the Athenian, nor were their commanders in a class with Phormio. He embarked on a daring maneuver: proceeding in column he formed a ring around the enemy formation and kept circling steadily about it. He thereby put his vessels in the most dangerous position possible—their broadsides exposed to the enemy's rams—but he figured he could rely not only on the quickness of his crews to spin and get out of danger in case of a charge, but also on the sluggishness of the enemy in mounting one. Moreover, like Themistocles at Salamis he cannily included the wind in his calculations. It was just after dawn and dead calm. But there was usually a morning breeze from the east in these quarters, and he reasoned that when it set in it would throw the dense Peloponnesian formation into confusion. He had reckoned perfectly. As soon as the wind sprang up, the enemy ships started to foul one another and had to be fended off with boat poles. Soon they were so close that the oars couldn't be worked. At that moment Phormio signaled the attack, and his ships turned from column to line and drilled in. In the very first charge they destroyed a flagship, and before the enemy could shake free and scuttle away they had seized a dozen prizes.

The Peloponnesians prudently waited until they outnumbered Phormio's little squadron by four to one before they set out to even the score. In a battle off Naupactus they lost again, but this time only because of a single piece of Athenian seamanship that was extraordinary even for Athenians. The Peloponnesians, with their overwhelming numbers, practically had the fight in their hands; they had captured nine ships and were savagely pursuing the remainder. One of their vessels pressed forward at the heels of a lagging Athenian craft. As it happened, a merchantman was anchored just ahead in an open road-stead right in the way. The Athenian captain headed straight for it— but, instead of continuing on past, made a lightning turn around it, which put him in perfect ramming position: he struck his pursuer square amidships. This was too much for the crews of the other enemy galleys. They sat at their oars stunned and, before they could get under way again, the Athenian squadron stopped its flight, wheeled, charged, and seized six craft.

No more than sixteen years after Phormio's spectacular victories, a bitter fight took place whose outcome presaged the end of the light, fast trireme's undisputed reign as queen of the seas. The locale was the harbor of Syracuse, far from Athens.

The Peloponnesian War was halted for a while by an indecisive treaty in 421 B.C. but erupted again a few years later. In 415 the Athe-nians took the first of a series of steps that was to lead to their defeat. Their navy was incomparable and they knew it. In an access of cock-sureness they voted to send an enormous armada—134 triremes and over 30,000 men—to capture Syracuse in Sicily. Before the attempt was over, two years later, it had not only cost them all their ships and men but had produced a new style of war galley and fighting that spelled the end of their naval supremacy.

When the huge fleet, including the finest units in the Athenian navy, sailed into the harbor of Syracuse in the summer of 415, there were probably few people on both sides who didn't think that the cam-paign would be over shortly. The Syracusans had a good-sized fleet; but nobody in it, from the admirals to the deckhands, reckoned that it had a chance against the Athenians.

But an important clue to the direction in which victory lay was sup-plied the Syracusans by what at the time must have been reported as merely a minor naval engagement. In 413, in the narrow waters of a bay near the western end of the Gulf of Corinth, a squadron of Athe-nian ships engaged one from Corinth. There were no more than thirty-three units in each, a far cry from the great fleets over one hun-dred strong that were facing each other at Syracuse. When they finally disengaged after a long struggle, three Corinthian craft had been de-stroyed and seven Athenian had been put out of action. To the Corinthians, to have come off this well was tantamount to a victory. The reason for their good showing was clear: before the battle they had taken pains to reinforce their ships with extra timbers on the bows as well as on the catheads forming the front face of the outriggers, and, during the battle, they had stuck to narrow waters where their opponents, with no room to maneuver, had to ram prow to prow. As a result, seven Athenian craft bashed in their outriggers against the enemy's newly installed massive foretimbers.

Taking their cue from this engagement, the Syracusans reinforced all their triremes in this way. The locale of the fighting was totally in their favor. Their harbor was an oval about two thousand by four thousand yards in extent, and they had succeeded in plugging the entrance with a line of linked vessels. The Athenians were securely bottled up. They had to battle in waters where there was no room for the style of fighting they had been trained in, their slender prows faced the heavily armored fronts of the newly reconditioned Syracusan fleet, and their sterns pointed to a shore that was mostly in enemy hands. Ramming could be only prow to prow, in which they were at a distinct disadvantage. What is more, their ships were waterlogged and hence sluggish, since they had been in action continuously for two years without ever being hauled out for reconditioning. The Athenian commander tried one last measure: he stationed extra marines in the bows with irons to grapple the Syracusan ships as they surged in; if his crews could back water quickly enough to ride out the first blow, the grapplers could hold the attackers fast, keep them from backing off for a second charge, and give their own men a chance to board. It was plainly a measure of desperation, for these were the very tactics Athens had never bothered with and had no competence in. As it happened, the Syracusans got advance word of the plans and covered their foredecks with hides so that the grappling irons would rip harmlessly through and not embed in the planking. When the fleets finally engaged, the Athenians fought gallantly but it was in a lost cause. Of the more than two hundred Athenian triremes that, in the course of the campaign, had made their way into Syracuse harbor, not one came out of it.

The Athenians had incredible stamina. Even this disaster didn't finish them off. In the following years, virtually starting from scratch, they were able to build up new powerful fleets and even win several victories, though their ships and crews were now often inferior to their opponents'. During these years, in a complete reversal, it was the Athenians who defended against the *diekplus* and *periplus* and the Peloponnesian fleets that executed them. The final defeat was almost anticlimactic. In September of 405 B.C. Athens sent her entire navy, 180 units strong, to the Dardanelles to make sure that freighters carrying grain from southern Russia to the city got through safely. The commanders drew the whole force up on a bare beach on the northern shore near Aegospotami, "Goat's Rivers." Because there was no settlement nearby, the crews had to straggle off to Sestus, the nearest place that had a market, almost two miles away, to get food. The enemy fleet camped on the opposite shore in front of Lampsacus, a well-stocked city. The next morning both sides manned their ships and the Athenians rowed up to the enemy formation and offered battle. Lysander, the shrewd admiral of the Peloponnesian fleet, held off and, after his opponents turned to go back to their beach, sent scouts to keep an eye on them, at the same time holding his own men at their battle stations. The same procedure was repeated for four days. On the fifth day, when his scouts signaled (by shields hoisted aloft to reflect the sun) that most of the Athenians had beached their ships and gone off for food, he pressed in at full speed and, without losing a man, seized 171 prizes, probably the most spectacular victory in the history of naval warfare. Only nine Athenian craft escaped. They happened to be under the command of Conon, an alert and able naval officer, who managed to man the banks and raise sail on his tiny flotilla quickly enough to make a getaway. The enemy, stripped for action, had no sailing gear aboard (p. 88), so Conon, boiling along toward the Aegean with the prevailing northeasterlies at his back, was able to show his heels to any pursuers. He had so much of a head start that, in a move which reminds one of the bandits in a Western film who turn loose their victims' horses to forestall chase, he took the time to cross the strait, stop at the Peloponnesian anchorage for a few minutes, and cart off all the sails that had been left there.

A few months later Athens, with no fleet to secure her lines of supply, was starved into submission.

In the Mediterranean where states of any size had to depend on overseas sources for food and the only feasible long-distance communications were by water, sea power was paramount. Its superb ships and tactics had given Athens unchallenged rule of the eastern sector for almost a century, from the moment Themistocles had brought them on the stage at Salamis to the ludicrous curtain at Aegospotami. When it tried to extend its arm farther, to the west, it lost everything. Complete control of the Mediterranean was something that had to wait until the Romans came along.

In the years after Aegospotami, Athens succeeded in rebuilding its fleet more or less on the old model. But changes were in the wind. For one, the weakness in cramped waters of the light trireme, built primarily to ram, was now apparent. For another, after the vast losses during the war on both sides, adequate crews in sufficient numbers were harder than ever to find and because of certain factors remained so. Another major development in naval design and tactics was soon to take place.

Chapter 9

THE MERCHANTS OF ATHENS

ONE DAY, sometime toward the end of the Peloponnesian War, a pair of Athenian bankers made their way to the slave market in front of the temple of Castor and Pollux at Athens. They needed another employee, and the personnel of the bank was mostly slave. That day they bought a young foreigner named Pasion—perhaps "Pasion" was as near as they could get to a name unpronounceable on a Greek tongue. This new purchase, who trotted dutifully behind as they tramped the five miles from the city to the office at the Piraeus, Athens' harbor, was eventually to take over their bank, become a key figure in the business circles of the port, and end up one of the richest men in Athens.

Pasion was lucky. He might have been bought by some estate owner and spent the rest of his life in a farmhand's unvarying round of chores, or by some contractor for mine labor and died after a few years of backbreaking work underground. Instead he landed as an employee of the Antisthenes and Archestratus Banking and Loan Company, a position that turned out to be uniquely suited to his talents. He probably started at the bottom as a porter who handled the heavy bags of coin but rose quickly to chief clerk in charge of a money-changing table at the port. He was quick, accurate, honest, and, above all, had a keen eye for spotting undesirable clients and bad credit risks. As the partners grew older they relied more and more on him; they granted him his freedom—it happened often enough in those days to slaves who had served their owners faithfully and well—and finally, when age kept them from playing an active part in the business, he took the bank over.

Pasion prospered. Some of the biggest men in Athens, military and political leaders, were his clients. With shrewd business sense and scrupulously kept books, he carried on the multifarious activities of a banker in the fourth century B.C. He received money from his clients and kept it on deposit for them. He supplied the ancient equivalent of a safe-deposit box by storing their valuables. He provided convenient methods of payment for them: although the written check had not yet been invented, a depositor could appear with a person to whom he wanted funds paid and Pasion would transfer the appropriate sum on his books, or, if the payee came from another city, arrange to have a business contact there hand over the money and debit the bank's account. This was no ordinary advantage, for it spared the client the risky business of carring cash around or, what was even more a concern, transporting it overseas.

With his own money as well as that on deposit as working capital, Pasion fattened on the profits from money changing, on the conservative interest from well-secured loans, and on the juicy returns from speculative loans to shippers. As time passed and his capital grew, he branched out: he bought ships to charter, and even went into the lucrative munitions business by founding a factory to manufacture shields. He was always keenly aware of the debt he owed the city that had opened up such unique opportunities to him. Once he gave the army an outright gift of one thousand shields. A rich man was often called upon to serve as trierarch, to undertake the expense of fitting out and maintaining a trireme for a year (Chapter 8); Pasion on one occasion voluntarily signed up for five ships. His service on behalf of the state was finally rewarded by the highest gift it had to offer, citizenship, something foreigners could gain only by a vote of the Athenian assembly. This helped business too, since Pasion could now add investment in real estate to the bank's activities. Aliens were not allowed to own property in Athens, and for a banker who wasn't a citizen it was too risky to invest in mortgages; he couldn't foreclose in case of nonpayment.

Eventually Pasion got too old to play an active part in the business. When he had to make the five-mile walk from his headquarters at the Piraeus to Athens on business, he found it a little too much for his aged legs. At this point he ran into the problem that so often faces a successful businessman. Of his two sons, one was still a minor and the other was too interested in his horses, clothes, and courtesans (the ancient equivalent of chorus girls) to be trusted with the business; the firm just couldn't become Pasion and Sons and prosper. So he did what his former masters had done years before: he turned the bank over to his general manager, Phormio, whom he himself had bought off the slave block, trained in the business, and freed. And, to make sure that the assets stayed in the family, he did what quite a few bankers did in those days: he stipulated in his will that Phormio was to marry his widow. The bank under its new management flourished as it had under Pasion and maintained its reputation for service and square dealing. Phormio, too, became one of the richest men in town.

Athens of the fourth century B.C. was just the time and place where a Horatio Alger career like that of Pasion or Phormio could happen. Commerce was more vital to the city's existence than it had ever been before. In the fifth century, Pericles, a soldier and statesman, had led Athens by virtue of his office as a member of the board of generals; one hundred years later its destinies were guided by men like Eubulus and Lycurgus, financial experts serving in the office of chancellor of the exchequer. A web of trade routes crisscrossed the waters between Marseilles and the Crimea, and bankers and shipowners and shippers cooperated in sending over them every conceivable sort of product, especially the basic commodities of the ancient world: wine, olive oil, and grain. Traders in Byzantium on the Bosporus cocked a wary eye on the crop in Sicily eight hundred miles away; rumors of a bad harvest in Egypt sent prices soaring on the exchanges of half a dozen Greek cities. At the center of this commercial activity stood Athens with its seaport town, the Piraeus.

When a skipper steered his vessel into the port of the Piraeus in the fifth or fourth century B.C., he headed for a narrow opening between two moles that formed the entrance to a capacious harbor. Here he was hailed and boarded by customs officials who looked over his cargo, checked the valuation, and levied a toll of two percent. Going and coming, ships paid this, even on transit goods headed for a further destination. It was not a protective tariff but simply a source of revenue; many a conveniently located Greek seaport was able to base a good part of its budget on the collections from harbor tolls. The officials kept such precise records that their ledgers could be produced in court as evidence of the exact nature and amount of cargo a ship had carried. After customs had taken its cut, agents came aboard to collect dues for the use of the port facilities. There was a way to avoid both tolls and dues if one wanted to run the risk: to the west of the port and outside its jurisdiction was a quiet cove so well known as a mooring point for smugglers that it was called "Thieves' Harbor."

Once clear of all the red tape, a skipper steered for the eastern side of the harbor. The southern side, as well as two smaller bays farther eastward, belonged to the navy and were given over to the long roofed sheds that housed the triremes and other war craft. But on the eastern side stood the *emporion*, the commercial part of the port. All along the water's edge ran a stone-paved quay where freighters made fast. Just behind, parallel to it, were no less than five colonnades. This is where business was done.

If the newly arrived skipper had a cargo of grain he unloaded at the "Long Colonnade," the biggest of the five even as grain was the biggest item in Athens' trade. Here he was met by the local grain wholesalers who came up bawling out the prices they were willing to offer, as well as by official supervisors who were on hand to make sure that governmental regulations were observed. Alongside the grain exchange were the colonnades where other products were dealt in: jars of Athenian olive oil or crocks of Athenian honey or carefully wrapped batches of ceramic ware decorated in the inimitable Athenian style, for export; jars of wine imported from Asia Minor or of preserved fish from the Black Sea; timber and pitch from Macedon for the shipyards; and so on. One area right alongside the quay was known as the Deigma, the "sample market" or "bazaar," and from here rose a babel in every language of the Mediterranean seaboard as traders laid out miscellaneous wares from all quarters and bickered with officials or bargained with dealers. Here one could buy carpets or pillows from Carthage, seasonings and hides and ivory from Libya, flax for cordage and papyrus paper from Egypt, fine wines and incense and dates from Syria, furniture from Miletus, figs and nuts from Asia Minor (slaves, too, from the same area), pigs and beef and cheese from Sicily and Italy. There was usually a seller's market, for, with all the intensity of the traffic, it was still the age of the small businessman, and the organization of supply was haphazard. Hundreds of small traders dumped their wares on the docks and haggled over prices with hundreds of dealers. Spotted here and there among the bewildering varieties of stalls were the tables of the money changers, and amidst the clamor of hawking and bargaining could be heard the clink of coins as sharp-eyed clerks exchanged darics from Persia or staters from Cyzicus or the coinages of Sicilian cities for Attic four-drachma pieces with the old-fashioned picture of Athena and her owl that Athens kept using since it was accepted everywhere as the mark of a trustworthy currency.

From April through the summer the hurly-burly went on at the Piraeus. With the coming of October, winds and weather put a close to the sailing season. Money changers folded their tables, shippers from abroad sailed for home, shipowners hauled out their craft onto the beach or bedded them down at the quays, stevedores wandered off to the city. Like a summer resort, the harbor shut down to wait for spring.

It was the Persian wars that launched Athens on its career as a center for shipping. Before this time cities on or off the coast of Asia Minor, such as Chios or Miletus, played the key roles in the trade of the east and Corinth in that of the west (Chapter 7). Aegina, a little island right at Athens' door, had a merchant marine that tramped all over; when King Xerxes was organizing his attack on Greece and was scouting the Dardanelles, the first thing that met his eye was a convoy of ships headed for Aegina, loaded with grain from southern Russia. But when, in the wake of the victories over the Persians, Athens created an empire that ensured her special privileges in the Greek cities of the Aegean, filled her treasury, and enabled her to build up a navy strong enough to police the seas, the Piraeus was gradually transformed into an international entrepôt. And Athens maintained its commercial domination despite the stunning defeat in the Peloponnesian War. Geographically it stood in the center of the Greek world: any trader who put in and unloaded would be sure to find a return cargo and not have to go home in ballast. It had one of the few good natural harbors in the eastern Mediterranean; its coinage was still one of the best in current use and was accepted in every port; there was capital available among its businessmen for investment in maritime ventures. So the Piraeus hummed with activity.

Far and away the biggest business in Athens was the importing of grain. The ancient Greeks lived principally off bread and porridge; if supplies weren't unloaded regularly on the quays of the Piraeus, the populace faced hardship. The same was true of most of the larger Greek cities. Intense commercial competition took place in this age, with many a clash of interests; it was not over markets in which to sell surplus products but over access to supplies essential for keeping a city going: grain for food, wine to drink, and olive oil which, by itself, did for the people of those days what soap and butter and electricity do for us—they cleansed their bodies with it, cooked in it, and burned it in lamps. Athens grew olives; wine could be got nearby; but the most important item, grain, was available in quantity in only three places, all of them far overseas: Egypt, Sicily, and southern Russia. In the Peloponnesian War, Sparta starved Athens into submission by destroying its fleet and blockading its port; a little over half a century later King Philip of Macedon, the able father of Alexander the Great, went about achieving the same result by occupying the city of Byzantium and closing the gates of the Bosporus, thereby cutting access to south Russian grain.

So, to feed themselves, Athens and the other major Greek cities required trade on an international scale. But it is necessary to get the nature and extent of their commercial activity in proper focus. The history of the Greeks in the fifth and fourth centuries B.C. is so important for its great contributions to the civilization of the West that we tend to lose sight of the actual size of the nations and the numbers of people involved. Athens, by far the largest city of Greece, was politically and culturally a mighty place, but its population was certainly not more than 300,000, slaves and foreign residents included—in other words, what in today's world would qualify as a center of quite moderate size. Less than 100,000 tons of grain, some eight hundred average-sized boatloads, were enough to feed the population for a year, and some of this, though relatively very little to be sure, was grown in its own fields. The activity in importing grain was intense—the actual shipping had to be crammed into the summer sailing season—but the totals involved were small. The day of massive shipments and government in business on a large scale lay ahead. In Athens of the fourth century, even a Pasion or a Phormio did not have the capital to finance big ventures. Most of the investing was done by small businessmen who often worked with partners, and they preferred to put limited amounts in a number of undertakings and thereby spread their risk. The trading was done by individuals who as a rule used borrowed funds, handled but one cargo a year, and frequently traveled on the ship with their goods to make sure everything went off without a hitch. But though the operations were small in scale, they were widespread. The banker or merchant at the Piraeus had business contacts in Marseilles or Syracuse or Byzantium. Once, during a period of acute grain shortage around 330 B.C., Cleomenes, Alexander the Great's governor in Egypt, cornered the market on his country's supplies. In Rhodes, a port of call for all ships from Egypt, he was able to establish a headquarters where his agents could collect, from contacts all over, the latest quotations and, as the loaded freighters arrived, divert them to whatever spot was offering the highest price.

It usually took four men of business, each playing a specific role, to bring a cargo from the wheat fields of southern Russia or Egypt or Sicily to the miller at Athens: shipper, shipowner, moneylender, and wholesaler; in many cases it took a pair or group of partners to provide the capital for each of these roles. The shipper practically always worked on credit and generally with a chartered vessel. He contracted with a shipowner for a ship or space on one, and then borrowed money from an investor or group of investors to pay for the freight charges and a load of merchandise. Those who owned their own ships pledged them as security. Those who did not—the majority—pledged the cargo they intended to buy. Obviously they must have been by and large men of integrity, for the investors never saw their security until months after the loan had been made, when the vessel with its load finally docked at the Piraeus. Interest for this service ran high, 22½ to 30 percent for the four to five months of the sailing season, that is, between 67½ and 90 percent per annum. That was only natural. There was no insurance in those days; the men who made the loans assumed total responsibility—if the vessel failed to come back, they, not the shipper, lost everything—so their reward had to be big, big enough to compensate for all risks. And these were considerable because, alongside the purely maritime ones, there was the ever present possibility of seizure by hostile men-of-war or attack by pirates. The same risks plus the lack of any system of insurance made the shippers anxious to work as much as they could with borrowed funds even when they had funds of their own; in this way they limited their personal loss when a venture ran into trouble.

Whether a shipper hauled grain to Athens from Sicily or the Crimea or Egypt, the voyage was difficult and slow one way, quick and easy the other. This is because of the prevailing winds in the eastern Mediterranean and Black Sea, which during the ancient mariner's sailing season are from the north; in the Aegean, for example, summer northerlies were so constant that the Greeks called them the Etesian, "annual," winds (the *Meltem* of the Turkish sailors today). A skipper leaving Athens on the Black Sea run had to fight his way out there but could boom home with a following breeze. For those who handled Egyptian grain, the reverse was true: they sailed downhill before northerlies from Athens to Rhodes and before northwesterlies from there to Egypt but had to work against them all the way back, and the best course they could lay was a roundabout one by way of Cyprus; it helped somewhat that between Egypt and Rhodes they were willing to sail all year round. A skipper headed for Sicily had the wind behind him only as far as the southern tip of Greece, and from that point on he had to work against it; conditions were, of course, just the reverse on the homeward leg. An ancient freighter could make between four and six knots with the wind, only two or a bit more against it. This meant that the round trip to Egypt or the Crimea involved about three weeks at sea, to Sicily about two.

After a vessel arrived at the Piraeus and the customs and port charges were paid, a shipper unloaded into the "Long Colonnade" and stood by while the wholesale grain dealers, who in turn sold to millers or consumers, bid for portions of his cargo. He had to get a good price, for this was his one chance of making a profit: what with the time consumed at sea and in loading up, generally only one round-trip could be fitted into the short sailing season. If the price had fallen between the time he purchased his cargo and the day he arrived at the Piraeus, he had to swallow the loss and wait until the following year to recoup. When he finally collected from the wholesalers, he paid principal and interest to the moneylender or moneylenders and chartering charges to the shipowner and pocketed as profit what was left.

In a system of credit such as this, a great deal depended on the integrity of the shipper. The Athenians were perfectly aware of this and, though in other fields they were free and easy in making loans, even to the extent of turning over cash without papers or witnesses, when it came to maritime loans they nailed everything down hard and fast in a written contract that tried to anticipate all contingencies. But businessmen are the same in all ages and places, and the Piraeus saw its share of shady operations. One favorite was to pledge a cargo for a loan from one moneylender and then, by repledging the same cargo, collect further loans from others. If a man could load, transport, and sell a cargo quickly enough to pay off the creditors in short order, there was a fair chance the fraud would never be discovered. If a shipper, after negotiating a series of loans in this way, could inveigle a shipowner into entering a deal to arrange a convenient shipwreck, either real if the boat wasn't worth much or pretended if it was, both could clear in one season more money than they could possibly make in years of legitimate business.

The great orator Demosthenes is best known for the fiery political speeches he made before the Athenian assembly. In private life he was a lawyer, and his clients included a good number of people who had lent money at one time or another to shippers who turned out to be unfortunate credit risks. In the gallery of rogues whom Demosthenes sued, the most lurid without question were a pair named Zenothemis and Hegestratus. Zenothemis was a shipper and Hegestratus a shipowner, a partnership which, if dishonest, could prove disastrous to investors in maritime enterprises. Both came from Marseilles; like so many of the men who did business at the Piraeus they were foreigners. The transaction involved in the case began as a perfectly legitimate one. Protus, a shipper of Athens, got a loan from Demosthenes' client, putting up as collateral a cargo of Sicilian grain which he was to buy at Syracuse. He chartered space on Hegestratus' ship, left Athens, arrived at Syracuse, bought his grain, loaded it aboard, and was ready to leave. So far everything was fine. But at this point Hegestratus and Zenothemis swung into action. Each made the rounds of the local moneylenders, raising as many loans as he could; when asked for collateral, each would glibly describe the cargo of grain that lay in the ship at the quay, merely omitting the slight detail that it was already pledged for a loan. When they had collected a sizable amount of cash in this fashion, they sent it off to be stashed away in their hometown of Marseilles.

This was one of those swindles in which a shipowner had to take part, since it was essential to the scheme to get rid of the grain: if that ever arrived at Athens and was sold by Protus, in the normal course of events the word would get back to the lenders at Syracuse and they would sooner or later catch up with the culprits. Zenothemis and Hegestratus laid their plans carefully. They waited until the ship was two or three days out of Syracuse en route to Athens and was coasting along not too far from the island of Cephallenia. On a dark night Hegestratus, leaving his partner to chat on deck with the passengers, stole down to the hold clutching a handsaw, made his way to the ship's bottom planking, and started to saw through it energetically. Apparently Zenothemis' diversion on deck wasn't loud enough, because some of the passengers heard the noise below, went down to investigate, and caught Hegestratus red-handed. He rushed on deck and, without breaking his stride, went right over the side, intending to grab the ship's boat, which was being towed behind, and cut loose; obviously he and his partner had in mind to use this means of saving their skins if the scuttling had gone off as planned. In the dark he missed it and, as Demosthenes comments, "met the end he deserved." Zenothemis, who was a quick thinker, tried a last-minute tactic: he raced about the deck hollering that the ship was going to go down at any minute and exhorting officers, crew, and passengers to climb into the boat and abandon ship. This might have worked except that Protus called to the crew that he would reward each one of them handsomely for bringing the vessel in and they stuck by their posts. When the voyage finally ended at the Piraeus, Zenothemis was far from through. At Athens he decided to claim that the grain was really his and, when Protus and his moneylender took it over, hired a sea lawyer to sue the two of them for the return of "his property." It is clear that Demosthenes, who represented the Athenian moneylender, had a tough case on his hands, especially since the creditors at Syracuse, realizing that they had been swindled and that they could recoup only if Zenothemis could acquire some assets, were zealously supporting the latter's story. What is more, it seems that at the end even Protus made a deal with Zenothemis, since the price of grain had dropped by the time he arrived, and, after paying off his debt and interest and the rewards to the crew, he faced a good-sized loss on the whole transaction. We do not know what the court's decision was, for all that is preserved is the speech Demosthenes wrote for his client.

Another case that Demosthenes took for an investor in maritime loans was against two Lycians who, like Zenothemis and Hegestratus, turned out to be lamentable credit risks. This pair borrowed money, offering as collateral both a cargo of wine, which they were to purchase in northern Greece and deliver to the Black Sea area, and a cargo of grain, which they were to purchase out there and bring back to Athens. The contract between the parties is still extant, and since it is the only document of its kind preserved it is worth quoting (I have added the rubrics and parenthetical notes):

Parties: Androcles of Athens [this was Demosthenes' client] and Nausicrates of Carystus

have lent to

Artemo and Apollodorus of Phaselis [in Lycia, in Asia Minor]

Amount: 3,000 drachmas,

Purpose: for a voyage from Athens to Mende or Scione [both in northern Greece] and thence to Bosporus [in the Crimea], or, if they so desire, to the north shore of the Pontus [Black Sea] as far as the Borysthenes [Dnieper], and thence back to Athens, on interest at
Interest: the rate of 225 drachmas on the 1,000—however, if they should leave the Pontus for the return voyage after the middle of September [that is, run the danger of hitting equinoctial storms], the interest is to be 300
Security: drachmas on the 1,000—on the security of 3,000 jars of wine of Mende which shall be conveyed from Mende or Scione in the ship of which Hyblesius is owner [that is, a chartered vessel].

They provide these goods as security, owing no money on them to any other person, nor will they make any additional loan on this security. They agree to bring back to Athens in the same vessel all the goods [certainly grain] put on board as a return cargo while in the Pontus.

Time of repayment   If the return cargo is brought safely to Athens, the
and permissible   borrowers are to pay the lenders the money due in
deductions: accordance with this agreement within 20 days after they shall have arrived at Athens, without deduction save for such jettison as the passengers shall have made by common agreement, or for money paid to enemies [the inevitable pirates], but without deduc-
Provisions in   tion for any other loss. They shall deliver to the lend-
the event of   ers all the goods offered as security to be under the
nonpayment   latter's absolute control until such time as they themselves have paid the money due in accordance with the agreement.

If they shall not pay back within the time stipulated the lenders have the right to pledge or even to sell the goods for whatever price they can get, and if the proceeds of the sale fall short of the sum the lend-

ers are entitled to in accordance with the agreement, they have the right to collect [the difference]
by proceeding, severally or jointly, against Artemo
and Apollodorus and against all their property
whether on land or sea, wherever it may be.

After several further stipulations the agreement closes with the sig-
natures of the parties and witnesses.

Artemo and Apollodorus neatly managed to break every provision
in the contract. First they loaded aboard only 450 jars of wine instead
of the specified 3,000. Next they proceeded to float another loan on
the same security. Then they left the Black Sea to go back to Athens
without a return cargo. Finally, on arrival they put in not at the port
but at the smugglers' cove, the Thieves' Harbor. Time passed, and the
creditors, seeing no sign either of their money or of any merchandise
which they could attach, confronted the pair and were blandly told
that the cargo had been lost in a storm and hence all obligations were
off. Fortunately the creditors were able to produce sworn depositions
from passengers and crew that no cargo of wine or grain had been
aboard. Again, we don't know how Demosthenes made out because all
we have is the speech he wrote for his client.

On top of all the dangers from acts of God and godless men, there
was yet another, the need to deal in cash, to carry about large and
heavy amounts of coin. A trader's method of procedure was more or
less as follows. First he made his way to the waterfront to line up a
shipowner who had space available and whose vessel was headed for
the destination he had in mind. He then ranged up and down the
porticoes in back of the quay at the Piraeus, where men with money to
invest or their agents gathered, until he found one or more willing to
grant him a loan. The two parties, after drawing up a written agreement, repaired to the office—the same as his home—of some banker
they knew and trusted. There, under his eye, the lender or lenders
passed over the coin, and the agreement was left with the banker for
safekeeping. No writing accompanied the transfer of the money, no
receipts were executed in duplicate or the like—something we feel so
necessary today. Greek businessmen of this age preferred to work
orally before witnesses. The trader had a slave shoulder the sack or
sacks of coin and accompany him to the ship. He either went aboard
himself or entrusted cash and mission to an agent; the latter might be
an Athenian who was an associate of his, or one of his slaves who
served as his man of affairs and had full authority to act in his name.
If the voyage ended successfully, the trader summoned his creditor(s)

to a meeting at the banker's office, and there, again with him as witness, handed over in cash the amount of the loan plus interest, and the parties wrote finis to the deal by tearing up the written agreement.

One of the surprising features of commerce in Athens at this time is that so many of the men involved were not Athenian. There was good reason for this. The form of investment that was safest and boasted the highest social tone was real estate. But ownership of real estate, whether land or houses, was open solely to Athenian citizens. This meant as well that only they could make loans secured by real estate. They turned to maritime ventures only when it suited them. Foreigners, on the other hand, had no alternative; however, since there was money to be made in the business, they were willing volunteers. Of the three roles involved—shipowning, trading, and moneylending—they almost totally monopolized the first: practically all the vessels that carried products in and out of the Piraeus belonged to men from Marseilles, Byzantium, the Greek cities in southern Russia, Asia Minor, and so on. Athenians, with more attractive possibilities open to them, preferred to leave to others a capital investment of considerable size that stood idle for half the year and could be totally lost in a few moments during the other half. In the second, trading, foreigners were easily in the majority, although there were plenty of Athenians taking part along with them; indeed, in the comedies of this period, a standard character is the Athenian father who goes off overseas on business, leaving a ne'er-do-well son free to sow wild oats and start the wheels of the plot spinning. And, in the third, the financing of maritime ventures, Athenians outnumbered non-Athenians by a good margin.

It was the size of the return that tempted them. Real estate was a fine form of investment, safe and prestigious, but it yielded no more than 8 percent. Keeping money on deposit in a bank or lending on good security brought 10 to 18 percent. Running a factory might produce 20 percent or more—but even though factories were small, they still forced an owner to tie up for life no small amount of capital in the work force of slaves. A maritime loan, on the other hand, could double a man's money within the few months of the sailing season; it was the one way in ancient Athens to make a quick financial killing.

Of the multitudinous foreigners who carried on business dealings in Athens or the Piraeus, a number became "metics," aliens who had officially established permanent residence in either place. The Athenians, like all Greeks, were too close-knit a community to share readily any of their privileges as citizens; but to mark the metics as a class a cut above out-and-out foreigners, they magnanimously extended to them the questionable joys of partaking in paying taxes and serving in the armed forces. Despite this, the metics had a genuine feeling of devotion to the city. For one thing, they were businessmen and there was money to be made at the Piraeus. It was one of the few places where, like Pasion and Phormio, a man could pull himself up by his own efforts from the bottom of the ladder; there were many other metics besides these two who, though they started out as slaves and never learned to speak Greek without an accent, ended up well-to-do and respected members of the business community. For another, these metics, as well as the various foreigners who traded at the Piraeus, were a vital link in the city's food supply, and Athens went out of its way to look after them. It had to make sure, for example, to provide swift and efficient justice for them. So, it opened up its courts to their cases between November and April, when ships stayed off the water and shippers had the spare time to bother with legal proceedings. The city held monthly hearings for complaints that involved them, and, if a complaint led to a trial, made sure it went on within a month; no trader was to prefer to sell his grain at Corinth or Samos just because Athens kept him waiting around for justice until his name came up on some overcrowded court calendar. And, whereas in other cases the penalty usually was a fine, those involving shippers carried prison sentences. This helped both parties: if a native Athenian won a case against a foreigner, the prison sentence guaranteed that the latter couldn't settle matters in his own way by taking off in his ship without paying judgment. Conversely, if the Athenian lost, the fear of prison made him pay up promptly and not compel the foreigner, whose home might be hundreds of miles away, to hang around Athens and go through all the red tape involved in collecting on the judgment.

The city was even prepared to grant some of the privileges of citizenship, or even citizenship itself, to those businessmen who had demonstrated over the years their loyalty and dedication to its interests. This was the way ex-slaves like Pasion and Phormio got to be citizens. It took a special act of the Athenian assembly to do it, but Athens found it prudent to be liberal with such acts. It had to be: there were plenty of other cities ready to come across, particularly when bad harvests gave the grain shippers even more leverage than they normally had.

The grain trade of Athens was too vital to the city's well-being to be left completely in the hands of private businessmen. Yet the government had neither the administrative machinery nor the desire to take over any part of the actual operations. It did the next best thing: it exercised careful control. The Piraeus, because of its location and fa-

cilities was, like London or Amsterdam or New York, a central clear-
ing point: loads of merchandise came into the harbor which were simply in transit, destined for consignees farther on. The government
passed a series of stringent decrees to make sure that enough grain to
feed the city resisted the lure of higher prices elsewhere. Of any cargo
of grain that entered the port, only one-third could be transshipped;
the rest had to stay on the dock. No Athenian, either citizen or metic,
was allowed to import grain to any place other than Athens: in other
words, only out-and-out foreigners could handle transit grain. No
Athenian, citizen or metic, could lend money on a grain cargo destined
for any place other than Athens: in other words, Athenian capital was
to be used for Athenian benefit. The regulations didn't end with the
shipper. When the cargo arrived, each wholesaler was allowed to buy
only fifty measures (probably about seventy-five bushels); this kept
ambitious dealers from cornering the market at any time. There were,
of course, dealers and shippers who were willing to break the law, but
it was risky business since the penalties were severe. At times even all
these precautions didn't ensure an adequate supply, and then the city
was forced to step in and take an active part. It appointed special
boards of grain purchasers to buy supplies at any cost in the open
market, which they then sold at normal prices to the citizen. The princelings who controlled the rich grainfields of southern Russia were
always collecting statues and elaborate expressions of thanks from the
Athenian government by giving the city cargoes of grain gratis, or
granting loading priority to ships headed for Athens, or canceling the
port dues for them. A surefire way for a foreigner to get honors at
Athens, or at any Greek city that lived off imported grain, was by con-
tributing to its grain fund, by giving it a gift of grain, or by just selling
some to it at the normal price during a scarcity. Here, for example, is
the text of a resolution that was moved and passed by the Athenian
assembly in 325 B.C. (the government recorded the bills it passed on
long-lived stone instead of perishable paper, and archaeologists have
dug up hundreds of them):

Motion put by Demosthenes, son of Democles:

Whereas Heracleides of Salamis [the town on Cyprus] has
   continuously shown his dedication to the interests of the People of
   Athens and done for them whatever benefactions lay within his
   power, viz.,
      on one occasion, during a period of scarcity of grain, he
         was the first of the shippers to return to the port, and he volun-
         tarily sold the city 3,000 *medimni* [4,500 bushels] at a price of 5
         drachmas per measure [the market price was probably in the

neighborhood of 16],

and

on another occasion, when voluntary contributions were
being collected, he donated 3,000 drachmas to the grain purchase fund, and

in all other respects he has continually shown his good will and
dedication to the people,

be it resolved that official commendation be extended to

Heracleides, son of Charicleides, of Salamis and

that he receive a gold crown for his good will and dedication to
the interests of the People of Athens,

that he and his offspring be declared an Accredited Representative and a Benefactor of the People of Athens,

that they have the right to own land and buildings, subject to the
limits of the law, and

that they have the right to undertake military service and the payment of property taxes in common with Athenian citizens.

Be it further resolved that the secretary currently in office

have a record of this motion and others ancillary to it inscribed on a
stone slab and set up on the acropolis, and that the treasurer provide
for this purpose 30 drachmas from the appropriate funds.

The stone, as the last section indicates, records as well a companion
motion, also passed, which includes two additional interesting pieces
of information: that the crown is to cost 500 drachmas, and that once,
when the ruler of the town of Heraclea on the Black Sea tried to keep
Heracleides' ship from departing for Athens by confiscating his sails,
the Athenians stepped in immediately and dispatched a representative (with fifty drachmas officially voted for expenses) to lay down the
law.

Obviously, Heracleides was a man to cultivate. In the cases Demosthenes took, the cargoes involved were never worth more than
7,000 drachmas and usually almost half that; here was someone who
handled cargoes worth 15,000 drachmas and, on behalf of the city, was
willing to forgo a clear profit of 33,000. No wonder Athens sent an
official representative at government expense when he got into
trouble.

Heracleides' little incident at Heraclea reveals another and very important problem that the government had to contend with. The grain
did nobody in Athens any good until it arrived at the Long Colonnade,
and there were unscrupulous competitors, like the Heracleote ruler,
and pirates loose all over the seas. One of the reasons the Piraeus was
so important a center for the grain trade was that Athens had a navy

large enough to supply escorts to convoy fleets of freighters, especially those that sailed from southern Russia through the Bosporus and Dardanelles. Although no serious battles took place during a large part of the fourth century B.C., the Athenian navy at this time counted more units than it ever did during the bitterly fought Peloponnesian War. No less than four hundred war craft of various sizes lay in the naval base at the Piraeus. To keep this armada in repair, the city controlled the trade in timber and naval supplies as carefully as grain. Because most of the wood and pitch came from the pine forests of Macedon and Thrace, Athens tried to force the local rulers there to sign treaties guaranteeing the sale of their products to her and no other state. A tiny island named Ceos had only one exportable product, ruddle, a substance used in paint; it was bound by treaty to turn its total output over to the city. The Athenians were thorough.

The size of Athens' naval forces is deceptive. Of its four hundred vessels, many were not in shape to put to sea and of those that were, many had to be left in their slips because there were no crews to man them. Athens and every other Greek city that maintained a navy was plagued by a shortage of rowers. The Greek citizen of the commercially minded fourth century wasn't as willing as his fifth-century ancestor had been to spend the better part of his days in military service. Athens' military leaders now included hired professionals, like the *condottieri* of Italy in the fourteenth and fifteenth centuries, who signed on with their own following of mercenaries. This meant that the labor force that used to be available only to the fleet now had a chance to enroll in the army, and they seized it with alacrity; the life was far easier than on the rowing benches, and a man stood a fair chance of fattening his salary with loot or booty. The trierarchs, those rich men who were required to equip and maintain a trireme in fighting condition for a year, were hard put to keep the rowing benches filled. "Many of my crew," complains a trierarch in 360 B.C., "jumped ship; some went off to the mainland to hire as mercenaries, some went off to the navies of Thasos and Maroneia which not only promised them a better wage but paid them some cash down in advance. . . . There was more desertion on my ships than on those of the other trierarchs since I had the best rowers. . . . My men, knowing they were skilled oarsmen, went off to take jobs wherever they figured they could get the highest pay." The situation grew so serious that it ultimately resulted in one of the greatest changes in fighting ships that took place in the ancient world. For the details we must leave Athens for the moment and turn westward.

Just about the time when Sparta and its allies were closing in on Athens for the kill that was to end the Peloponnesian War (Chapter 8), off in Syracuse an astute, hardheaded political opportunist was taking the first steps in building up a powerful and sizable empire. Dionysius was a canny statesman, a practical and unscrupulous politician, and, above all, a soldier who regarded warfare as a science. In the field he reorganized the traditional army unit and devised new tactics for it; he learned the techniques of oriental siege craft from his Carthaginian enemies and bettered them by designing enormously powerful catapults. And, on the sea, in 399 B.C. he revolutionized the makeup of navies by including in his own types of warship larger than the trireme, namely quadriremes and quinqueremes; indeed, the latter was his own invention (Carthage seems to deserve the credit for the former). With such an army and navy he was able to fashion a realm that covered nearly all of Sicily and much of southern Italy. His galleys swept the Tyrrhenian Sea and the Adriatic free of pirates; traders from the Piraeus were able to import Sicilian grain without molestation.

The new types of warship—we shall treat the details later (Chapter 11)—did not catch on immediately. Although Athenian naval observers must have kept a careful eye on what was going on in the Syracusan shipyards, there was no need for them to urge quick changes. Dionysius was too occupied in the west to be any threat himself, and Athens' enormous fleet of triremes had no serious rival in the east; there was no pressing reason to undertake the expense of immediate wholesale conversion. But the new types were gradually introduced into the squadrons: the inventory records of the Athenian dockyards are preserved for the year 330 B.C. and they list 392 triremes and 18 quadriremes; by 325 B.C. the number of triremes had dropped to 360, there were 43 quadriremes, and, in addition, 7 quinqueremes. Within a few decades the new types had become standard in all navies.

What of the merchantmen of this age? We know in detail what a small freighter of the times looked like and how it behaved, thanks to the fruitful collaboration of the marine archaeologist Michael Katzev and the historian of naval technology, J. Richard Steffy. In 1968 Katzev undertook the excavation of a wreck lying off the north coast of Cyprus. Not only was the cargo (chiefly wine jars) carefully removed, but the considerable remains of the hull were painstakingly lifted from the seafloor, brought to the nearby town of Kyrenia, and there restored and reconstructed. Pottery and other indications revealed that the vessel was a Greek craft that had gone down sometime between 310 and 300 B.C. It was of modest size, about forty-five feet long and twelve to fifteen broad, with a capacity of around thirty tons. It was built of pine in the standard ancient fashion (Chapter 3), shell-first with the planks carefully pinned to each other by means of close-set mortise-and-tenon joints, and was powered by a sail set well forward of amidships. So much of the hull was preserved that it was possible, under Steffy's exacting supervision, to create a precise replica. The sail and lines, of course, had all been lost, so the vessel was given the standard ancient rig, a squaresail equipped with brails. In 1986 it made a maiden voyage, from the Piraeus to Cyprus, and the following year it sailed back (Pl. 30). Its performance was outstanding: under a strong favorable wind it reached speeds as high as eleven knots, and it weathered with no difficulty storms in which the wind rose to gale force. It triumphantly demonstrated the ability of the ancient shipwright to design a hull that was seaworthy and massively strong and a rig that was efficient, safe, and easy to handle.

The *Kyrenia II*, as the replica has been dubbed, was but a small coastal craft, the kind that no doubt tramped from port to port along the shores of Cyprus and Asia Minor. The freighters that brought grain to Athens or were the standard carriers for overseas transport of wine and oil were much bigger, capable of holding 100 to 150 tons on the average, while vessels capable of hauling 250 or more were not uncommon. (What the dimensions of the last were is anybody's guess; the smaller American coastal packets of the first half of the nineteenth century, which had a carrying capacity in the neighborhood of 250 tons, ran 80 to 85 feet long, 23 to 25 wide, and 11 to 12 feet deep in the hold.) These bigger merchantmen were, to be sure, the queens of the sea: they made their runs with a minimum of stops en route, they sailed in fleets, and they were often given an escort of warships which, besides protecting them, would throw over a line when the wind was feeble or foul and tow them to make sure they got through. The ordinary workhorse freighter of the Mediterranean was not so large nor so well treated: it probably carried about 80 tons or so on average; it tramped leisurely from port to port, picking up and delivering any and every sort of cargo; and it took its chances on wind, weather, and pirates.

A shipowner might accompany his vessel on voyages, but even if he did he would leave its handling to the *kybernetes*, his captain. The crew, right up to and including the captain, were generally slaves (a factor that added no inconsiderable sum to a shipowner's investment). The speed of his craft, since its sole propulsion was its sails, depended on the direction and strength of the wind: when it was favorable, blowing over the quarters or stern, an ancient ship on average could do between four and six knots or, if it were particularly strong, even better; against it, only about two or a bit more. Skippers still navigated by stars at night and by landmarks and wind direction and "feel" by day, but now they had one useful aid: sometime about the middle of the fourth century B.C. a geographer named Scylax the Younger published the first *Periplus* or "Coast Pilot," a volume that described the circuit of the

Mediterranean, naming ports and rivers, giving distances between points, indicating where fresh water was available, and so on.

For shorter hauls and general coastal work there were merchant galleys, roomier and heavier and slower relatives of the sleek warship and, of course, lacking the ram. As we would expect, they were of all sizes, some being little more than large dories with a handful of oarsmen, some having as many as fifty. The rowers were all in one level; multiple levels were hardly needed on galleys that carried oars mainly to ensure arrival at a destination even when there was no wind or it was contrary.

In 322 B.C., the year after Alexander the Great died, Athens fought two major actions in the Aegean. In the second, the battle of Amorgos, its fleet, outnumbered 170 to 240, was shattered and, with startling abruptness, Athens' role as a great sea power came to a close forever.

The victor was Alexander's fleet, now under the control of one of his successors. Alexander's blazing career profoundly affected the world of the fourth century B.C. In the wake of his conquests there came into existence almost overnight great new nations and with them new trading centers and routes. Business went on at the Piraeus—the city, after all, had an excellent harbor and its populace still had to eat. But the focus of commerce had shifted forever, leaving Athens on its edge and no longer at its center.

Chapter 10

BEYOND THE PILLARS OF HERCULES

JUST ABOUT the time that Athens' sea power was disintegrating in battle in the Aegean, far to the west, in the harbor of Marseilles, maritime history of a different kind was being made: Pytheas, the most gifted of the ancient mariners, was setting off on a voyage of exploration that for daring and length was not to be matched until the days of Da Gama and Columbus.

Pytheas' expedition did not come out of the blue. It came, as a matter of fact, toward the end of a series of bold ventures out of the Mediterranean into the ocean.

After Jason had led the way into the Black Sea (Chapter 6) and the Phoenicians had opened up Spain (Chapter 7), the tide of exploration ebbed for a while. Skippers busied themselves investigating the nooks and crannies of the newly opened areas. In the west, Phoenician and Carthaginian traders in tin from Cornwall poked their noses past the Pillars of Hercules, those landmarks that flanked the Strait of Gibraltar, only as far as Cadiz and left the ocean portion of the transport for native craft. In the east no one tried to challenge the monopoly of Indians, Arabs, and other locals who plied the Indian Ocean (Chapter 2). Then, from the beginning of the sixth century on, seamen, as if they had had their fill of the Mediterranean, turned their attention to the waters that lay outside it.

In the seventh century B.C. Egypt, which up to then had gradually become suspicious of foreigners, opened its doors to Greek and Phoenician traders. Pharaoh Necho (610–594 B.C.) went further and began to dig a canal between the Nile and the Red Sea in order to provide access from the Mediterranean into the southern seas. For some reason he gave up the project and turned instead to a bold exploration of an alternative way to get from the one into the other: he fitted out an expedition to undertake nothing less than a circumnavigation of Africa from east to west, from the Red Sea clockwise around the continent, through the Strait of Gibraltar, and back to Egypt. He entrusted it to Phoenicians, presumably the best qualified to carry out such a voyage.

Homer had described the world as an island encircled by a river called Ocean, and Greeks in Necho's day were convinced that water surrounded Europe and Africa; it is hard to say whether this was de-

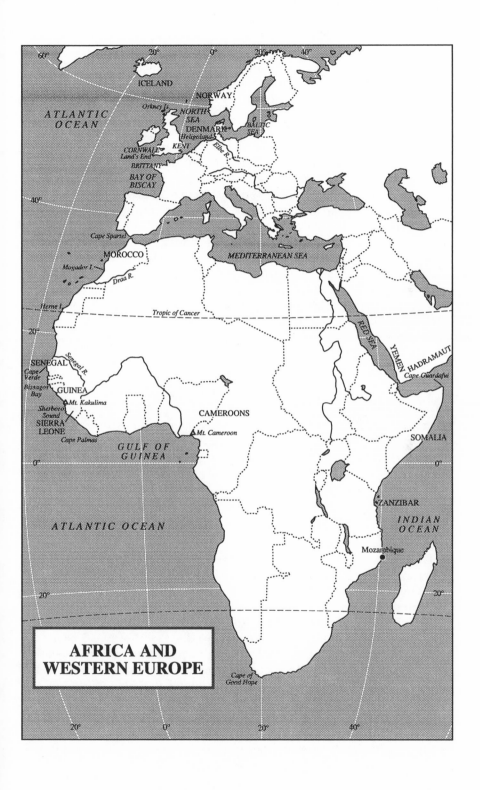

ATLANTIC
OCEAN

ICELAND

NORWAY

Orkney Is.
NORTH
SEA
DENMARK
Heligoland
KENT
BALTIC
SEA

CORNWALL
Land's End
BRITTANY
BAY OF
BISCAY

Elbe R.

MEDITERRANEAN SEA

40°

Cape Spartel

MOROCCO

Mogador I.

Draa R.

RED SEA

Herne I.

Tropic of Cancer

20°

YEMEN
HADRAMAUT
Cape Guardafui

SENEGAL
Cape
Verde
Bissagos
Bay
GUINEA

Senegal R.

Sherboro
Sound
SIERRA
LEONE
Mt. Kakulima

CAMEROONS

SOMALIA

Cape Palmas
Mt. Cameroon

GULF OF
GUINEA

0°

0°

ATLANTIC OCEAN

ZANZIBAR

INDIAN
OCEAN

Mozambique

20°

20°

AFRICA AND
WESTERN EUROPE

Cape of
Good Hope

20°

0°

20°

40°

duced from sailors' reports or whether, since Homer was their bible, they just took his word for it. However, they had no idea that Africa extended as far south as it does; they conceived of it as a rectangle running east-west, and thought that once a ship got a little beyond Ethiopia it could make a right turn and skirt, along the bottom of the continent, a shore that paralleled the Mediterranean coast along the top. No doubt Necho's Phoenicians believed this too, and agreed to attempt the expedition partly, at least, because they considerably underestimated its length. (One of the reasons for Columbus' confidence was that he reckoned the circumference of the globe one-quarter less than its true size.)

The only ancient writer to describe this remarkable voyage is Herodotus, the Greek traveler and historian, who had a keen nose for interesting and unusual bits of information; his wanderings included a tour of Egypt and he could well have picked the story up there. Here are his words (with modern equivalents substituted for his geographical names):

> Africa, except where it borders Asia, is clearly surrounded by water. Necho, pharaoh of Egypt, was the first we know of to demonstrate this. When he left off digging the canal between the Nile and the Red Sea, he sent out a naval expedition manned by Phoenicians, instructing them to come home by way of the Strait of Gibraltar into the Mediterranean and in that fashion get back to Egypt. So, setting out from the Red Sea, the Phoenicians sailed into the Indian Ocean. Each autumn they put in at whatever point of Africa they happened to be sailing by, sowed the soil, stayed there until harvest time, reaped the grain, and sailed on; so that two years went by and in the third they doubled the Pillars of Hercules and made it back to Egypt. And they reported things I cannot believe, though others might, namely, that in sailing around Africa they had the sun on the right side.

Hundreds of pages have been written about this bald paragraph, debating the truth of the story, questioning whether such a tremendous feat had actually been accomplished. Three centuries after it was written, Polybius, one of the finest ancient historians and an African explorer himself, registered his doubts. Many, perhaps a majority, of modern commentators are also unconvinced.

On one point most agree: such a voyage is perfectly feasible. There is no reason why a crew of Phoenicians could not have carried it out in the span of time and in the fashion Herodotus describes. Necho by chance sent them the best way: the circumnavigation of Africa from east to west has wind and current in its favor more than from the opposite direction. By starting in late summer or early autumn they would catch favorable northerlies to bring them down the Red Sea, and the last of the summer southwest monsoon would carry them east through the Gulf of Aden to Cape Guardafui. They could easily have reached this point by the beginning of November, when the northeast monsoon would be starting to blow steadily along the east coast of Africa, and that would speed them on their way as far as Mozambique; from there they would have a wind on the port beam as well as a favorable current almost to the southern tip of the continent. They would round the tip against the prevailing westerlies but with a favorable, though at times dangerous, current. By now almost a year would have gone by and they would be in the southern hemisphere's autumn. They could have landed just past the tip, where climate and soil would permit the growing of wheat, sown, awaited the crop, reaped it, and resumed the voyage. They would have wind and current with them as far as the Gulf of Guinea, where Africa's great western bulge begins. From this point on, however, they would have their work cut out for them, first putting in long stretches at the oars under torrid heat to get past the calms of the Gulf of Guinea and then rowing constantly against wind and current right up to the Strait of Gibraltar. The Moroccan coast is an area suitable for wheat, and here, by now well into autumn of their second year, they could have planted and reaped a second crop. Then, during what was left of the third year they could easily have made it through the Strait of Gibraltar and on to Egypt.

Yes, say the skeptics, theoretically possible but most unlikely. The Phoenician mariners not only lacked the compass but, once past the equator, would no longer have had available the North Star, the Great Bear, and all the other northern stars that they had always depended on. They would be sailing most of the time in totally unknown waters, and they would have traversed an unbelievably long distance, far more than any other voyage known from antiquity. Herodotus' detail about the sun, which to nonskeptics appears to be solid proof that they had gotten far enough south to have the sun constantly to their north, can easily be explained away.

But even the skeptics do not deny that Necho did send out such an expedition. And, despite their assertions, the probability is that it did get south of the Tropic of Capricorn where throughout the day the sun would be to the north of the ships. Possibly it made the complete circuit as Herodotus describes—but only possibly, and we will never know for sure.

The next attempt to sail around Africa was made in the other direction, from west to east, and there is no doubt whatsoever that it was a failure. Again Herodotus tells the story, and this time he indicates his informant, although he is reticent about his name: when the explorer died, one of his eunuchs absconded to Samos with a lot of his money and there, writes Herodotus, "a certain Samian got his hands on it. I

know the man's name perfectly well but I shall willingly forget it here."
The voyage, it seems, started as the result of a scandal at the court of
King Xerxes (485–464 B.C.), the same one who spent that unsettling
day watching the defeat of his fleet off Salamis (p. 81). His cousin
Sataspes had violated one of the court ladies. Xerxes was ready to
carry out the appropriate punishment, namely impaling, but Sataspes'
mother suggested he be sent on a trip around Africa instead. The king
had no objection to this—he probably figured the end result would be
the same—so

> Sataspes went to Egypt, got a ship and crew there, and made for the Strait
> of Gibraltar. Passing through it and doubling Cape Spartel, he headed
> south [all the ancient geographers were convinced that the Atlantic coast
> of Morocco trended south, even southeast, instead of southwest]. After
> sailing for many months over a vast amount of water and always finding
> that he had to keep going further, he put about and made his way back
> to Egypt. From there he returned to Xerxes and reported that, at the
> farthest point he reached, he sailed past little people who wore clothes of
> palm leaves and abandoned their villages to flee to the mountains when-
> ever the boat put in at the shore, and that he and his men, when they went
> in, did them no harm but only took some of their cattle. Moreover, the
> reason he didn't sail all around Africa was that the ship stopped and
> couldn't go any further.

This turned out to be most unfortunate for Sataspes personally since,
on the grounds that he had not completed the assignment, Xerxes
went ahead with the original sentence and had him impaled.

It sounds very much as if Sataspes got south of the Sahara, as far as
Senegal or even Guinea, where he saw Negro tribes, perhaps Bush-
men living farther north at that time than they do today, and then
either ran into the calms and adverse current of the Gulf of Guinea or
the combination of adverse wind and current beyond. As we have
noted, wind and current make the circumnavigation of Africa from
east to west, the way Necho's Phoenicians set out to do it, easier. Although a number of ancient mariners after Sataspes tried the west to
east voyage, they all failed. Vasco da Gama at the end of the fifteenth
century was the first to turn the trick.

Necho's expedition and Sataspes' were purely voyages of exploration, probably launched with an eye to opening up new trade routes.
About a century after Necho—some scholars think before 500 B.C.,
others after 480—another venture outside the Strait of Gibraltar was
made, this time part of a grandiose scheme for colonization. A number
of ancient writers mention it, providing a few and not always trustworthy details, but fortunately there also exists, written in Greek, a full-
scale account that purports to be the verbatim report of the com-

mander of the venture, Hanno, king of Carthage. He had it inscribed on a bronze plaque, which he set up in a temple at Carthage; some Greek visitor must have seen it there and drawn up the translation that has come down to us.

"The Carthaginians commissioned Hanno to sail past the Pillars of Hercules and to found cities of the Libyphoenicians [Phoenicians residing in Africa]. He set sail with sixty vessels of fifty oars and a multitude of men and women to the number of thirty thousand, and provisions and other equipment." So begins Hanno's report, a document of less than 650 words, which over the centuries has provoked several hundred thousand of explanation, comment, and argument.

If the whole expedition had been put aboard sixty penteconters, the ships would have quietly settled on the harbor bottom instead of leaving Carthage; a penteconter barely had room to carry a few days' provisions for its crew, to say nothing of a load of passengers with all the equipment they needed to start life in a colony. The penteconters must have been the escort of warships and scouting craft; the colonists must have tagged along in a good-sized fleet of merchantmen. Very likely there were far fewer than thirty thousand. The Greek manuscripts that we have today are almost all the result of successive copyings over the centuries by scribe after scribe, and numerals, since they can rarely be checked by the context, are particularly liable to miscopying.

In following Hanno's narrative, the prime difficulty lies in identifying the places he records. Almost all the names he uses mean nothing to us today; there was no system available to him of fixing points by latitude and longitude (not used by geographers until over two centuries later); and the physical details he records are not always numerous and specific enough to make identification certain. His first leg was through the Strait of Gibraltar and along the Atlantic shore of Morocco where he kept dropping off batches of colonists who planted half a dozen settlements. At the mouth of what is probably the Draa River (28°30′N) he found a local tribe of nomads, very likely Berbers, and he took some aboard as guides and interpreters, since they were familiar with the coast farther south.

Some time after the interpreters joined him, Hanno led his fleet into a deep gulf in a recess of which he came upon "a small island with a circuit of five stades (about half a mile). Here we founded a colony named Cerne. We estimated from the distance traversed that it lay in a line with Carthage; for the distance from Carthage to the Pillars and from there to Cerne was the same." A number of commentators are convinced that Cerne is to be identified with Herne Island, which lies just a little north of the Tropic of Cancer (23°50′N); its location well suits the author's dscription, and the relative distances, from Carthage to Gibraltar and from there to Herne Island, are just about the same.

Others, pointing out that Hanno's estimate of the mileage he covered could well be mistaken since it was based solely on elapsed sailing time and his best guess as to his average speed, argue in favor of sites either farther away from Gibraltar than Herne or nearer. Several prefer a site considerably nearer, namely, Mogador Island (31°34′N), where archaeological excavation has revealed unmistakable remains of Phoenician occupation.

From Cerne, Hanno made two voyages farther south. During the first, he reports, after "sailing through the delta of a big river, named the Chretes, we came to a lake containing three islands larger than Cerne. From there, after a day's sail, we came to the head of the lake. Beyond it rose extremely lofty mountains full of savages wearing animal skins who pelted us with stones and kept us from landing. Sailing on from that point we came to another deep and wide river, which was infested with crocodiles and hippopotami. There we turned around and went back to Cerne." The crocodile-filled river can only be the Senegal; perhaps the first river Hanno came to, the Chretes, was one arm of it and the second, the "deep and wide river," another arm. The "extremely lofty mountains" pose something of a problem, since there are none such in the vicinity. The Senegal reaches the coast at 16°45′N, so, presuming Cerne was Herne Island, Hanno had a long ride back. Why he chose to go back is not stated.

Again he left Cerne to follow the coast south. He passed Negro tribes who fled at his approach and whose speech his interpreters could not understand. He took two days to pass by an area marked by wooded mountains; commentators take this to be Cape Verde, which suits such a description. He pushed onward and forthwith encountered a series of strange and perilous adventures. He came to

a great gulf, which according to the interpreters was called the Western Horn. In it lay a large island, and in the island a marine lake containing another island. Landing on this, by day we could see only forest, but by night many fires being kindled, and we heard the noise of pipes and cymbals and a din of tom-toms and the shouts of a multitude. Fear gripped us, and our soothsayers ordered us to leave the island.

We left in a hurry and coasted along a country with a fragrant smoke of blazing timber, from which streams of fire plunged into the sea. The land was unapproachable because of the heat.

So we sailed away in fear, and coasting along for four days saw the land ablaze by night. In the center a leaping flame towered above the others and appeared to reach the stars. By day it was revealed to be a mountain of tremendous height; it was called the Chariot of the Gods.

Sailing by the rivers of fire for three further days, we reached a gulf named the Southern Horn. In a recess lay an island like the previous one:

it had a lake and within this was another island. This was full of savages, of whom by far the greater number were women with hairy bodies. Our interpreters called them "gorillas." We gave chase to the men but could not catch any, for they scampered up the cliffs and held us off by throwing stones. We did catch three of the women, who bit and scratched and resisted as we led them off. However, we killed and flayed them and brought the hides to Carthage.

We sailed no farther, owing to lack of provisions.

Most commentators are convinced that Hanno succeeded in making his way a considerable distance down the coast. They point to phenomena he records that today are commonplace in explorers' accounts of journeys to Africa: the jungle, the beating of tom-toms, the enormous grass fires that natives kindle to burn off stubble and help the following year's crop, the ubiquitous monkeys. What his interpreters called "gorillas" must be some kind of large ape, but hardly what we know by that name; his men were tough but not up to going after gorillas barehanded, even females. Chimpanzees or baboons have been suggested. (It was an American missionary, Thomas Savage, who in 1847 applied Hanno's term to the mighty apes that now bear it.)

Exactly how far did he get? Conservative commentators think that he stopped short of the calms and heat of the Gulf of Guinea and pushed no farther than Sierra Leone, that the Western Horn is Bissagos Bay, that the Chariot of the Gods is Mount Kakulima in French Guinea which, although relatively low (ca. 3,000 feet), stands out in the midst of low-lying ground, and that the Southern Horn is Sherboro Sound. Others, more bold, take him as far as the Cameroons, arguing that the Chariot of the Gods is better identified with Mount Cameroon, the tallest peak in West Africa (13,370 feet) and a volcano to boot.

Finally there are the skeptics who feel that Hanno actually got only a short way down the coast and that the part of the voyage during which his dramatic experiences took place—the river full of crocodiles, the Western Horn with a fiery zone that extended all the way to the Southern Horn, the flame that seemed to reach the stars—were added by armchair geographers writing centuries later who attributed to Hanno their own fantasies about the shape and nature of *Africa incognita*. As in the case of the Phoenician circumnavigation of Africa, we will never know for sure. And, like that venture, Hanno's had no effect on subsequent history. Most of the west coast of Africa was to remain outside of European knowledge right up to the fifteenth century, when Prince Henry the Navigator successfully pressed his captains to sail ever farther south along its shores.

For over a century after Hanno's return, mariners stayed within the Mediterranean. The Carthaginians were satisfied to exploit the settlements Hanno had founded, and their hold on the Strait of Gibraltar kept others out of the Atlantic. Then, as the fourth century B.C. drew to a close, Pytheas of Marseilles entered the picture. He slipped through the blockade and was off on a unique and daring voyage of discovery.

"In fact there is no star at the pole but an empty space close to which lie three stars; these, taken with the point of the pole, make a rough quadrangle, as Pytheas of Marseilles tells us." It is only through stray notices such as this, scattered among the writings of ancient astronomers and geographers, that we know of this remarkable mariner, so accomplished a navigator that he was the first to observe that the pole-star did not mark true north, and so skillful a seaman that he sailed to a quarter of the globe as unknown then as America was in Columbus's day, and returned safely.

Pytheas was a native of Marseilles, the city which those doughty seamen, the Phocaeans, founded (Chapter 7) and which grew and stayed rich through overseas trade. He completed an all-important pioneering voyage, but nothing written about it in his own hand survives, just excerpts made by those who had access to his writings, many of whom were convinced he was an out-and-out liar and only mentioned what he said to scoff at it. They would have done better to take him seriously. Pytheas was no charlatan but the most scientific seaman of the ancient world.

Besides determining the true position of the polestar, he calculated the latitude of his hometown and came within a shade of getting it right (43°3′ instead of 43°17′ N). He took observations of the sun during his voyage that helped later geographers to establish a number of parallels of latitude. He was the first to notice the connection between the moon and the tides. He was the first to use the name "Britain." For centuries, whatever was known of the northern regions—Brittany, Ireland, the British Isles, and the North Sea—was derived from what he had reported.

Sometime during the decades before 300 B.C., Pytheas sailed out of the harbor of Marseilles, headed his prow westward, and got under way on a voyage that was not to end until he had gone around Spain to the British Isles and beyond. One of his reasons for going was certainly scientific, to explore and collect astronomical data, but this cannot have been the whole explanation. He was not wealthy enough to finance such an expedition on his own, so he must have gotten backing from the merchants of Marseilles. Yet it's hard to imagine that they would put up hard cash in return for some abstruse geographical findings. It is more than likely that they did it in order to get information about the source of tin. This was one of their prized objects of trade. It reached the city from somewhere up north but only overland through France; the cheap sea route around Spain was a monopoly of the Carthaginian merchants of Cadiz (Chapter 7). If Pytheas could come up with some way to circumvent them or somehow to increase the supply, his trip would more than pay for itself.

Like all ancient voyages of exploration, Pytheas' is full of problems, and the very first is how he managed to evade the Carthaginian blockade at the Strait of Gibraltar. Possibly his timing was right: he may have picked one of the years between 310 and 306 B.C. when Carthage, locked in a bitter struggle with the Greeks of Sicily, may have dropped her guard at the strait. Like Hanno's, the first leg of his journey is clear enough. He skirted the Atlantic coast of Spain and the shores of the Bay of Biscay, doubled the northwest tip of Brittany, and reached the Breton coast. From here he crossed the channel to Cornwall and absolved some of his obligations to his backers by reporting on the tin mining there. He watched the workers excavate ore along galleries, smelt and refine it, and hammer it into oblong ingots for shipment.

Probably his next step was to circumnavigate Britain. This enabled him to report, correctly enough, that the island was shaped like a triangle, its three points being Belerion (Land's End), Kantion (Kent), and Orca (the northern tip of Scotland just below the Orkney Islands). He estimated the length of the sides of this triangle, getting the proportions right (3:6:8) but just about doubling their total extent. The only means for measuring at his disposal was by reckoning the time spent in sailing, and he must have overrated his speed; most ancient explorers did. He established the location of Britain ("it extends obliquely along Europe") and probably of Ireland, and made several visits into the interior of the former to observe the inhabitants.

So far it has been relatively easy to follow Pytheas' track. Now the trouble begins. At some point during his voyage he heard of—or perhaps even visited—an "Island of Thule" which, he reported, lay six days' sail north of Britain and only one day south of the "frozen" sea, and the sun there went down for only two or three hours at night. It was surrounded by some mysterious substance which he actually saw but of which he gives an obscure and puzzling description; he may possibly be referring to the heavy sea fogs common in these regions. No known place fits his description in all respects but there are only two real possibilities: Iceland or Norway. In one part of his report Pytheas observed that some of the people in the northern regions brew a drink of grain and honey and grow millet. By millet he probably means oats; a crop of cooler climates, it would have been unfamil-

iar to someone from Marseilles. If he is referring to the people of
Thule, then Thule must be Norway because Iceland is too far north
for oats. That Norway is not an island poses no problem; discoverers
of new regions often mistake a piece of the mainland for an island.

Pytheas crossed the channel from Britain back to the Breton shore
and then proceeded to skirt the coast eastward, a journey that took
him past an enormous estuary and to an island where amber was so
plentiful the natives used it for fuel. This part of his travels has led to
the wildest guesses of all; some commentators have taken him right
around Denmark into the Baltic, a source of amber since prehistoric
times. But it is more likely that Pytheas got no further than the North
Sea, that his estuary was that of the Elbe and his island Helgoland, also
a depot for amber.

When Pytheas finally dropped anchor in the harbor of Marseilles,
he had covered between 7,000 and 7,500 miles, as much as Columbus
had on his first voyage. He had completed one of the most daring feats
of navigation made in any age and, from the point of view of the
world's knowledge, a highly important one: for centuries geographers
depended for information about northern countries on his data. He
opened their eyes to the fact that lands that lay so far north that
everyone believed they were barren wastes were habitable. It is not
surprising that armchair geographers, knowing nothing of the effect
of the Gulf Stream and the moist Atlantic winds on climate, found the
facts he reported hard to believe.

There are some slight indications that his backers received divi-
dends on their investment: the tin trade, from Cornwall across the
channel to Brittany and from there across France to Marseilles, seems
to have increased somewhat after his return. But nobody followed in
his footsteps. The Carthaginians once again closed the gates of Gibraltar and shut off the Atlantic to further exploration.

Even after the tide of Roman power had reached to the western-
most parts of Europe and opened them up, the ocean route around
Spain never was regularly utilized nor even thoroughly investigated.
Tin mines were discovered nearer home in Spain, and for communications with Britain the Romans preferred the overland route
through France and across the Channel. Over three hundred years
after Pytheas had reported on Ireland, a respectable geographer
could still babble about the Irish custom of eating dead parents and
having intercourse with mothers and sisters. It was on the Indian, not
the Atlantic, Ocean that the ancient mariners next concentrated; but
that story belongs to a later century.

Chapter 11

THE AGE OF TITANS

AT SUNSET of June 13, 323 B.C., Alexander the Great lay dead in a room of what had once been Nebuchadnezzar's palace in Babylon. Behind the scenes his staff officers were already laying plans to pick up the reins of his power. They were no ordinary men themselves, and they had worked in harmony only while a greater man had been alive to direct them. In the desperate contest that followed, two were to make maritime history: eagle-beaked, jutting-jawed Ptolemy, who laid the foundation of a fleet which his son expanded into the mightiest of the ancient world; and grizzled, one-eyed Antigonus, who grasped the surpassing importance of sea power in the struggle with his rivals and whose son became a sea lord par excellence, a brilliant admiral and a daring innovator in the design and use of men-of-war.

Alexander was born into a small world; he left it a big one, setting the stage for a new era, the Hellenistic Age, which lasted three centuries after his death. There was but one great empire in his day, the Persian, and that lay off to the east and was playing only an indirect role in the history of the Mediterranean. The Greek who lived in Greece or in any of the colonies that Greeks had planted was a citizen of a city that by itself made up his nation. It was in this world of little city-states that Athens had reached its heyday as a naval and commercial power in the fifth and fourth centuries B.C.—a little frog, but bigger than all the others in the pond. Alexander changed all that. In one swoop he built up an empire that stretched from Greece to India. And when, on his death, it disintegrated, as was inevitable without his genius to keep it whole, it did not break into city-state fragments but into large chunks: one, centered on his home state of Macedon, constantly trying to exercise overlordship upon the cities of Greece and the Aegean isles; another, centered on Egypt, constantly trying to control the coasts and islands of the eastern Mediterranean; a third, centered upon Syria, constantly contesting the advances of its Egyptian neighbor. The history of the century after Alexander's death is, by and large, the story of the bitter struggles among his former officers and their successors, the rulers of these new empires.

The creation of such states brought a new dimension into Greek history: bigness. Not only did large political units replace clusters of little ones, but a widespread common culture came into being. Alexander's officers were Greek and, to help them in the enormous job of ruling and policing widespread areas containing varied peoples and cultures, they brought in numbers of their fellow countrymen. They settled them as a trusted and favored upper class the length and breadth of their new kingdoms, and founded dozens of cities to accommodate them. As a result, a common Greek culture pervaded lands that had hardly known Greeks before: one language now took a traveler from Italy to India. Men read the same books, saw the same plays, looked at the same sort of paintings and statues at Seleucia in the heart of Meso-potamia, at Alexandria in Egypt, Antioch in Syria, Athens in Greece, Syracuse in Sicily. Commerce became big: caravan tracks stretched hundreds, some thousands, of miles to Arabia and India; long sea routes crisscrossed the Mediterranean and capacious freighters sailed over them.

Athens, even at its height, had operated on a tight budget with little left over for luxury; the new rulers could indulge in extravagance completely beyond the ken of a Greek city-state. Like the pashas of Persia, whom they supplanted in many places, they maintained elabo-rate courts, centers of luxurious living, which kept busy an army of merchants and shippers and caravaneers; there were excellent profits to be made in furnishing this newly created nobility with rich textiles, perfumes, gems, spices, rare woods, imported delicacies. They planted great new cities, which they proudly named after themselves or mem-bers of the family and decorated opulently with public buildings. Al-exander's young cavalry officer, Seleucus, founded Seleucia, near Babylon, as his capital and Antioch in Syria, named after his father, Antiochus. Egypt supplied Ptolemy with the income to make the city his former commander had created, Alexandria, into an architectural glory and the intellectual center of the Greek world; when, three cen-turies later, Cleopatra pressed an asp to her bosom and the dynasty came to an end, there was still an enormous amount of money left in the treasury. Even the descendants of Antigonus in Greece, where the pickings were necessarily slimmer because of the barren nature of the country, were able to found cities with imposing buildings and keep up a presentable court.

The greatest drain on the treasuries of all these kingdoms, one which eventually bled them into financial anemia, was the military budget. Ptolemy's successors in Egypt, Antigonus' in Greece, those of Seleucus in Syria, watched one another like hawks, never daring to drop their guard; when, at the slightest sign of weakness one attacked, another hurried to help the victim, in order to preserve the balance of power. Huge armies clashed; the seas saw the largest warships ever to be built and some of the mightiest fleets ever to be collected in the ancient world.

Alexander started without a navy. As he swept over the Greek coastal cities of Asia Minor and the seaports of Phoenicia, he picked up their squadrons and patched together a force that eventually reached the respectable total of 240 units and ended Athens' days as a sea power off Amorgos in 322. Like the empire that he had built up, it was dismembered after his death and the parts taken over by his successors. Seven years later the bulk of it came into Ptolemy's hands.

Ptolemy's chief rival at the moment was Antigonus the One-Eyed, founder of the dynasty that was to rule over Macedon and much of Greece until the Romans came in a century later. He worked closely with his son, Demetrius; the two present an example of harmony and affection unusual in an age that even saw fathers murdering sons and vice versa for political advantage. Antigonus, a tireless worker who rarely wasted a minute, was able to maintain an attitude of ironic tolerance toward his young partner's penchant for taking time out to play. A story is told that once, hearing Demetrius was ill, he walked to his bedroom and at the door a beautiful girl brushed by, obviously just departing; when his son greeted him with, "I've been sick; I just got rid of a fever," "I know," replied the old man, "I met it on the way out." When, in 301 B.C., father and son fought their last battle together, Antigonus, trapped in a corner of the field, held fast to his post, repeating over and over, "Demetrius will rescue me." For once he was wrong; the odds were too great and he was cut down.

The two made a perfect team. Antigonus was aware of the importance of sea power, and Demetrius was not only a brilliant tactician but a gifted and bold designer of ships. In 315 B.C. they set out to build a fleet that would match what Ptolemy had taken over of Alexander's— and touched off the greatest naval arms race in ancient history.

Antigonus turned to the dockyards of Phoenicia. They were conveniently located near the cedar and pine forests of Lebanon, and their shipwrights had been at their trade for literally thousands of years. But for designs he turned to the west: Antigonus wanted a fleet, not of triremes like the Athenian, but of the newer quadriremes and quinqeremes which, having proved their worth in the navy of Dionysius of Syracuse at the beginning of the century, were gradually making their way into eastern navies (Chapter 9). Demetrius' ideas were even more grandiose: if quadriremes and quinqueremes, that is, "fours" and "fives," could be built, why not larger still?

Under his watchful eye, in 315 B.C., the Phoenician shipyards turned out some "sixes" and "sevens" for him. By 301 he had "eights," "nines," "tens," an "eleven," and even one great "thirteen." A dozen years later he added a "fifteen" and a "sixteen." When he was ultimately defeated in 285, Ptolemy got the "fifteen," and the "sixteen" passed to another of his rivals. But somehow it wound up in the fleets of Demetrius' successors; when the Romans conquered Macedon in 168 they found the old ship there; it was no longer of any use in battle but they sailed it home, rowed it up the Tiber, and moored it at one of the city docks as a trophy.

The race did not stop here. Demetrius' rival Lysimachus, to match the "sixteen," built an even bigger ship, perhaps a more powerful type of "sixteen" (see below). Ptolemy's son countered this with not only a "twenty" but two gigantic "thirties." The climax was reached toward the end of the third century B.C., when Ptolemy IV built a Brobding-nagian "forty." It was over 400 feet long and 50 wide; the figureheads on prow and stern towered more than 70 feet above the water; its benches were manned by 4,000 rowers and its deck accommodated 400 deckhands and other crew members and 2,850 marines. But this behemoth never saw action and may have been meant only for display; the fourth Ptolemy had a penchant for building floating showpieces (p. 158).

Just what kind of ships were these supergalleys? Seamen and scholars have wrangled over the question for centuries. The quadriremes and quinqueremes—"fours" and "fives"—that Athens added to its fleet toward the end of the fourth century B.C. were housed in the same slips as its triremes, so they could not have been very different in size. Indeed, the simplest explanation is that both were just beefed up triremes, the quadriremes, say, with two rowers to each oar in the uppermost bank and the quinqueremes with two to each oar in the middle bank as well. Such an arrangement would still permit the men to row in the way they always had, from a seated position.

But what about the still larger sizes? For these the Greek naval architects, willy-nilly, must have turned to the long sweep manned by multiple rowers, so familiar to us from its widespread use in later ages, in the galleys that ruled the Mediterranean from the sixteenth to the eighteenth centuries. This involved a clean break with the past, for the rowers of such sweeps cannot remain seated, they must rise to their feet to dip the blade and throw themselves back on the bench for the pull. It is an arduous stroke, yet it has the great advantage of requiring a minimum of trained personnel: only the man at the tip of the loom need be skilled; the others merely supply muscle. This was no small advantage to the naval recruiters who, at a time when trained oarsmen were in short supply (cf. p. 112), were faced with the problem of filling the benches of ships that were bigger than ever in fleets that were bigger than ever.

Once naval architects had taken this innovative step, they would be in a position to design differing versions of the various sizes of galley, either a one-banked version or a two-banked or a three-banked (the ancients never went beyond three banks), depending upon circumstances. If a state had a fleet of seaworthy triremes and lacked the money to scrap them and replace with new heavier units, the architects could convert the triremes into three-level quadriremes and quinqueremes in the manner described above. If a state had the money but lacked skilled rowers, like the Romans when they entered the First Punic War (Chapter 12), the architects could supply one-level versions: quadriremes powered by a line of four-man sweeps, quinqueremes by a line of five-man sweeps. If faster types were wanted, they could supply two-level versions: quadriremes with two men to each oar in both banks, quinqueremes with three men to each oar in the upper and two in the lower. "Sixes" might be three-level with two men to an oar throughout, or two-level with three to an oar, or one-level with a line of six-man sweeps. Pictures reveal that the architects also introduced a new way of arranging the oars, a modification of the outrigger: on some ships they set all the oars in a projecting oar box that ran in a straight line from prow to stern (Pl. 31). Two thousand years later, designers of galleys turned to the same device.

By assuming multiple-rower sweeps in one, two, or three levels, we can satisfactorily explain the oarage of the various new supergalleys right up to Demetrius' great "sixteen." This could have had two banks of eight-man sweeps or three banks with, say, eight men to each oar in the topmost, five to each in the middle level, and three to each in the lowest. But eight is the most we may allot to an oar, for such was the experience of later ages: their very largest galleys have that many and no more. How, then, are we to explain the "thirties" of Ptolemy II? Or the "forty" of Ptolemy IV, a ship whose benches accommodated no less than 4,000 rowers and whose deck no less than 2,850 marines? The "forty" was so unusual a craft that an ancient writer drew up a detailed account of it, and this luckily has survived. It had three banks, he reports, and the oars of the uppermost were fifty-seven feet long. Actually that is not so extraordinary, not much longer, as it happens, than the six-man and seven-man sweeps used by the galleys in the navy of Louis XIV or of the Knights of Malta. Such oars would be just right for eight rowers, the maximum possible, as we have seen. Yet even if we allocate eight to the oar in all three banks, we still fall short, we arrive at only a "twenty-four." How could the ship possibly be a "forty"? The clue lies in certain very special features that we are told it possessed: it was "double-prowed" and "double-sterned" and it had four steering oars instead of the standard two. This can only mean that Ptolemy's architects designed for him a twin-hulled craft, what we

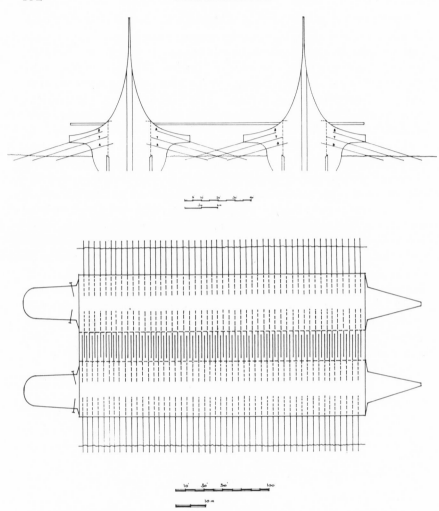

FIG. 5. Reconstruction of Ptolemy IV's "forty."

would call a catamaran (Fig. 5). The deck that spanned the two hulls
would offer a broad expanse, like that of an aircraft carrier, and this
would explain how there could be space for a complement of 2,850
marines, a veritable regiment. And the catamaran structure will explain how the galley could be classified as a "forty." Let us assume
there were eight men to each oar in the topmost bank, seven to each in
the middle bank, and five to each in the lowest. Let us further assume
that there were rowers on each side of the hull, the inner as well as the
outer. Each hull, then, would be a "twenty." Yoked together, they
would make a "forty."

The "forty" was not the only war galley that was twin-hulled. The "thirties" of Ptolemy II must have been twin-hulled also. And the ship that Lysimachus designed in order to match Demetrius' "sixteen" seems to have been a catamaran-style "sixteen." All these oversize vessels, whether catamaran or not, with the sole exception of the behemoth of Ptolemy IV, were neither kings' playthings nor misguided experiments. They were ships that saw service and proved their worth in action. Ptolemy II regarded the architect of his two "thirties" so highly that he honored him with a citation carved on stone that has survived to this day. The great ships, as one would expect, brought about a rise in power all the way down the line in the navies they belonged to. A well-balanced force in Demetrius' or Ptolemy's day was led by one of these superdreadnought, generally carrying the flag; it included a group of battleships, anything from "sixes" to "tens"; its ships of the line were "fours" and fives"; and triremes were reckoned among its light craft.

The size as well as the power of fleets grew. In the battles between Demetrius and Ptolemy or their sons, each side could put 150 to 200 ships into the line. At one time, about 313 B.C., Demetrius and Antigonus had a navy that totaled 330 units. Fifty years later Ptolemy II topped this with one even greater: he had 336 units with an average power of a quinquereme. It was made up of

2	"thirties"
1	"twenty"
4	"thirteens"
2	"twelves"
14	"elevens"
30	"nines"
37	"sevens"
5	"sixes"
17	"fives"
224	"fours," "threes," and smaller types
336	

His father had depended chiefly on "fives," and Demetrius' newly designed bigger ships had beaten him. The son learned the lesson: he cut down the number of "fives" to seventeen and built his fleet around a powerful core of heavier craft.

Demetrius' contribution to naval warfare did not end with the introduction of the supergalley. He has yet another one to his credit: a proper appreciation of naval artillery. Demetrius had always taken a keen interest in all the devices available for besieging walled towns—battering rams, storming towers, protective mantlets, and especially catapults for firing darts and stones; indeed, his contemporaries gave him the sobriquet Poliorcetes, "Besieger of Cities." He not only exploited catapults for siege warfare but mounted powerful versions on his warships. Very likely one of his reasons for designing ever bigger craft was to support the weight and withstand the recoil of these heavy weapons. In the bows of some of his vessels he set catapults capable of shooting darts at least twenty-one inches long. It wasn't size that mattered so much as range: as his forces approached a hostile fleet, his naval artillery could fire a preliminary barrage from perhaps four hundred yards away while the enemy would have to wait to get within bow shot to reply. Like his other novelties, it was quickly adopted elsewhere. Soon men called "catapultists" became a standard rating in all navies.

Artillery and bigger ships naturally had their effect on naval tactics, and sea battles were different in this age from what they had been a century earlier. They still took place near shore (p. 92); a supergalley was even harder to keep at sea than a trireme. But a fight now opened with a heavy barrage from catapults and bowmen. Lighter craft, triremes and quadriremes, still concentrated on maneuvering for position and the chance for an effective blow with the ram; but larger units, which had massive reinforced snouts (cf. pp. 94–95), were not afraid to meet each other prow-to-prow, and this often resulted in close-packed mêlées in which the marines on the decks, hurling javelins or thrusting with special long spears, decided the issue. To aid in this sort of fighting turrets were added to the ships' armament, lofty wooden platforms that could be quickly set up at bow and stern when a vessel went into action; their height gave sharpshooters a chance to fire down on the enemy's decks (cf. Pl. 38).

To maintain their expensive fleets, the new rulers adopted the system of using trierarchs. Athens, of course, had been able to call only on its own population; Ptolemy or Antigonus had the upper classes in every city in their empires to turn to. They needed them: the sums poured into their navies were enormous. But even the pockets of the rich weren't inexhaustible, and the difficulties that arose are attested to by a document, written on papyrus, that is one of the rare pieces of firsthand evidence we have for ancient maritime history. Like Wenamon's report (Chapter 5), it was found in the sands of Egypt and owes its preservation over the centuries to the perennial dryness of that country's climate.

It is a letter that was written in October 257 B.C. by Apollodotus, a bureaucrat in Egypt's finance ministry; his clerks must have sent out many others like it. The addressee was Xanthippus, a resident of Halicarnassus (a city on the southwestern coast of Asia Minor which Egypt controlled at the time) who apparently was wealthy enough to have been chosen trierarch for nothing less than a "nine." The date reveals that the ship belonged to the navy of Ptolemy II. Xanthippus, it appears, did not have the ready cash to meet the expenses involved, so Apollodotus arranged a loan for him. He writes:

> Apollodotus to Xanthippus, greetings. In addition to the 2,000 drachmas which I have written to you about in a previous letter, I have forwarded to Antipater, who is representing you as trierarch of the "nine," 3,000 drachmas which must be made good to Apollonius, Minister of Finance. Will you therefore kindly arrange to remit to him in accordance with the enclosed. Goodbye.

Enclosed was a memorandum with all the particulars of the trierarch's debt. It was probably difficulties like these that induced the business-like Ptolemies to cast their net wider and get more than just the rich to share in the burden: they passed a "trireme tax," the proceeds of which were for the upkeep of the fleet.

Recently some unusual archeological finds have made manifest what vast amounts of money the upkeep of such fleets demanded. Save for the description of the monster showpiece of Ptolemy IV, we have but haphazard, scattered information about the warships of this age, derived from random remarks of ancient writers and what we can deduce from these. There is now one all-important exception: in 1980 Israeli divers recovered from the sea off Athlit just south of Haifa a warship's ram in perfect condition and with the wooden parts of the bow that it enclosed still in place inside (Pl. 32). It is a mighty casting, with an overall length of a little under seven and one-half feet (2.26 meters), a maximum width of two and a half feet (76 centimeters), a maximum height of a little over three feet (95 centimeters), and a weight of somewhat more than one thousand pounds (465 kilograms). To judge from the wooden remains, the ship had wales running its length at or near the waterline that were massive timbers nine to ten inches high and seven thick, and its planking was at least two inches thick, and more likely four. The planking, like that of the wrecks of ancient merchantmen that have been investigated (Chapter 3), was fastened with close-set mortise-and-tenon joints. In other words, the ship from which this ram came required not only a formidable amount of top quality timber that had to be cut, fitted, and assembled by highly trained craftsmen, but also half a ton of bronze that had to be made into a shape whose casting would be considered a major project even today.

The divers found no other remains on the site, so there are no clues as to what class of war galley this ram belonged. But another remarkable archaeological find helps supply an answer. Ancient historians state that Augustus, after the battle off Cape Actium in 31 B.C. (Chapter 16), commemorated his great victory by setting up in the neighborhood a monument, one element of which was a display of rams taken from the ships that he had vanquished. Remains of the monument came to light in 1913. A number of years later it was noted that among its features was a series of sockets, diminishing in size, cut into a long retaining wall. The purpose of the sockets remained a mystery until 1986, when William Murray, an archaeologist and historian, was struck by the similarity their shape bore to the outline of the Athlit ram looked at head on. He excavated them carefully, took their measurements, and demonstrated their reason for being: they were to hold the display of the rams; each ram had been anchored in one of them. They diminished in size because they held the rams from warships of different classes, presumably from that of a "ten," which we know was the largest unit in the defeated fleet, on down. And they reveal the striking fact that the Athlit ram, massive as it is, came from at most a "five," perhaps even from a "four." The ram that fitted into the largest socket, three times as wide and proportionately bigger all around, must have been a gargantuan casting.

Thus, not only did each of the great ships of this age carry a ram, but that ram very likely was its single most costly piece of equipment. The addition of catapults to the ships' armament and the large increase in the number of marines aboard point unmistakably to the heightened importance now given in naval combat to closing with an enemy ship in order to let the men on the decks decide the issue. But the presence of these mighty, highly expensive rams is a reminder that ramming was by no means obsolete, that commanders must have been just as ready to smash head first into an enemy as to grapple and board him.

In 306 B.C. the opening move took place in a seesaw struggle for control of the eastern seas that was to last a century: Demetrius, at the head of the squadrons recently built for himself and his father and riding one of the new "sevens" as flagship, clashed with Ptolemy's fleet off the city of Salamis on the eastern coast of Cyprus. Ptolemy had about 150 ships and Demetrius at least that many and very likely more; moreover, his aggregation was heavier: Ptolemy had nothing bigger than "fives," while Demetrius had no less than seven "sevens." The fleets formed up face to face in two long lines at right angles to the shore. Demetrius, who always planned with meticulous care, on this occasion adopted an unbalanced line. He deliberately made his seaward wing very strong, putting into it a fine squadron of thirty

Athenian "fours" and all his "sevens," including his flagship, and he deliberately left his shoreward wing weak, even though it faced the wing of the enemy where Ptolemy himself was in command; for reasons that will become apparent in a moment, he put the fleet's chief pilot in charge of it. And so, when, after a preliminary barrage from his catapults, he collided with the enemy, the two lines pivoted about the center like a huge swinging door as Demetrius' powerful seaward wing annihilated the enemy ships facing it and Ptolemy's shoreward wing pushed back the weak forces opposing him. This was exactly what Demetrius counted on. For, when Ptolemy had finished with his own immediate job and turned to help out his seaward wing, he found himself in an unhappy bind: where his seaward wing should have been, all he could see were Demetrius' mighty galleys bearing down on him, while at his rear was Demetrius' shoreward wing; under the command of the fleet's best pilot, it had made a measured withdrawal in the face of Ptolemy's attack, nothing more. Ptolemy managed to escape with his life and eight ships, and Demetrius wound up with forty captured intact, eighty that had been put out of action and were successfully towed ashore, and the mastery of the seas for the next twenty years (cf. Pl. 33). In a sense he never lost it. When he was finally cornered in 285 B.C., it was on land while he was desperately trying to get back to his ships; he was captured and one of his admirals handed over the bulk of his fleet to Ptolemy.

Five years later his son, Antigonus Gonatas, tried to win the sea back. His father's gigantic "sixteen" now carried the flag for the enemy and he had nothing to match it; he was defeated and the eastern Mediterranean became an Egyptian lake. The shipyards and squadrons of the Phoenician ports of the Levant and of the Greek cities of Asia Minor were now securely in Ptolemy II's hands; he controlled the Aegean islands north to the coast of Thrace. Antigonus had to wait until the middle of the century before he could try again. By this time he was firmly established as the ruler of Macedon and held the ports of Greece with their shipyards. They built him a new fleet. It was still weaker than Ptolemy's, but he was willing to gamble, and the gamble paid off: in two clashes with the Egyptians, one near the island of Cos off the southwestern coast of Asia Minor and the other on the opposite side of the Aegean near Andros, he beat them both times. No one knows how, for all details of the fighting have been lost. Yet even after this comeback on the part of Macedon, Egypt was still strong on the sea. The Ptolemies kept control of much of the eastern coast of the Mediterranean, and their squadrons moved at will in the waters north of Egypt. But both sides by now had to slacken their pace: the money and effort that had been expended just couldn't be kept up. Their supergalleys, the most costly to maintain, like the great dinosaurs became extinct; they were dedicated as monuments or just left to rot. When in 168 B.C. the Romans found the "sixteen" in a Macedonian dockyard, it was a fossil; it hadn't been to sea for seventy years. The two rivals had succeeded in canceling each other out, and the stage was set for the entrance of a new naval power.

Rhodes, located on an island off the southwestern coast of Asia Minor, was a small nation compared with the mighty kingdoms that surrounded it. As an island state, its whole life was bound up with the sea and it had built up a small but highly respected navy. Now, toward the end of the third century B.C., by holding the balance of power on the water, it was able to step forward as the key figure in the eastern Mediterranean.

The two great rivals, Egypt and Macedon, from the very outset had been caught in a vicious circle. The Ptolemies needed a navy to defend their shores against Demetrius' or Antigonus' fleet—and, to maintain one, just like the pharaohs whom they had replaced, they had to have access to the Levant or the southern coasts of Asia Minor, where pine and cedar forests supplied ship timber; the kings of Macedon had their native pine forests to draw on for timber and naval stores (they exported both, carefully raising the price for all pro-Egyptian customers), but they needed the dockyards of Greece to turn out and maintain their ships—and they had to have ships or else Egypt's fleet would sail brashly across the Aegean and incite Greece to revolt. And so the struggle, largely political, went on. But Rhodes needed a navy because its economic life depended upon overseas trade. It was an international port and banking center, and its merchant marine was one of the largest in the ancient world, out of all proportion to its size, like Norway's or Greece's today.

Freedom of the seas was Rhodes' keynote, so that its freighters could travel where they wanted in safety. Yet the seas could hardly be called safe if a skipper had to sail with the jittery feeling that the other side of the headland he was passing hid the sleek black hull of a pirate craft. Rhodes bravely shouldered the burden and single-handedly kept the eastern Mediterranean free of its ancient scourge. Athens in the great days of its commerce had shied away from the job—but then Athens depended upon foreign shipping (p. 108) and did not have the investment in a merchant marine to protect that Rhodes did.

There was more involved than chasing pirates, difficult as that was, in keeping the seas free. When the city of Byzantium in 220 B.C. tried to levy a toll on the traffic through the Bosporus, it was to Rhodes that shippers who were affected sent their complaint, and a Rhodian fleet was at the trouble spot in short order. Most important of all, Rhodes had to see to it that no nation grew powerful enough to turn the Aegean or Levantine waters into a private preserve. So, when Antigonus Gonatas built a new fleet to challenge Egypt's control, Rhodes joined him. The Ptolemies were practically its business partners—its merchant marine carried most of their vast exports of grain—but allying with the Ptolemies' enemy gave the island a chance to restore the balance of power on the sea. From the long-term point of view—and Rhodian leaders were as farsighted statesmen as they were businessmen—this was safer than becoming a dependent, even a prosperous one, of Egypt.

Holding down pirates and upholding the balance of power on the sea demands a first-rate navy; the one the Rhodians maintained was the most efficient of its time. It was small: it averaged about forty major units—no match, for example, for Ptolemy's aggregation of over three hundred. But it was not intended for such a challenge; the statesmen would see to it that the admirals had powerful allies at their side when the time came to take on an enemy. Its units were small: there was nothing in the slips larger than a quinquereme, but the Rhodians had neither the budget nor the need for anything bigger. They particularly favored the quadrireme. The fastest type of major unit afloat, it suited perfectly their style of fighting, which depended on maneuver and use of the ram; some of their most spectacular victories resulted from the lightninglike moves they carried out in these craft (Chapter 12). They even came up with a new naval weapon, the last one to be invented until the very end of the ancient world. In 190 B.C. a squadron of about thirty of their ships was hopelessly trapped; but seven ran the gantlet safely because they had been fitted out experimentally with a new device, containers of blazing fire slung at the ends of two long poles that projected from the bows. If an enemy attacked, the fire pots were dropped on his deck, and if he flinched he laid himself open to a stroke of the ram.

But sea duty for the Rhodians nine times out of ten meant not fighting formal actions but tracking down pirates, and this called for light, swift vessels. Rhodes fought the devil with fire: its fleet included a large number of a special type of craft called the *triemiolia* or "triremehemiolia." Long before, pirates had remodeled the two-banked galley into the *hemiolia*, the "one and a half," a craft designed for the particular purpose of chasing down merchant shipping; it allowed them to run under sails as well as oars during pursuit and yet provided room to stow the rigging away when the time came to board (p. 78). A trireme could outfight any such ship if it could catch it—but the standard model was made to go into action without any sailing gear aboard (p. 78). Rhodian architects created the triemiolia to chase down hemiolias. It was simply a fast type of trireme revamped in the manner of the vessel it was intended to fight. It was made so that, during a chase, all banks could be manned and sail carried; when the time came to close in, it became a "two and a half": the thranite oarsmen abaft the mast quitted their benches, leaving a space into which mast and sail could be quickly lowered.

To keep this fleet with all its varied units in a constant and perfect state of repair, Rhodes maintained an extensive, complex navy yard. It was the only one in the ancient world that we know had a security system: certain portions were closed, on pain of death, to all but authorized personnel.

Good ships are useless without good men; Rhodian crews were the best there were. Athens had filled the benches with citizens of the lowest class and with hired rowers. The Ptolemies and their Macedonian rivals used whatever they could get—island Greeks, Asia Minor Greeks, Phoenicians. But in Rhodes the navy was the senior service, and every galley in it was commanded and rowed by its citizens. They made it possible for the fleet to specialize in maneuver and the ram at a time when inferior oarsmen were compelling its neighbors to reduce the emphasis on such tactics. Moreover, the Rhodians were indomitable fighters. In 305 B.C. Demetrius tried to take the city of Rhodes by storm. He moved up a fleet of 200 warships and 170 transports loaded with 40,000 men and the very latest in heavy–siege machinery; large numbers of pirates gleefully joined him. The Rhodians, though desperately outnumbered—they had about 7,000 men, not counting slaves—fought him to a standstill: with courage, stubbornness, and ingenuity they repelled attack after attack; under brutally heavy fire some of their light craft dashed across the harbor and upset the barges carrying Demetrius' siege weapons, while others broke his blockade of the entrance to gain the open sea and harry his lines of supply. After a year he finally called the siege off.

The officers who commanded these men were thoroughly trained; many had made their way up through the ranks. Archaeologists have found on the island a stone monument that the crew of a quadrireme set up in honor of Alexidamus, one of their officers. Pridefully they recorded his naval career: enlisted man first on destroyers (triemiolias), then on heavier units (cataphracts; p. 90); boatswain; bow officer on a triemiolia (*prorates*, his first commissioned rank); bow officer on a quadrireme. They carefully noted that he had seen action in the last two assignments. Another monument sets forth the career of a certain Polycles. He was a member of the island's aristocracy and did not have to climb the ladder like Alexidamus; he started with the command of a flotilla of destroyers (aphracts). His next assignment was command of a quinquereme and then, after a tour of duty with the army, appointment to the staff of the commander in chief of all of Rhodes' naval forces. Subsequently he was trierarch of a quadrireme and led it in action. Officers like Alexidamus and Polycles literally devoted their lives to the sea. Other navies scrambled to hire them whenever they were available, and every now and then an occasion arose when a fleet of Rhodes found itself pitted against an enemy line commanded by one of its sons.

Rhodian crews respected their commanders and frequently honored them with monuments like the two described above. Excavators have dug up a number of similar citations, and because of them we know more about the complements of Rhodian men-of-war than of any other. The personnel assigned to a quadrireme, for example, included

Officers:	trierarch or *epiplus* (qualified officer selected by the trierarch to substitute for him)—captain
	grammateus—chief administrative officer
	kybernetes—executive and navigating officer
	prorates—bow officer
	keleustes—chief rowing officer
	pentekontarchos—assistant rowing officer
Ratings:	boatswain (*hegemon ton ergon*, literally "leader of the activities")
	carpenter (*naupegos*)
	quartermaster (*pedaliuchos*, literally "steering-oar holder")
	oiler (*elaiochreistes*, literally "oil anointer," probably in charge of issuing oil to the crew for rubbing down)
	doctor (*iatros*, just a rating, not an officer, and generally a foreigner; many came from the island of Cos, the home of Hippocrates)
	oar-thong man (*kopodetes*, literally "oar binder"; probably in charge of straps that secured the oar to the tholepin)
Nonrated personnel:	bow deck watch (*ergazomenoi en prora*, "workers in the prow," for handling sails and lines; at least 5)
	stern deck watch (*ergazomenoi en prymne*, "workers in the stern," for handling sails and lines; at least 5)
	rowers
Fighting personnel:	artillerymen (*katapeltaphetai*, literally "catapultists"; at least 2)
	archers (*toxotai*, at least 6)
	marines (*epibatai*, at least 19)

Probably triremes and quinqueremes carried the same officers and ratings, the only real difference being in the number of rowers and of fighting men. Smaller units like the hemiolias perhaps had to forego the luxury of a ship's doctor.

History relates in its impersonal way that Rhodes built up a fine navy and worked hard to sweep the seas clean of pirates. An inscription has been discovered on the island which tells, vividly and pathetically, what this meant in the lives of men. It is on a gravestone that once stood over the burial place of three brothers. As so many of their compatriots must have done, the boys entered the navy. They had done well. One had risen to commissioned-officer rank (*prorates*). The second, though just a rower, served on a flagship. The third was captain of a unit of marines; he had come up the hard way, for, in another inscription set up some years earlier, his name was cited along with a number of others for gallantry in action and he had then been only a *katapeltaphetes*, an artilleryman. All had been killed in different actions, not in major battles against enemy fleets but in the grinding daily work of the Rhodian navy, engagements with pirates. Two of these actions are merely mentioned, but the third is localized: it took place in the narrow waters between Crete and Greece, near Cape Malea, a spot so favored by pirates that ancient Greek mariners had a proverb that ran, "Round Malea and forget about getting home," and modern Greek sailors until relatively recently still sang, "Cape Malea, Cape Malea; help me Christ and all the Saints!"

Late in the summer of 201 B.C. a Rhodian galley nosed into the Tiber, far to the west, and rowed slowly upstream to Rome. It was carrying special envoys from the island and one of its neighbors to place before the Roman Senate a request for help. Antigonas Gonatas' grandson had just finished building a powerful fleet and was making friendly overtures to Antiochus III, ruler of Syria, who also had naval ambitions. Egypt, Rhodes' traditional ally, had fallen upon hard times and what was left of its once great fleet was no longer fit for sea duty. So Rhodes, following as always its policy of maintaining the balance of power on the sea, was inviting the major power of the west, monarch of the western waters, to mix into the politics of the east. At the time it looked like a shrewd maneuver; a generation later it had become discouragingly clear that the guest had moved in to stay. And Rome was a most formidable guest. At one time it had built up, off in the western Mediterranean, a navy almost the equal of any in the east; and there were over two hundred galleys in its slips the summer that the Rhodian embassy arrived.

1. The earliest example of a sail, ca. 3200 B.C.

2. Clay model of probably a skin boat, ca. 3400 B.C.

3. Egyptian seagoing vessel of the mid-third millennium B.C.

4. Minoan galleys in procession, ca. 1600 B.C.

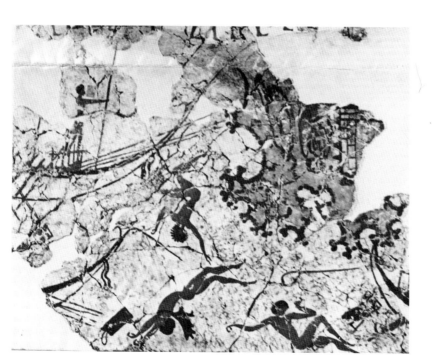

5. Minoan galleys in action, ca. 1600 B.C.

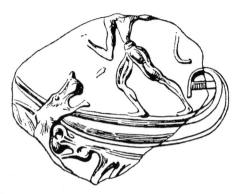

6. Minoan seal picturing a sailor fighting a
sea monster, ca. 1600 B.C.

7. Divers excavate within a plastic grid frame a wreck of the late fourth century B.C. found off Cyprus.

8. The Ulu Burun wreck, ca. 1350 B.C. A diver clutching an amphora clambers over a mound of copper ingots; note the identification tags.

. Shipwrights add a plank to the hull of replica of a wreck found off Cyprus see Pl. 7).

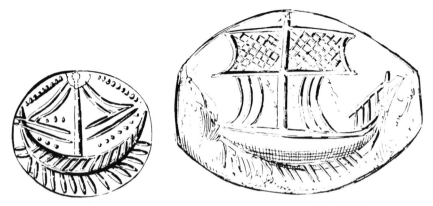

10. Galleys on Minoan seals; left, 1600–1200 B.C.; right, 1300–1200 B.C.

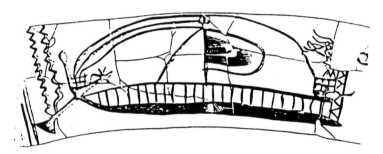

11. Galley on a clay box found at Pylos, 1200–1100 B.C.

12. Galley on a vase from Asine, 1200–1100 B.C.

13. Galley on a "frying pan" from Syros, third millennium B.C.

14. Galley on a cup from Eleusis, 850–800 B.C.

15. Warship cruising, ca. 750 B.C.

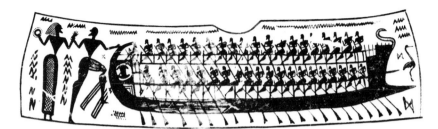

16. Warship, probably fifty-oared, preparing to leave, 750–700 B.C. The vessel actually has but one bank of oars; the artist, wanting to include both port and starboard rowers but unable to handle the perspective, portrayed the one above the other.

17. Forward part of a warship showing the keylike tholepins, ca. 750 B.C.

18. After part of a galley in action, ca. 750 B.C.

19. Galley, probably twenty-oared, cruising, 520–480 B.C.

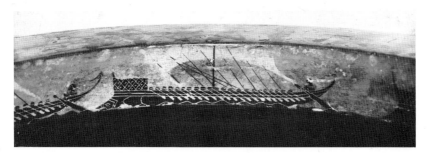

20. Galley, probably fifty-oared, cruising, 550–530 B.C.

21. Galleys cruising under sail, ca. 530 B.C.

22. Two-level Phoenician warship, 705–681 B.C.

23. Dionysus with satyrs and maenads cruising on a two-level warship, ca. 510 B.C.

24. Hemiolia, fifty-oared, overtaking a merchantman traveling under short-ened sail, ca. 510 B.C.

25. Detail of a second scene: the hemiolia has secured the upper oars abaft the mast preliminary to lowering it (it already leans slightly aft). The mer-chantman now has all its canvas drawing in the effort to escape.

26. Sailing ship on a Hebrew
seal, eighth–seventh centuries
B.C.

27. Reconstruction of a wall painting of a two-masted sailing ship, early fifth
century B.C.

28. The *Olympias*, replica of a fifth-century Athenian trireme.

29. Interior of the *Olympias* showing the arrangement of the three levels of rowers.

30. The *Kyrenia II*, replica of a Greek merchantman of the late fourth century B.C.

31. Hellenistic galley on the Nile, early first century B.C.

32. Warship's ram found off Athlit, Israel, probably first half of second century B.C.

33. Victory on the prow of a galley pictured on a coin of Demetrius Poliorcetes, ca. 300 B.C.

34. Amphoras from one of the Grand Congloué wrecks, early second century B.C.

35. Stevedores unloading wine jars, third century A.D. On the quay are the shipping clerks, one of whom hands each stevedore a tally piece from a pile in front of him while another makes entries in a ledger.

36. Pile of amphoras marking the site of a wreck off Cyprus (see Pl. 7).

37. Wreck showing how the cargo of amphoras has preserved the bottom of the hull, first century B.C.

38. Two-level Roman galley, perhaps a quadrireme or larger, second half of first century B.C. In the boxlike niche on the bow is a head of the deity after whom the vessel was named.

39. Roman warships, A.D. 113. In the center is a trireme carrying the artemon, to port and starboard are two-level galleys, probably liburnians; the one
to port has its sailing rig lowered and resting on crutches.

40. Roman warships carrying marines, first century A.D.

41. Seagoing merchant-
man entering port, first
century A.D.; a hand on
deck hauls on the brails
and two aloft prepare
to furl the canvas.

42. Scene at Portus, the harbor of Rome, ca. A.D. 200. At left a seagoing merchantman sails past the lighthouse into the entrance; the artemon has been removed and the brails are being tightened to shorten the mainsail. At right a sister ship (or perhaps the same ship) moored to the quay, with sails furled, unloads a cargo of amphoras of wine.

43. Seagoing merchantmen of two different types sail past the lighthouse at Portus, ca. A.D. 200. Decoration of the office of the shippers of Syllectum, Tunisia, at Ostia.

44. Merchant galley with a deckload of amphoras, second or third century A.D.

45. Scene at the entrance of the harbor of Portus, third century A.D. Three sailing vessels maneuver in an attempted rescue.

46. Shipwright, having completed a hull, adzes a frame to insert in it, late second or early third century A.D. The inscription reads, "Longidienus pushes ahead on his work."

47. Galley unloading beasts transported for the gladiatorial games, fourth century A.D.

48. Merchantman in an Adriatic port, A.D. 113.

49. Lateen-rigged craft, second century A.D.

50. Sprit-rigged craft, second or third century A.D.

51. Detail of the center ship in Pl. 45 showing the sprit.

52. A small freighter, the *Isis Giminiana*, loading sacks of grain, second or third century A.D. Farnaces, the commander (*magister*), stands at the steering oars. Stevedores carry the sacks aboard and empty the goods (*res*) into an official measure under the eye of the vessel's owner, Abascantus, and of a government inspector (holding an olive branch). A stevedore who has emptied his sack (marked *feci*, "I'm done") rests in the bows. The mast is stepped far forward; the ship was probably sprit-rigged.

53. Skiff warping a vessel, third century A.D. Note the towline that goes from the stern presumably to the prow of the vessel being pulled. Note the oversize steering oar to provide leverage to direct the clumsy tow. The mast, stepped right in the bow, must have carried a sprit-rig.

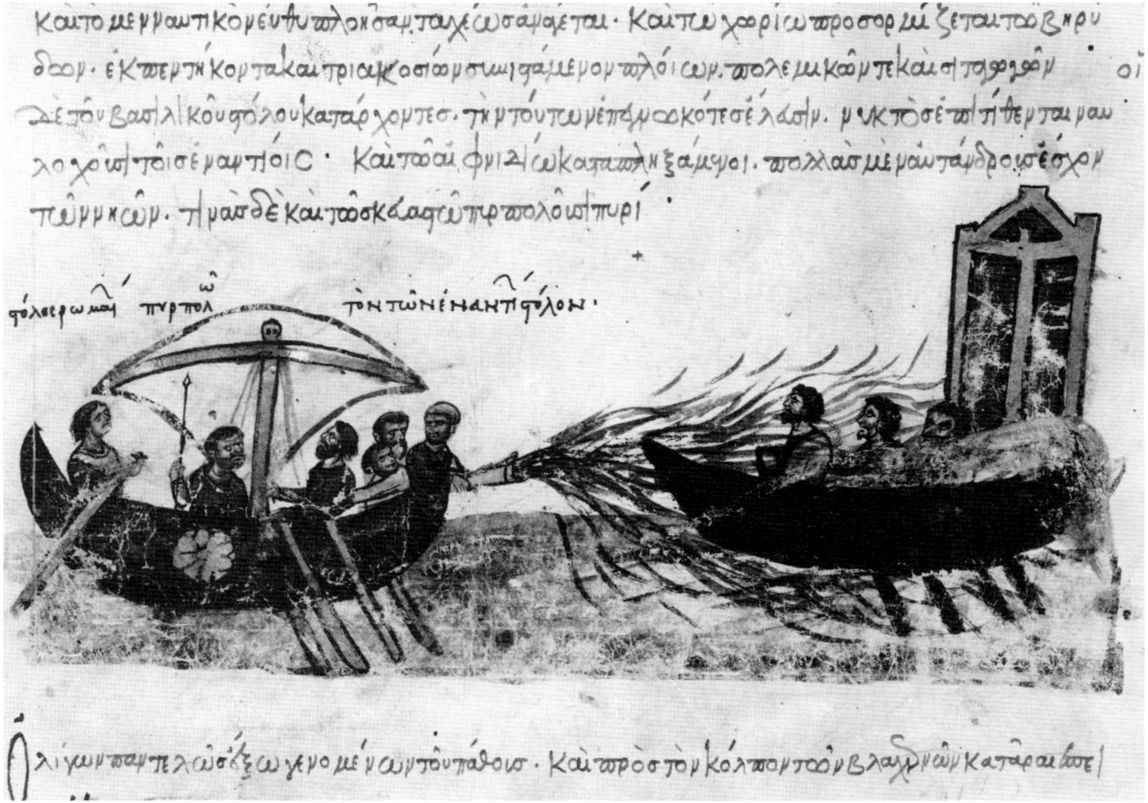

54. Dromon using Greek fire, A.D. 820–829.

Chapter 12

LANDLUBBERS TO SEA LORDS

THE ROMANS are an anomaly in maritime history, a race of lubbers who became lords of the sea in spite of themselves. Only a nation of born landsmen would have dared, as they did, to pit against one of the greatest navies afloat a jerry-built fleet, manned by green crews fresh off the farms, and commanded by admirals who lost four ships to the weather for every one to enemy action. When they ultimately became the chief naval power of the Mediterranean, they felt so uncomfortable in the role that they let a mighty navy rot in the slips and for a full century exercised their control with hardly a vessel to their name.

Around 500 B.C., not long after Carthage had settled its dispute with the Greek colonists and marked off the western seas as its private preserve (Chapter 7), the inhabitants of an obscure village on the banks of the Tiber in central Italy began to flex their muscles—and within two and a half centuries became the masters of the peninsula from the Po Valley to the tip of the boot. They were a nation of hard-working, thrifty peasants who drew their livelihood from the land and were among the toughest fighters in the world—on land. They left the waters around their newly acquired realm strictly alone, to Etruscans and Greeks and, of course, to pirates.

Across the Mediterranean lay Carthage, literally living off the sea. It ruled a far-flung empire and defended it with a navy whose traditions reached back beyond the times of King Solomon (p. 64). In its early days, Rome had no bone to pick with Carthage. Hundreds of miles separated it from the nearest Carthaginian colonies in the western part of Sicily, and it cheerfully signed and renewed treaties in which it gave up trading rights in western waters—in return for a promise to keep hands off its own sphere of interest. It was an easy gesture: the Romans got nothing out of, and wanted nothing to do with, the sea.

But, as time went on, the lubbers found that, like it or not, they had to try the water. Their march up and down Italy had brought under their subjection the seaports of Etruria to the north and the Greek coastal cities to the south. All these lived off maritime trade—and the pirates that infested the Tyrrhenian Sea were a particularly virulent breed. So, in 311 B.C., Rome equipped two squadrons of ten triremes each to police the local waters. Twenty years later one of these fledglings decided to try its wings in formal combat, attacked the fleet of the Greek town of Tarentum in the far south, and got clobbered so thoroughly that the Romans hastily reverted to type: they scrapped even this miniature navy and arranged to guard the sea lanes by simply requisitioning ships from the Greek cities of southern Italy. Though these were subject to Rome and the city was responsible for their defense, its attitude had a rough justice about it: what seaborne trade there was lay largely in their hands; let them chase the pirates themselves.

But it soon became apparent that there was a more serious problem than piracy to worry about. A scant two miles from Italy, across the Strait of Messina, lay the island of Sicily. The eastern half was occupied by independent Greek city-states, but the western belonged to Carthage. Separated by several hundred miles, both parties had found it easy to abide by their treaties; now that Rome reached down to the Italian side of the strait, relations became strained. And when, through a complicated set of circumstances, the Carthaginians moved eastward and garrisoned the town of Messina on the Sicilian side of the strait, the two found themselves eyeball to eyeball. This could not be kept up for long; in 264 B.C. the First Punic War broke out. Both sides had no inkling that it was to last twenty-three years, and the Romans certainly none that the issue, almost from the first, would be fought out on the sea.

Rome's prime objective was to remove the Carthaginians from eastern Sicily. It ferried armies into the island across the strait—an enemy squadron was on hand to intercept, but no ancient blockade was ever airtight (p. 92)—and for three years campaigned with fair success. But Carthage refused to call it quits. It didn't need to: it had an impregnable position on the western coast of Sicily, a series of ports ringed with fortifications, too strong to be stormed from the land side alone and which, if besieged from there, could always be supplied by sea from the metropolis in Africa; from them, once the enemy relaxed its guard, Carthage could always strike out again to regain what it had lost. To complete the job Rome had to push its opponent out of Sicily. But this could not be done by the army alone; somehow control of the water had to be wrested from Carthage's hands in order to cut off its forces in Sicily from home. In 261 B.C. Rome's statesmen and generals faced a dismaying reality: sooner or later they had to take the plunge and create a navy; David had to fight Goliath but not with a slingshot, with the giant's own weapons.

In the early spring of 260 B.C. the Senate—the body which at Rome at this time handled foreign policy and national defense—called for the construction of one hundred quinqueremes and twenty triremes to be ready in time for the summer campaigning season; it must have sounded as fantastic to Rome as Roosevelt's call for fifty thousand airplanes in the grim spring of 1942 did to the United States. Since the standard unit in the Carthaginian navy was the quinquereme, the new fleet perforce consisted mostly of these, in all probability the single-banked version—that is, powered by five-man sweeps, since Rome was manning the benches with the rawest possible recruits, and for this kind of sweep only one man out of the five had to be experienced (p. 130). Carthage may well have been using the two-level or three-level versions, but Rome simply did not have the time to train crews capable of rowing these.

The miracle was accomplished. The vessels were turned out "from the tree," as an ancient writer put it, to the last detail of rigging in sixty days. No Roman knew how to design or make war galleys, so the Senate must have requisitioned naval architects and shipwrights from the subject Greek coastal cities of southern Italy as well as from Syracuse, which, with a sizable navy of its own, had joined the cause. Four years earlier when the Carthaginian squadron on blockade duty in the Strait of Messina had attacked a Roman convoy, one of its galleys ran aground, and the Romans dragged it ashore. The architects used this as a model but avoided following it to the letter. Carthage favored a light, fast vessel designed to maneuver and ram, which only a crack crew could handle; to put green men aboard such a craft was useless. So they adapted the design to a slower, bulkier, heavier ship that was far more foolproof and had spacious decks to carry a powerful force of marines.

But this was only half the problem. Each quinquereme was going to need three hundred oarsmen and each trireme 170. It was out of the question to think of training crews for the latter, so the hard-working Greek allies were called on to supply them, and the Roman commanders addressed themselves to the job of recruiting and readying the thirty thousand necessary to man the bigger ships. They could not look to the city, for Rome, going further even than Athens, refused to assign a citizen to the benches. They turned to the only other available source—the various Italic peoples who, over the centuries, had been conquered and made subject allies. Soon, on makeshift rowing frames set up on land, young huskies fresh from the farms up and down Italy were sweating and grunting in mock oarsmanship. Then, as each galley came off the ways, they were tumbled aboard and given a taste of what the real thing was like. The whole program must have been under the direction of naval officers from the Greek allies; they very likely did as much swearing in those hectic two months as Baron von Steuben in his famous two at Valley Forge. In June 260 B.C., the new fleet left the harbor of Ostia at the mouth of the Tiber and sailed down the southwestern coast of Italy to rendezvous at Syracuse. Only Romans, with the courage that comes of ignorance, could have entertained the thought of sending it into action against the superb ships and veteran crews of Carthage.

Then a second miracle took place. While the fleet was lying in the harbor of Syracuse, someone came up with an idea that was to change the whole complexion of things; possibly it was one of the Roman officers, more likely a Syracusan. The city had a tradition of naval inventiveness: its architects had designed the heavy triremes that destroyed the flower of Athens' navy and its onetime ruler, Dionysius, had invented the quinquereme itself. Possibly, just possibly, the author was that renowned ancient scientist and engineer, Archimedes; he had been born in Syracuse twenty-seven years earlier and very likely was in residence there the day the fleet arrived.

The Romans were unbeatable fighters on land; the problem was to come up with something that would allow them to turn a sea fight into a land fight, some sure-fire device to enable them to grapple and board. The anonymous inventor designed what came to be known as the *corvus*, "raven," probably the sailors' slang term for it; we would call it a "crane" rather than a "raven" (Fig. 6). It was nothing more than a gangplank, thirty-six feet long and four feet wide, with a heavy spike at the outboard end and at the other a long slot that fitted around a pole set up like a mast in the bow of the ship; when raised, it stood upright snugly against the pole and, when lowered, it projected far over the bow. One tackle between the further end and the head of the pole controlled the raising and lowering, and two, made fast to the deck on either side, swiveled it from side to side. A vessel so equipped would warily keep its prow headed toward the enemy and, as soon as he closed in to ram, drop the "raven"; the spike would embed in his deck, and a boarding force would rush over the plank. Originally each Roman ship had been assigned a permanent force of forty fighting men, drawn from the lowest class of citizens, to carry on the defensive duties normally handled by marines. Now an additional eighty first-line troops from the legions were put aboard; their job was to charge the moment the "raven" landed.

About August 260 B.C., the test came. The Carthaginian fleet, superbly built and trained—much like the great Athenian fleets of the fifth century B.C. except that it was made up of quinqueremes instead of triremes and its flag was carried on a huge "seven"—anticipating a slaughter was out to provoke an encounter as quickly as possible. It

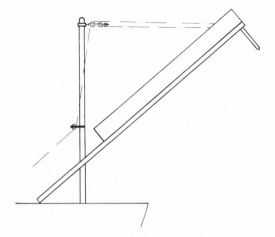

FIG. 6. Reconstruction of the *corvus*.

swooped down on Mylae on the north shore of Sicily and started to
ravage the coast. Caius Duilius, the Roman commander, took up the
challenge: his clumsy galleys, the poles and planks of the ravens standing out grotesquely on the bows, crept around to Mylae. He had about
140 ships, slightly more than the enemy.

When the Carthaginian admiral sighted the Roman fleet wallowing
along, he confidently let his captains surge forward to attack on their
own without bothering to form a proper line of battle. They sighted
the queer rigs on the Roman prows and hesitated, but only momentar-
ily. Each ship pressed forward smoothly but swiftly, moved in for a
thrust of the ram—and, with a screeching of blocks as the tackles were
let go, the gangplanks came clattering down, the spikes thudded into
the decking, and the Roman crews gasped and swore as they frantic-
ally backed water to keep the enemy from running on past and
wrenching the ravens loose; seconds later, legionaries spilled over the
Carthaginians' decks. When the two sides pulled clear, no fewer than
thirty-one ships, including the "seven" that carried the flag, were in
Roman hands.

The Carthaginians, stunned but far from beaten, immediately regrouped for a second attack. This time they took no chances: they
formed up to carry out a coordinated maneuver, the dangerous
diekplus (p. 91). Giving the enemy's prows with their deadly ravens a
wide berth, they raced like greyhounds past the sluggish Roman craft
to take them in the quarter and stern. But Duilius was no fool and, if
he had had no personal experience, he had read the books. He had
started with a slight advantage in numbers and now, after Carthage's
disastrous first attempt, he held at least a three to two edge. So he was

able to draw off some units and hold them as a reserve in a second line, a standard defense against the *diekplus*. When the Carthaginians attacked his main line in flank and rear, he gave the reserves the signal: they lumbered forward and dropped their ravens on the enemy's sterns. Carthage broke and ran. It had lost in all forty-four ships and ten thousand men. The outcome was incredible: a rank amateur had climbed into the ring with the champion and knocked him out. In Rome one can see today a column erected to commemorate what happened, either the one actually set up at the time or a copy made a few centuries later. The monument is covered with carved anchors and bristles with adornments in the shape of ships' prows. On the base the Romans proudly recorded that Duilius

> was the first Roman to perform exploits in ships at sea. He was the first to fit out and train ships and crews and, with these, he defeated in battle on the high seas all the Carthaginian ships and their mighty naval personnel, under the eyes of Hannibal, their commander in chief. By his strength he captured one "seven" and thirty quinqueremes and triremes along with their crews, and he sank thirteen. . . . He was also the first to bring the people booty from a sea battle and the first to lead free-born Carthaginians in a victory parade.

But the Romans were not the sort merely to sit back and gloat over their accomplishment. The Senate knew that the enemy was far from being down for the count, that one reason for the success had been the novelty of the new weapon, and that a second had been Duilius' superior numbers. They could do nothing about the novelty but they could do something about the other: from this time on they did their best to outbuild Carthage.

During the following years without letup, shipwrights turned out galleys and rowing masters trained crews; some small engagements in the meantime gave the men a taste of action. By 256 B.C. the fleet was brought up to circa 350 units, most of them quinqueremes, which just about achieved parity with the enemy. This figure turned out to be the high-water mark for both sides. Rome's number gradually diminished because of severe losses to weather and enemy action that were only partially made up. The Carthaginians, less successful in making up losses because of a lack of manpower, fell further and further behind.

As soon as the enlarged navy was ready, the Senate determined on a bold stroke. Why not have it convoy a powerful expeditionary force to Africa to storm the enemy's home base and, as it were, cut the war off at its roots? In the summer of 256 B.C. a huge armada of warships and transports laden with troops left port to carry out this assignment. Carthage intercepted it off the promontory of Ecnomus, about the midpoint on the southern coast of Sicily, and a mighty battle erupted between the two fleets. Carthage's fleet had circa 350 war galleys, Rome's about twenty less. The Roman vessels, arranged in a triangular formation, were moving ahead slowly, their speed held down by the lumbering transports. The Carthaginians, facing the tip of the triangle in line abreast, launched the initial moves in a carefully planned pincers movement. The foremost Roman units reacted by charging headlong into the center of the enemy line—and, in so doing, broke their triangle into two parts: the tip, consisting of the ships that made the charge, the fastest and best manned, forged ahead while the base, mostly slower units and encumbered by the transports, fell steadily behind, leaving an ever widening gap between them and the tip. This confronted the Carthaginians with an unexpected situation: there was now no possibility of their closing a pincers about the entire fleet. So they had to abandon their plan of action, and, with no time to concert another, they let themselves get involved in a free-for-all battle which divided into three separate engagements all going on at the same time, one around the tip of the triangle, and two around the base. This was a lucky break for the Romans: defending themselves against an enemy assault that was neither planned nor coordinated, they were able, by fighting savagely and tirelessly, to win a signal victory, destroying or capturing almost a hundred Carthaginian craft. The expeditionary force landed safely.

But on their home grounds the Carthaginians fought like animals at bay. The Senate, fearing it had bitten off more than it could chew, decided to evacuate the army. So, in the spring of 255 B.C., the grand fleet once more made its appearance off the African coast. Carthage dispatched 200 ships to Cape Hermaeum to attack. This time they were heavily outnumbered and, what is more, the vessels and crews, having been hastily assembled, were below the accustomed standard. To make matters worse, the commander chose a fatally weak position, with his back to the shore. His men had no room in which to maneuver, and the heavy Roman fleet, moving in ponderously with ravens at the ready, thrust his ships implacably toward the beach. It was a shattering defeat: 114 of his craft were captured and 16 sunk. The Carthagians were now almost without a navy. It was their turn to need a miracle.

The miracle came. As a matter of fact, considering Rome's inexperience on the sea, the wonder is that the misfortune it suffered had not happened earlier. As the victorious fleet sailed back home, its ranks swelled by 114 prizes, it ran into a gale off Camarina, a town near the southeastern tip of Sicily. When the skies cleared, the shore was littered with wrecks. Only eighty ships limped into port; hundreds of vessels and well over 100,000 men had been lost. It was a staggering blow. Another was soon to follow: just two years later the Romans, having with dogged energy rebuilt the fleet, saw most of it go down in a storm off the southern Italian coast.

Replacing the ships was not the big problem: there were plenty of trees, shipwrights, and dockyards. But replacing the crews was another matter. Suitable recruits were growing scarce, and those available were hardly eager to serve under admirals who knew so little about the sea that they could not tell when to come in out of the weather. The Senate had given up all thought of cutting off the war rapidly by striking at Carthage's heart in Africa. There was only one thing left to do: gradually build up the fleet again until it could blockade the enemy's ports in western Sicily and starve them out. By 250 B.C. there were enough ships, and the army and navy were sent to strangle the key Carthaginian base at Lilybaeum.

But blockading a port, the Romans quickly found out, was a branch of naval science they also had to learn from the beginning. Carthage, too, had been active during the lull, constructing ships of a new model, even lighter and faster than those it had used before and yet just as seaworthy. They were ideal for blockade running and, manned by experienced crews, could sail even when the wind was strong. Picking the right time, blustery days that kept the blockaders shorebound, whole squadrons slipped in and out carrying quantities of supplies and men. The clumsy Roman craft did not have a chance of overtaking them, much less of dropping a raven on their decks. If the Romans were to win out, they had to scrap their present navy, ravens and all, and start again from scratch. The decision was made for them when, in 249 B.C., one of their admirals lost most of his fleet in a misguided attempt to attack one of Carthage's ports from the sea and, almost simultaneously, another lost his in a gale at the very point, Camarina, where the first storm disaster had taken place; a Carthaginian squadron had been in chase but the commander prudently pulled in and let the weather do the job for him. Rome was now down to twenty ships.

Sometime earlier a crack Carthaginian trireme, trying to get through the cordon around Lilybaeum, had gone aground. The Romans dragged it off, refitted it, and when Carthage's best blockade runner, the fastest quinquereme afloat—very likely a two-level type, perhaps even three-level—and manned by a picked crew, tried to slip out, they gave chase in their new ship and caught it. Roman oarsmen by this time were just as good as those of Carthage: all they needed were the ships. This prize was to serve as the model for a new fleet. It took time—fifteen years of war had taken their toll of men, materials, and money—but the time was available, for Carthage providentially had its hands full at the moment, putting down revolts in its African empire. In 242 B.C. the new navy was finally ready, two hundred quinqueremes of the latest, fastest, most seaworthy type. Near the Aegates Islands, off the western tip of Sicily, the crucial battle took place on March 10, 241 B.C. A strong wind was blowing, the sort that fifteen years earlier might have torn a Roman fleet apart or at least kept it from using the ravens. But the tables were now turned: the Romans had the better ships and crews and, as usual, superior numbers (200 to 170). They attacked; fifty enemy ships were destroyed and seventy captured with their crews.

The war was finally over. At the end of its twenty-three long years, the roles were completely reversed: Carthage, the erstwhile naval power, went into the last round with old vessels and raw crews; Rome, the nation of lubbers, ended with a navy of two hundred of the finest war galleys afloat, manned by veterans.

Between 218 and 201 B.C. the two powers fought another bloody war. But it was of a totally different character, one which, because of Rome's virtually uncontested control of the western Mediterranean, was waged on land; there were no great sea battles in the Second Punic War. Everyone knows the story of how Hannibal, Carthage's most famous son, led a powerful army, elephants and all, overland from Spain to Italy, crossing the Alps when snow already blocked the passes. He did not do it that way because he wanted to end up in the history books but simply because the water route, the natural way of transporting an army from Spain to Italy, was closed to him. His military genius enabled him to range over the Italian peninsula, destroying Roman army after Roman army. Without a fleet to control the seas he could not count on the essential steady arrival of reinforcements and supplies for his troops. He could ravage the farms of Italy, but merchantmen brought in all the grain Rome needed from Sicily and Sardinia, once from as far off as Egypt. Rome even learned to organize its control of the sea by setting up naval stations with permanent squadrons in Spain, Sicily, and the Adriatic. Sea power and his opponent's bulldog trait of never giving up ultimately wore Hannibal down. He shipped the remnants of his forces out of Italy back to Africa. Rome ferried a mighty army of its own there and, in 202 B.C., brought to a close Carthage's role as an important state.

In 201 B.C. the nation that sixty years earlier had no fleet of its own was the greatest sea power in the Mediterranean. There were two hundred galleys in its slips, all of them quinqueremes, more than double the size of any other navy afloat. A century later it was still the greatest power in the Mediterranean—but it had hardly a ship to its name. The Romans were a gifted people who, when hard necessity pushed them, were able to master the sea. But salt water was not to their taste and, as soon as they could, they gave it up.

It was in 201 B.C. that the envoys from Rhodes and its neighbor on the Asia Minor coast, Pergamum, arrived to speak to the Roman Senate (p. 142). The grandson of Antigonus Gonatas, Philip V, King of Macedon, was out to win back his ancestor's position in the eastern Mediterranean. But Rhodes stood in his way. So he stirred up the pirates from that eternal breeding ground of piracy, Crete, to prey on the island's commerce, sent an agent to sabotage Rhodes' fleet (he managed to set a fire in the navy yard which destroyed thirteen triremes), and readied a navy of his own, a formidable one with more than fifty major units, most of which were at least quinqueremes and a number were heavier—"sixes," "sevens," "eights," "nines," even a "ten." To all of this Philip added something new in naval tactics, the use of squadrons of *lembi*. These were light, extremely fast galleys, some single-banked and some double-banked, that the Illyrians, his neighbors on the Jugoslav coast, used so successfully for piracy and plundering. Like modern torpedo boats their job was to race in close to the enemy's heavy galleys and disable them by damaging whatever they could get at, particularly the oars. In two battles near Chios off the Asia Minor coast, Rhodes' home waters as it were, Philip held his own against the forces of Rhodes and Pergamum combined. This was serious; it looked as if the balance of power that the island had worked so hard to maintain was on the point of being shattered. Rhodes invited the dominant power of the western waters to take a hand in the east.

A short time before the first war with Carthage, the Romans had gone through a savage struggle with one of the Greek kings of the east who, looking for a new world to conquer, invaded Italy and fought his way to within fifty miles of their capital. He was ultimately driven off, but the memory was bitter and the Romans thereafter viewed the moves of the Greek monarchs to their east with a suspicious eye. Against Philip they had a special score to settle: during the second war with Carthage, when their fortunes were at low ebb, he had jumped in to take advantage of the situation—he had his own suspicions of Rome's intentions—and concluded a treaty with Hannibal; it looked for a while as if he was going to open up a second front, but Rome, by sending a squadron to the Adriatic and embroiling him with hostile neighbors, managed to keep him at home. The offer brought by Rhodes and Pergamum now provided an opportunity to square accounts, and the Senate grabbed at it. When it came to sending out the grand fleet, however, they held back. Of the two hundred galleys available, only fifty were dispatched. Why use more when there were the crack fleets of its new allies, Rhodes and Pergamum, to depend on? The Romans, after one of the most spectacular achievements in the history of naval warfare, at this point took their first step backward, a return to the old system of relying on the forces of nautically minded allies.

The move hardly affected the war Rome was to fight now. Its squadron of fifty, matched by twenty from Rhodes and twenty-four from Pergamum, not only bottled up Philip's fleet for the duration of the war but provided convoys for the steady ferrying of men and supplies to Greece. The enemy never had a chance on the sea, and the issue was decided on land. In 197 B.C. Philip gave in; the peace terms included loss of his whole fleet.

Rome was now an acknowledged participant in the affairs of the east. Almost without taking a breather it rushed right into another war, with Antiochus III, king of Syria, a descendant of Alexander's cavalry officer, Seleucus. During the years that Macedon and Egypt had been dueling for control of the eastern Mediterranean (Chapter 11), the rulers of Syria by and large refrained from mixing in; they had troubles of their own to keep them busy in the interior of their vast empire. But Antiochus had other ideas and, when he started to build up a navy, his neighbors, Rhodes and Pergamum, grew uneasy; then, when he welcomed Hannibal, that *bête noir* of the Romans, to his court, the Senate joined in the feeling. The year 192 B.C. found the three allies once again lined up, this time to combat Antiochus.

And this time there was more for the naval arm to do than just slog along convoying ships and transports. Antiochus had no mean fleet and it was commanded by a skilled admiral, Polyxenidas, a Rhodian, who, after learning his trade in that best of academies, the island's naval service, for some reason had been exiled. The allies had to remove this obstacle before they could safely ferry an army into Asia Minor to strike the king at home. Eight years earlier, against Philip, Rome had supplied half the naval forces; this time it furnished even less: of the 160-odd ships required to beat Polyxenidas, only about 75 were Roman.

The first round took place in the summer of 191 B.C. off Corycus, a point on the western coast of Asia Minor just northwest of Ephesus, and it went to the Romans. They had 105 major units in action, most of them quinqueremes, and Polyxenidas could match this with only seventy triremes; he had some 130 light craft of various types but apparently they weren't of much help. He locked himself up in the harbor of Ephesus and reported to the king that he needed more and heavier vessels. When he reappeared the following year it was with two fleets, both of them among the heaviest to be seen in the Mediterranean in half a century. In Ephesus he had an aggregation of ninety units; over half were bigger than triremes and there were two "sevens" and three "sixes." And coming up from the ports of Phoenicia, which Antiochus controlled in these years, was another of fifty units, including three more "sevens" and four "sixes," under the command of the redoubtable Hannibal. If the two ever joined they would outweigh and outnumber the whole allied force. The crucial job of preventing this was turned over to Rhodes.

Every ship that the island had available was mustered. It wasn't much, thirty-two quadriremes and four triremes; but the officers and men were the cream of the service, and the commander, Eudamus, was a skilled and astute veteran. Word reached him that Hannibal and his ships, having worked their way up the Syrian coast, were slogging westward under Asia Minor in the teeth of the prevailing northwesterlies. This gave him plenty of time to pick a point of his own choosing at which to intercept. Sometime in July or August of 190 B.C. the two drew near each other off the town of Side on the Gulf of Adalia in southern Asia Minor.

Eudamus had a reputation for caution but this was one time when he had to take chances: if the fleets formed up facing each other in two long lines as was usual, the enemy's superior numbers would outflank him. Hannibal, aware of that, had already drawn up his line. Eudamus took a deep breath, led his column out from the shore, and suddenly, before the rest of his ships had time to set themselves fully in line behind him, darted ahead with part of his force to engage the enemy's seaward wing, where Hannibal himself was stationed. It was a gamble designed to attract Hannibal's main attention until Eudamus could get in one telling blow somehow and even up the odds a bit. He was relying on the speed and skill of his crews and the initiative of his subordinates, and they did not fail him. His rearmost ships, without taking time to line up formally, in a split-second maneuver swung into a *diekplus* aimed at the enemy's shoreward wing. It was executed perfectly: when they regrouped after the attack, every vessel that had faced them was disabled; one Rhodian quadrireme had even single-handedly knocked out a "seven." Then, in a spectacular burst of speed—among the larger units there was nothing faster than a quadrireme—they raced to seaward to help out their commander, who naturally was having heavy going. Hannibal signaled the retreat; none of his ships had been sunk but over half had been put out of action. He threw over towlines to them and crept off. Eudamus took only one prize, the "seven" that had been knocked out in the first assault, but he had achieved his objective, had kept the enemy's two contingents from joining hands. It was a magnificent victory, reminiscent of the great actions fought by the Athenians in the Peloponnesian War (pp. 93–94): Antiochus, thinking to take a leaf from the Romans' book, had gone in for heavier ships, and the Rhodians had shown him that light vessels and trained crews could not only beat them but give them odds to boot. Eudamus turned to join the allied fleet off Ephesus. If he entertained the notion that his troubles were now over, he was wrong; there was one serious one left.

When the Romans took to the sea in the First Punic War they had had to put in command men who knew nothing about the water. The hair-raising losses suffered in storms forced them to work out some sort of system, and thereafter the squadrons were more or less kept in the hands of competent if not brilliant commanders. But in the war against Antiochus, the naval amateur made his appearance again, and with a vengeance: even in Rome's well-filled gallery of boneheaded admirals, there was none to match Lucius Aemilius Regillus, the man who in the spring of 190 B.C. had been entrusted with the fleet and now commanded the forces blockading the harbor of Ephesus. Before departing to take over his duties, he had been told that the prime naval objective was to keep the strait of the Dardanelles open so that the Roman army, marching around from Greece, could cross unmolested into Asia Minor and attack Antiochus on his home grounds. So long as Hannibal's force was licking its wounds somewhere on the southern coast of Asia Minor and Polyxenidas' was securely bottled up in Ephesus, this objective was automatically attained; anyone with any sense could see this, Eudamus for example, or Polyxenidas himself, much to his dismay. Moreover, the Romans already had a squadron posted at the strait. But Regillus had no sense. He was jittery: his place, he felt, was at the Dardanelles—even though it was still summer and the army, wearily tramping through Thrace, would not make its appearance until November. And he would actually have led the fleet up there, neatly uncorking Polyxenidas, had not Eudamus talked him out of it. The Rhodian had just risked his life and his nation's whole navy to win a victory against heavy odds and he wasn't going to stand by and watch all his hard-earned results go to waste. But he had to pay a price: Regillus agreed to stay put, but only on condition that twenty-three ships be detached and sent up north to reinforce the squadron there. There was nothing Eudamus could do about it; but he must have sworn some lurid Rhodian oaths since, by this move, Regillus was handing over superiority in numbers to the enemy on a silver platter.

To Polyxenidas it was like being proffered a reprieve when the noose was already around his neck. Sooner or later he would have had to send his fleet out of the harbor in a desperate move to win back the seas and block the crossing of the Roman army; now he could do it with the odds in his favor. Sometime in September he led his ships out, eighty-nine units against the allies' eighty, and drew them up in a long line off Cape Myonnesus to fight it out.

Regillus, having made the enemy a gift of the advantage in numbers, almost handed him the battle as well. He took his place at the head of the allied line, and ordered the Rhodian squadron to the rear to ride herd on stragglers. Luckily Eudamus was ready to disobey orders sooner than lose a fight. Knowing that Regillus was bound to get into trouble, he held his squadron of twenty-two quadriremes at the ready. On some of them he ran out the fire pots that had proved their effectiveness earlier in the year (p. 139). Just as he anticipated, Polyxenidas, with his superior numbers, began to crumple up Regillus' seaward wing. At precisely the right moment, Eudamus sent his ships racing from the rear to the rescue. The enemy vessels turned away from the fire pots, the Rhodian rams caught them in the sides, and the battle was won. Polyxenidas crept back into Ephesus and his fleet was still there when the war was decided in a great land battle the following year.

The nation which, seventy-five years before, had hardly a ship to its name now ruled the Mediterranean from the Strait of Gibraltar to the coast of Syria. It treated the sea like an unwanted child. It pulled its fleet out of the eastern waters and left them to Rhodes and Pergamum; in the west, where it had no maritime allies to share the burden, it resuscitated the plan of two miniature squadrons of ten ships apiece that it had used over one hundred years earlier (p. 144). When, in 171 B.C., Rome had to wage a second war with Macedon, against Philip's son Perseus, it fitted out just fifty quinqueremes and relied chiefly on Rhodes and Pergamum, whom it had bound by treaty to furnish naval forces. Perseus, with nothing more than a catch-as-catch-can aggregation of Illyrian pirate craft, was able to wreak havoc with Rome's lines of supply. In a brief third war with Carthage in 146 B.C., fifty ships, most of them probably old, turned up again. By the end of the century Rome's naval position seemed so secure that it shucked off even most of these.

But for Rhodes it was the end of an era. It had called in Rome to counter first the threat of Philip, then that of Antiochus. Both kings had to give up their navies and there was now no one left to challenge the Rhodians on the sea. Rome had even rewarded them with some territory on the Asia Minor mainland to administer. But for all that, they had lost the game. They had called in Rome for the same reason they had built up a superb fleet, to maintain their proud independence—and that was gone, as they were very soon to find out. When the blow came, it was launched not at their navy but at their merchant marine. To understand the circumstances, we must turn to the story of what was happening to trade on the sea in this age.

Chapter 13

EAST MEETS WEST

AMONG THE THOUSANDS of papyrus documents that have been found in Egypt (p. 46), there is one tattered piece whose battered lines of writing are the remains of a contract that was drawn up in Alexandria some time around 150 B.C. One party to the contract was a group of five merchants who were planning a trip down the Red Sea to the "incense lands," as Egyptian traders had been doing for millennia (Chapter 2). Like most ancient shippers they were working with borrowed capital: the party of the second part was a Greek who was putting up some of the money. The five partners too were Greek; one, as it happened, was from Sparta and a second from far-off Marseilles. Five other men endorsed to guarantee repayment. One of these was a traveling merchant from Carthage, the other four were soldiers stationed in Alexandria; quite possibly they had some of their spare cash invested in the venture. Of the soldiers, one came from Marseilles, another from Elia in southern Italy, a third from Salonika. The funds were handled through a banker. He was a Roman.

The document is almost unique; hardly any others like it have survived. It offers a picture in miniature of the key characteristics of trade in the Hellenistic world—the wide-flung world, run by Greeks, that Alexander opened and that lasted until the first century B.C. when Rome finally swallowed it. Its commerce was international in scope and, as a consequence, its business relations were complex and its business methods highly developed; to the age-old exchange of commodities that the Mediterranean had always known it added a lucrative trade in exotic luxuries; and, during it all, Egypt managed to play a major role.

Big cargoes require roomy ships and harbors, and far-ranging trade routes a knowledge of geography and navigation. The Hellenistic world met the challenge: its progress in the peaceful arts of the sea matched what it had accomplished in naval warfare (Chapter 11). The average merchantman now carried at least two hundred to three hundred tons of cargo, and many were larger. There is a description preserved of one leviathan that could hold over nineteen hundred tons—so big, in fact, that only capacious ports, such as Alexandria's, could accommodate it. In a bravura display of technical skill the shipwrights of Alexandria turned out an elephantine houseboat, a barge upon which a whole sumptuous villa was mounted, to enable King Ptolemy IV to ride the Nile in appropriate style. Bigger ships meant bigger rigging. It was probably at this time that three-masters were introduced, ships with artemon, main, and mizzen. The only superimposed sail that the ancients ever used was a triangular topsail set above the main; the earliest example does not appear until later under the Roman Empire (cf. Pl. 42), but it was very likely invented in the Hellenistic period. It is a misfortune that good pictures of the merchantmen of this age are lacking, and all the naval historian has to go on are vague clues scattered here and there in miscellaneous writings.

Good harbors were needed to handle the increased volume of trade and the bigger ships. Few Greek city-states with their limited resources could carry out such projects, but the Hellenistic rulers had funds at their disposal. They improved their ports by building huge breakwaters to create protected anchorages, by setting up lines of warehouses for storage, and by replacing the sand beaches that had served the smaller ships of an earlier day with stone quays. Of the seven wonders of the ancient world two, the colossus of Rhodes and the lighthouse at Alexandria, adorned harbors of this age.

Skippers must have had available to them new up-to-date "coast pilots" as a result of the spectacular progress in scientific geography that was taking place. Eratosthenes, the renowned mathematician-astronomer-geographer, calculated the circumference of the earth and arrived at a figure that came within two hundred miles of the true one; he pointed out that all the oceans were one, and concluded that a ship could eventually reach India by sailing westward from Spain—thereby influencing the thoughts of an imaginative Genoese lad who came across an echo of his words some seventeen centuries later. Maps of the known world were constructed with parallels of latitude and meridians of longitude; in the best-known areas, for example, the parallel that runs from Gibraltar through Rhodes, they were remarkably accurate. Sophisticated instruments were developed to help in this work, as we now know from the discovery in an ancient wreck of a complicated astronomical reckoner (p. 23).

In the third century B.C. Egypt played the leading role in commerce that Athens had in the one previous. Like its predecessor it had the products to export, controlled the major trade routes, and maintained a powerful navy to enforce its control. It had one great additional advantage: its rulers at the time, the first three Ptolemies, were shrewd and hard-driving businessmen.

What they were after was simple: export as much and import as little as possible, and keep the profits for themselves. They achieved it by a remarkable system of taxation, monopolies, and tariffs. The basic commodity of the ancient world was grain; it was in those times what oil is today. Egypt had always produced and exported large amounts. The Ptolemies reorganized agriculture to yield the absolute maximum, taxed it so that the peasant was left with just enough of his harvest to live on, put the rest in the royal silos at Alexandria, and, exporting it all over the eastern Mediterranean, pocketed the proceeds. This did not cut into the sales of other producers, such as Sicily or southern Russia, but simply made available more grain; it was the basis of the ancients' diet and there was always a seller's market in it. When the king of Syracuse, for example, launched a huge grain carrier (the nineteen hundred-tonner mentioned above) and then discovered it was too large to enter the harbors he shipped to, he made a present of it to Ptolemy III. Next in importance to grain in the international market were olive oil and wine. Neither of these was produced in any quantity in Egypt: the people traditionally washed and cooked with vegetable and seed oil, and drank beer. The Ptolemies saw to it that they continued to do so by levying a tariff of 50 percent on imported olive oil and 33 $\frac{1}{3}$ percent on imported wines, and took over brewing and the manufacture of oil as government monopolies. The ancient world's writing paper was either papyrus or parchment; papyrus was cheaper, practically all of it came from Egypt, and its manufacture and sale belonged to the crown. So too did the textile industry, which, using native flax, produced for export not only fine fabrics but very likely much of the linen that went into sailcloth. It was from sources such as these that the income came that enabled the earlier Ptolemies to build their capital into a magnificent showplace and an intellectual center, and the later to indulge their taste for such extravagances as floating villas. When ancient writers tried to describe the family's wealth, they could not find terms lavish enough.

Egypt's trade was not completely a one-way affair. There were certain things it had to import, but even here the Ptolemies were in luck, for territories under their control produced most of what was needed. Timber for the navy came from the pine forests of southern Asia Minor and the cedars of Lebanon, at least until 200 B.C., when these territories were lost to the Seleucids. Pitch had to be bought; although one possible source, Macedon, was out of the question for political reasons, the kings of Pergamum who controlled the rich producing area around Troy were friendly. Cyprus was an Egyptian possession, and its prolific mines supplied all the copper that was required. Tin and iron had to be imported, the first very likely from Carthage, the second from the southeastern shore of the Black Sea and possibly from central Italy. There was a brisk trade in delicacies for the gourmet tastes of the wealthy Greeks of Egypt: honey from Athens, cheese from the Aegean islands, nuts from the southern shore of the Black Sea, figs from Asia Minor. This class of course would not condescend to drink the peasants' beer and insisted on the fine wines of Syria and of western Asia Minor and its offshore islands. They paid the heavy tariff with no more reluctance than the American who today buys French champagne. What they imported, however, was strictly for their own tables; if they tried to sell any it was subject to confiscation.

To make sure nothing was smuggled in or out, the Ptolemies rigidly regulated their harbors. Ships had to have permission to enter, were assigned berths, had their cargoes checked item by item against cargo manifests, took on a return load under equally careful supervision, and left only after receiving clearance from the harbormaster. An example of a cargo manifest has actually been preserved. Apollonius, a high-ranking financial and administrative official under King Ptolemy II around 250 B.C., had as secretary a certain Zenon who was the sort that never threw away any papers. By great good luck part of his voluminous files were discovered, preserved from decay by Egypt's perennially dry climate. One of the documents happens to be the manifest of two small coasting vessels that had loaded up at some Syrian port to discharge at Alexandria. They were carrying a cargo that included many expensive delicacies clearly intended for the tables of the rich, perhaps even for Apollonius himself. Among the items listed are

table wine	138 jars, 6 ½-jars
dessert wine	5 jars, 15 ½-jars
olive oil	2 containers
dried figs	9 jars
honey (6 varieties)	14 ½-jars, 1 crock
wild boar meat	4 containers
Black Sea nuts	1 jar
pomegranate seeds	4 baskets
venison	2 jars
goat's meat	2 crocks
Chian cheese	1 crock
rough sponges	1 basket
soft sponges	1 (?) basket
pure wool	22½ lbs. in a box

The Mediterranean from very early times had maintained some commercial relations with India and Arabia and the coast of eastern Africa below Egypt (Chapter 2), but the great period of such trade dates from this age. Around the middle of the fourth century B.C. Theophrastus, the famous Lesbian botanist, knew pepper, which came from India, only as a medicinal drug; three centuries later a rich Athenian had so much that he could give away four quarts. The new wealthy class—the great kings, the commanders of their armies or powerful bureaucrats in their administrations, the prosperous merchants and bankers and shippers—wanted and could afford exotic luxuries. During the third century B.C. much of the traffic in them passed through the hands of the Ptolemies or their agents.

From Ethiopia and Somalia in Africa and from Yemen and the Hadramaut in southern Arabia came the myrrh that was a favored base for perfume and the frankincense that smoked on thousands of altars all over the Mediterranean; from all along the African coast as far as Cape Guardafui came ivory and from the waters off it tortoise shell. The products from southern Arabia traveled by camel caravan north to Gaza or even farther to the ports in Phoenicia; Egypt controlled all these terminal points, at least until 200 B.C., when they passed into the hands of the Seleucids. African products went by ship up the Red Sea, were unloaded at ports there, transferred to camel caravans for the haul across Egypt's eastern desert to the Nile port of Koptos, and from there went by boat downstream to Alexandria. This commerce was as old as the pharaohs (Chapter 2), but the Ptolemies gave it their characteristic efficient organization. They improved the caravan tracks across the eastern desert, set up numerous new ports on the western coast of the Red Sea, and launched attacks to hold down the pirates who haunted that body of water then and for long thereafter. In Arabia the traffic was almost wholly in the hands of Arabs, in particular the Nabataeans whose capital at Petra, located near a nexus of caravan routes, embarked on its prosperous commercial career at this time. Only at the terminals did it pass to Egyptians, Syrians, or Phoenicians.

From India came such luxuries as pearls, gems, tortoise shell, and silk, which Indian merchants imported from China and transshipped to the west. But the big trade derived from the plants and trees that produced prized cosmetics and spices—nard, costus, cinnamon, ginger, and, above all, pepper, which swiftly became a standard entry in ancient recipes; in a world of hot temperatures and no refrigeration, a strong seasoning unquestionably was welcome. There were a number of ways of getting these exports to the Mediterranean. One, the overland caravan route, ran through northwest India and Afghanistan and Iran to Seleucia, the capital the Seleucids had founded northeast of Babylon, near modern-day Baghdad. From here it followed the tracks along the Tigris and Euphrates rivers to northern Mesopotamia, where it split in three directions, either south to end up at the Phoenician ports of Tyre and Sidon, or west to Antioch, or on through lower Asia Minor to reach the sea at Ephesus. A second route, in use for millennia (Chapter 2), combined sea and land: ships loaded at India's northwest ports, coasted westward, and turned up the Persian Gulf to discharge at its head; from here camels took the merchandise to Seleucia, where it merged with what came via the overland route. A third was all by water. The greater part of it was in the hands of Arab and Indian shippers: their vessels left from India's northwestern ports and coasted westward but, instead of going into the Persia Gulf, continued on past and followed the southern shores of Arabia as far as where Aden now stands; there they unloaded and the cargoes were shifted to Greek craft for the voyage up the Red Sea. Once the goods arrived at Egypt, they were caught in the Ptolemies' web of commercial control: all had to be sold to the crown at prices set by the crown and, if it was raw material, was processed in workshops owned by the crown. In some of these, the incense factories for example, workers were stripped naked on leaving to make sure they departed with nothing more valuable than their skins. The Ptolemies left little to chance.

Of these numerous imports, a small amount remained in Egypt while the greater part was shipped out of Alexandria for distribution all about the Mediterranean. The large-scale and varied activity of Alexandria's waterfront, from the stevedoring of Egypt's voluminous bulky exports of grain to the transshipping of carefully packaged precious spices and incense, demanded the best in harbor facilities; the Ptolemies created there the finest port of the Mediterranean. Breakwaters strengthened and extended the arms of a natural lagoon, and the whole expanse was split into two harbors, an eastern and a western, by a huge mole, three-quarters of a mile long. It led at the seaward end to the island of Pharos, on which during the reigns of Ptolemy I and II was erected the famous lighthouse. This was a massive polygonal tower that rose in three stages to a height of over three hundred feet; its light, from a blazing fire backed by polished metal reflectors, could be seen, it was said, thirty miles out at sea. It quickly came to symbolize the city, and tourists brought back souvenirs adorned with its picture as enthusiastically as today's visitors to Paris collect gimcracks showing the Eiffel Tower. As time passed, its influence spread: it was hailed as one of the seven wonders, Roman architects modeled their major lighthouses on it, and it very likely had some influence on the form of Arab minarets. It stood nearer the eastern division of the harbor, which was the more important; here the waterfront was ringed by the fine gardens that surrounded the royal residences, museum, and library, as well as by the rows of warehouses and dockyards. The western harbor was for smaller craft, and channels leading out from it enabled them to sail through from the Mediterranean to the Nile.

Three hundred and twenty-five miles north of Alexandria lay another great port which, in the first half of the Hellenistic period, moved into a position of wealth and commercial importance, partly by riding Egypt's coattails. Rhodes had a fine geographical position near the center of the eastern Mediterranean's trade routes, a large merchant marine, a powerful navy to protect it, and a business-minded aristocracy with ample capital at its disposal. Most of the thousands of bushels of grain that the Ptolemies shipped out yearly, as well as much of their other exports, left Egypt in Rhodian bottoms and proceeded to Rhodes for transshipment to the ultimate destinations. But Rhodes' commercial relations were limited neither to Egypt nor to freight charters. It had two other sources of profit: banking and the wine trade. The island was one vast vineyard that produced lavish quantities of cheap wine. This was shipped out in large clay shipping jars of distinctive shape, and archaeologists have found remains of literally hundreds of thousands of them in ancient sites from the Black Sea to Sicily and Carthage. They turn up in quantity, as one would expect, in Egypt and the Aegean isles. But many have been found in southern Russia; Rhodian ships must have been busy in that area, ferrying in wine for return cargoes of grain to be distributed to the Greek world (cf. p. 101). Wherever Rhodian cargoes went, Rhodian bankers and agents followed; when, for example, a sheikh of what is today Algeria decided to try to enter the international market with some of his surplus grain, he worked through a Rhodian agent. Nothing shows more clearly how crucial a role the island played in the international economic scene than what happened when, in 228 B.C., a disastrous earthquake hit it. All of the great powers and some of the smaller ones rushed in handsome grants of aid. Ptolemy IV, in particular, sent thirty thousand tons of grain, the second largest single shipment recorded in antiquity—Rhodes was, after all, his best customer. The island collected an annual return of one million drachmas from the 2 percent tax on all merchandise that went in and out of its harbor (cf. p. 99), five times what Athens had netted from the same source two hundred years earlier. It is no surprise that the first organized code of maritime law, one that contains some of the seeds from which our present law of the sea has grown, was laid down and codified by the Rhodians.

Three characteristics in particular marked the island's way of doing business: efficiency, fair dealing—and Rhodes for the Rhodians.

Athens had been forced to depend heavily on foreigners (p. 108); it had the capital to invest but few citizens interested in the shipping trade. Rhodes had both. The foreigners to be found there were chiefly Greeks from Asia Minor and Egypt and Phoenicians, men whose presence business required. None were granted full citizenship. The citizens made the profits and with them maintained their superb navy, constructed a port that was a model of efficiency, and adorned their city with imposing public buildings and expensive works of art, among them (until the earthquake toppled it) the famous colossus that was one of the seven wonders of the world, a huge statue of the sun god set on the seaward end of an arm of the harbor.

Rhodes and Alexandria were in a class by themselves. Together they handled a vast trade in grain that no other port could match, and to this they were able to add a share of the lucrative transit trade in caravan goods. This was the icing on their cake of commerce: it gave extra work to sailors and longshoremen, opened new sources of profit for bankers and brokers, and, through the standard fee of 2 percent on harbor traffic, helped fill the public treasury. But the two were merely the greatest among a dozen rich and active Mediterranean entrepôts. Ephesus shipped out fine Asia Minor wines, Sidon expensive glassware, Tyre its traditional purple-dyed fabrics, and all three at the same time served as terminals for the caravans that originated in India and Arabia. Others, too, had their share of this traffic—Gaza, Beirut, Seleucia, the port of Antioch. Athens fell behind in this age because, although it still did a brisk business in exporting olive oil and importing grain, the transit trade largely bypassed it: to reach Athens ships from most of the caravan ports had to detour to the north and buck the Etesian winds in the process. Far off in the western sector of the Mediterranean, Carthage was still going strong on transit trade: the forwarding of British tin and Spanish minerals to customers all over the Mediterranean.

By 150 B.C. or a little later Rhodes' trade had been dealt a bruising blow, Egypt was almost shut out of the caravan trade, and Carthage lay in ashes. A new character had come upon the stage, and its entrance changed the commercial *mise en scène* as much as the political: Rome became not only the east's acknowledged master but its best customer as well.

It was not Egyptian grain or Greek olive oil or Asia Minor wines that the newcomer bought; Rome exported such products itself, and the trade in these commodities in the eastern Mediterranean went on much as before. The powerful senatorial families who ran Rome and its conquered territories at this time were now rich men living on vast estates and able to afford whatever luxuries were available. They wanted two things above all else: slaves to run their plantations, and art and exotic wares to add grace to their way of life. The east was ready to supply both, and the business-minded Greeks of southern Italy were ready to step in and act as middlemen. The flow of goods from India and Arabia, which had been steadily growing since the Hellenistic period opened, now channeled itself toward Italy. Rome's unceasing wars, first with Carthage and then with the Greek powers of the east, had thrown thousands of prisoners on the slave markets. The movement of this commodity, too, now turned toward the west and when, with the end of hostilities, the supply started to run low, pirates stepped in to replenish it. And Athens got a new lease on commercial life by mass producing works of art for the Roman market, both originals as well as copies of old masters; some of the ancient statuary in museums today was turned out in its workshops at this time. Luxuries and art and slaves for Rome were outstanding ingredients of trade in the second half of the Hellenistic age. But Rhodes' harbor saw very few such cargoes, and Alexandria's fewer than heretofore.

Rhodes was a proud nation run by an exclusive group of aristocrats who found it hard to flatter the new ruling power and followed as independent a line as possible. In 167 B.C. the Romans brought the Rhodians sharply to heel by hitting them where they were the most vulnerable.

In the middle of the Aegean lies the tiny island of Delos. Despite its size, it was from earliest times important as the site of a sanctuary of Apollo where a great yearly festival took place. During the first part of the Hellenistic Age the island was independent and in a small way started to develop some sidelines to its annual pilgrim trade. Rhodes in particular used it as a distribution point for grain shipments to nearby islands and as a branch banking center. Delos was the instrument the Romans used to teach Rhodes a lesson. In 167 they handed it over to their faithful ally Athens—with the stipulation that it was to be a free port, that no harbor or customs dues were to be collected there.

Within a year harbor receipts at Rhodes plummeted from one million drachmas to 150,000. The island did not go bankrupt. It still had its merchant marine and there was still money to be made hauling Egyptian and southern Russian grain and selling wine. But its harbor revenue was now limited to the big ships carrying bulky cargoes of commodities, which found it convenient to use Rhodes' capacious and secure port; the trade in slaves and caravan goods went to the free port of Delos. The funds available for maintaining the fleet and its vital anti-pirate patrols were no longer as ample as they had been formerly, a turn of events that quickly proved disastrous for international commerce; perhaps the Rhodians got some belated satisfaction when the Romans eventually turned out to be the chief sufferers (Chapter 15).

By about 130 B.C. Delos hit its stride. The harbor was far from large and was poorly protected, much inferior to Rhodes' or to any number of others nearby, but that hardly mattered. Slave ships were built to put in anywhere, and small freighters could carry a fortune in spices and perfumes. French archaeologists have completely excavated the island, and they have discovered that its long lines of warehouses were connected only with the quays, not with the town behind—striking evidence that Delos' trade was strictly transient: the merchandise moved in, unloaded, reloaded, and moved out. The slave market could handle thousands daily, and business was so good that the locals had a saying: "Merchant, sail in and unload! Everything's as good as sold."

There was more than merely the free port to bring the trade in luxuries and slaves to Delos. Rhodes prided itself on fair dealing, was ruthless with pirates, and maintained a standoffish attitude toward foreigners. Delos was frankly devoted to making money. Shrewd southern Italian dealers, sharp Near Eastern traders, and raffish pirate slavers found its unalloyed commercial atmosphere and its society, where money gave entrée to the best circles, far more to their taste than that of the stiff-necked city that had created an effective sea police and laid down the world's first maritime code. It was the difference between doing business in Macao, say, as against London.

Like filings to a magnet, there flocked to the island Greeks from Asia Minor and Alexandria, Phoenicians, Syrians, Jews, even far-distant Arabs—Nabataeans from Petra, Minaeans and Sabaeans from Yemen and the Hadramaut. To meet them came Rome's middlemen, the southern Italians, who soon formed the largest group on Delos. All brought their gods with them, as foreigners always do, and archaeologists have uncovered shrines or statues of Asia Minor's Cybele, Syria's Hadad and Atargatis, Phoenicia's Melqart; Apollo was sharing his sacred island with some curious colleagues. Inscriptions have been found in Latin and Greek and Semitic characters; the port must have heard a babble of tongues. The various groups formed associations— "Merchants and Shipowners of Tyre," "Italian Oil Dealers," "Merchants, Shipowners, and Warehousemen of Beirut"—primarily for religious and social reasons but, just as many a deal today is consummated at the bar of a golf club, they no doubt served business purposes as well. They actually became the government after a time: when the Romans made Delos a free port, they gave it to Athens to administer. Three decades or so later a coalition of these associations governed it.

From the great terminals at the end of the caravan routes, merchants brought to Delos their precious wares, and from everywhere, but particularly from Syria and Asia Minor, slavers brought their pathetic cargoes. The lion's share was turned over to the southern Italians who paid for it partly in Italian olive oil and wine but mostly in cash, and forwarded it to Puteoli, Pozzuoli today, the port of Naples. In the background were local shippers, wholesalers, shopkeepers, and the like who were needed to supply with all the necessities of life a motley population of twenty to thirty thousand souls packed in an area a little over one square mile in extent. It was only in this traffic in goods for home consumption that Rhodes now played any part: it sold the island grain and wine. Egypt kept its hand in by forwarding the luxury products that came to it via the Red Sea.

Ever since the end of the third century B.C. Egypt had been in a decline. The complex administrative machinery so painstakingly built up by the first Ptolemies began to run down. Macedon broke their command of the sea (Chapter 11), and Rhodes and Pergamum now shared the waters they once had ruled. More important, Egypt lost many of its extraterritorial possessions. The worst blow came when, in 200 B.C., the Seleucid ruler Antiochus III administered a defeat that resulted in Egypt's loss of Syria and Phoenicia, through which so much of the caravan traffic passed. It was reduced to what Arabian and Indian products came to it by the all-water route, and competition from the alternative caravan routes cut deeply into this. Help was needed; it came in an unexpected way.

The sea voyage between India and Egypt is actually relatively simple because of the phenomenon of the monsoon winds of the Arabian Sea and western Indian Ocean. During the summer the winds blow from the southwest. A skipper can leave the mouth of the Red Sea, stand off the southern coast of Arabia, and then strike boldly across open water, and the wind, coming steadily astern or over the starboard quarter, will carry him directly to India. But he must have a sturdy and dependable ship, for the southwest monsoon is blustery and violent, often rising to gale force. By delaying his return until any time during the winter, when the monsoon shifts to exactly the reverse direction, the northeast, he can make the voyage back. Moreover, it will be a pleasant voyage, since the northeast monsoon is as gracious and balmy as the other is difficult and violent. Arab dhows, which are lightly built, traditionally have avoided the southwest monsoon altogether and crammed both legs into the mild northeast monsoon.

Arab and Indian seaman had plied the waters between India and the Persian Gulf as early as the third millennium B.C. (Chapter 2). Unquestionably they learned about the monsoon winds. But they kept the knowledge strictly to themselves; why divulge such useful information to potential competitors? The seamen of Ptolemaic Egypt may well have known of the long coastal route to India, but this would have done them little good: the whole shoreline involved was controlled either by Arabs or subjects of the Seleucids or Indians, and even the most adventuresome skipper was not going to risk a voyage where there was no place to take refuge either from the weather or from attack. What was needed was a way to reach India that would bypass these obstacles. The answer came sometime around 120 B.C. A half-dead Indian sailor alone on a ship that had run ashore somewhere in the Red Sea was picked up and brought to the court of King Ptolemy VII. Nursed back to health and taught Greek, he told how, having set sail from India, he missed his way and landed on Egypt, the sole survivor since the others had all died of starvation. In return for his rescue, he undertook to act as pilot on a voyage to India for any group the king chose. He must have meant the voyage over open water, for the coastal voyage along consistently hostile shores would have been too dangerous for a Greek expedition. And in a voyage over open water he would inevitably have revealed to his passengers the nature of the monsoon winds.

Eudoxus, a daring and energetic explorer, happened to be in Alexandria at the time (he was a native of Cyzicus, a rich commercial city on the Sea of Marmora), and Ptolemy selected him as the leader of the expedition. He made two round-trips to India. On his return from the second he ran straight before the monsoon instead of keeping it on his starboard quarter and landed well south on the eastern coast of Africa where, in the best explorer tradition, he made friends with the natives by giving them strange delicacies (bread, wine, and dried figs apparently did the trick). On both trips he brought back a load of spices, cosmetics, and gems, only to see them confiscated by the royal customs officials. To avoid such humiliation a third time, he made the decision, drastic but characteristic, to sail to India by going around Africa and thereby bypass Egypt's inquisitive agents. He got together a well-equipped and well-planned expedition (there were even dancing boys and girls aboard, whether for the harems of Indian rajahs or to help while away the long days at sea, we can't be sure), and made it as far as the Atlantic coast of Morocco, where a mutiny turned him back. Undiscouraged, he fitted out a second expedition just as carefully—like Necho's Phoenicians (p. 118) he included in his arrangements stops en route to sow and reap crops—and it vanished without a trace. Bad luck dogged him even after his death. It must have been he who brought back to the Greeks the knowledge of the monsoons, but later generations gave the credit to a pilot named Hippalus. Nothing else is known about this figure. It's a shrewd guess, but only a guess, that he was Eudoxus' navigator.

Eudoxus' voyages put the Ptolemies' merchants in possession of a quick route, relatively safe from attack—warships and pirate craft were too light to operate far from shore—which could successfully compete with the caravan tracks. As it turned out, not too many of them ventured to use it, but it did keep at least a part of the Indian trade in Egyptian hands.

The second half of the Hellenistic Age was the heyday of the southern Italian businessman. Delos was not the only place where he was found: he followed the Roman armies into Greece, Thrace, Asia Minor, and Syria. Nor did he stick to the coast. He was a banker and investor as well as a merchant, and was willing to put his money into anything that promised a profit. He bought and ran farms, invested in mortgages, lent money to businessmen, to cities, even to kings. It is no surprise to find in the contract mentioned at the beginning of this chapter that the funds were handled by a banker with the good Roman name of Gnaeus.

In 88 B.C., during a bitter war between Rome and Mithridates VI, one of the powerful kings of Asia Minor, Delos was sacked. It had just about staggered to its feet from this blow when, in 69 B.C., a band of pirates overran and utterly devastated it. The island never recovered. It had served its purpose. When the dealers in caravan goods were first sensing the new drift in the current of their trade, toward Italy, they needed a convenient clearinghouse; moreover, Delos was perfectly located for the traffic in slaves from Thrace, Syria, and Asia Minor. But when the current of trade established itself and the supply of slaves began to peter out, the island lost its reason for being. Italians and foreigners moved out and set themselves up at Puteoli, which they made into a second Delos. The abandoned site lingered on as a ghost town to become eventually an ideal subject for the excavator's spade.

In the west the merchants of Italy had a bonanza: they fell heir, jointly with the merchants of Marseilles, to the rich traffic that had once passed through Carthage. But this was not all. There was another phase of their activity that remained all but unknown to history until recently, when archaeology's newest branch, marine archaeology, uncovered it.

Chapter 14

NEW LIGHT ON ANCIENT SHIPS AND SHIPPING

IN EARLIER CHAPTERS we told of the invention of SCUBA diving and the effect it had on the development of marine archaeology, and we cited some notable examples of how the examination of ancient wrecks has supplied totally new information about vital aspects of ancient maritime history. As it happens, for various reasons the greatest number of wrecks that have been found date to the period just reviewed, the second and first centuries B.C., the years in which the Romans gathered up well-nigh the whole of the Mediterranean in their political embrace.

What made possible the discovery of most of these was a humble artefact, the container the ancients used for transporting liquids. They put them not in wooden containers such as barrels or tuns, the way later ages did, but in amphoras. These were special clay jars that had a narrow neck and mouth, a bottom ending in a point, and a pair of handles placed vertically on opposite sides near the mouth (Pl. 34); when filled they were sealed by a stopper of cork or, more often, fired clay, set in mortar. The handles, positioned distinctively one across from the other, are what gave the jar its name: it was originally called in Greek *amphiphoreus*, "[jar] that was carried (*-phor-*) on both sides (*amphi-*)." *Amphiphoreus* was later shortened to *amphoreus*; this was borrowed by Latin transformed into *amphora*, and English took over the Latin word. The shape of the jars enabled them to be wedged tightly in a ship's hold in space-saving fashion: they were stowed upright in superimposed layers, with the bottom points of an upper layer fitting into the spaces around the mouths of those in the lower and cushioned by means of dunnage of small branches or the like. A large vessel might have as many as five layers.

Amphoras were big: they usually stood over 3 feet high (1 meter) and held between 5 and 10 gallons; a very common size was just under 7 gallons (26 liters). Since they were made of clay, they had the disadvantage of being heavy: the common 26-liter size weighed empty about 50 pounds or a little more (23–24 kilograms), and the contents more or less doubled the weight; stevedores could handle only one at a time, balanced on the shoulder (Pl. 35). Barrels, kegs, and the like are much lighter and more efficient, and such containers were known in ancient times; but, since wood was in short supply and costly, they were too expensive for large-scale use. That shippers of antiquity transported liquids overseas in amphoras has proved a priceless boon to marine archaeology, since wood is perishable, whereas clay is all but indestructible. When an ancient ship went to the bottom, the deck and topsides over time got eaten away, exposing the cargo. Had this been of barrels, they too would have disappeared—but amphoras will lie on the seafloor unaffected, forever flagging the presence of an ancient wreck (Pl. 36). Made strictly for a lowly utilitarian purpose, bulky and clumsy, these ugly ducklings of archaeology are as precious to the underwater excavator as pottery is to the excavator on land.

For, just like pottery, they supply vital indications of date and place. This is because different localities used different styles of amphoras, and these styles changed over the years. An expert can tell from the shape of a jar and of its handles, the fashioning of the lip of the mouth or of the tip at the bottom, analysis of the clay, and other such clues, what region it was made in and what century or even half-century it belongs to. A keen-eyed German scholar named Heinrich Dressel in the late nineteenth century got the idea of putting the Roman jars in a chronological sequence based on these various characteristics. His system is still in use: thus the type of amphora that was manufactured in Italy from the middle of the second century B.C. to the end of the first is still called "Dressel 1," other types "Dressel 2," "Dressel 3," and so on. A good number of amphoras bear stamps, generally on the handles, and these too help determine place and date. Amphoras manufactured in Rhodes, for example, are often stamped with a rose, the logo of Rhodes, and the name of a magistrate. Many Dressel 1 amphoras are stamped SES, short for Sestius, the name of a Roman family that in this period monopolized the wine trade of the western Mediterranean.

Three commodities figured the largest in ancient overseas transport: grain, wine, and olive oil. Grain, which was truly the staff of life in antiquity, much more so than today, traveled either in bulk or in sacks (Pl. 52), so ships in this trade that sank will forever remain unidentified since their cargo disappeared soon after they came to grief. Wine, too, was much more important then: it not only served the ancients as it does us but also took the place for them of coffee, tea, soft drinks, and so forth, all of which they lacked. And they used vastly more olive oil than we do since, as indicated earlier, that did for them what soap, butter, and electricity do for us. Wine and oil were shipped in amphoras, and if a vessel carrying a load of them went down in waters frequented by divers, whether sponge fishermen earning a livelihood or archaeologists searching for remains, there is every chance its wreck will be spotted—a stack of amphoras jutting up from the seafloor (Pl. 36) is a veritable signpost.

The finds of amphoras have revealed another object of overseas trade, which in volume was runner-up to wine and oil—*garum*. This was a fish sauce for flavoring food, apparently much like the fish sauces that are widely used in Indonesia today. It was made by taking whole fish, guts and all, or parts of fish, mixing them with salt, putting the mass in the sun to ferment, and keeping it there, with occasional stirring, for one to three months. A clear liquid formed at the top, and this, creamed off, was the garum. The smell was not for delicate nostrils, but strong smells, whether of ancient garum or modern limburger cheese, never deter the dedicated diner. It ranged in quality from grades priced at little more than ordinary olive oil to a premium grade that cost as much as the finest perfume and was solely for rich gourmets. The number of garum amphoras that have been found testify to the sauce's widespread popularity. Italy was a particularly good customer, receiving large-scale shipments manufactured on the Spanish coast.

The underwater discoveries illustrate graphically how great was the volume of overseas shipment of commodities, particularly wine. Marine archaeologists have excavated a big freighter that foundered off the coast near Toulon in the first century B.C. and they estimate that it was carrying at least 4,500 amphoras of wine and quite possibly as many as 7,800—between 225 and 390 tons. The vessel found off Albenga (Chapter 3), of the same date, had even more, between 11,000 and 13,500—500 to 600 tons. Every year hundreds of such ships must have arrived at Rome and Alexandria and Marseilles and the other major ports and stood at the quays while an army of stevedores, in lines like trains of ants, emptied them of their burden of amphoras (cf. Pl. 35).

There is yet another object of trade that bulked large in ancient overseas transport and, being almost as durable as clay, lasts under water to catch a diver's eye—building stone. The extant ruins of temples, baths, law courts, and the like are witness to the Roman penchant for enhancing the impressiveness of their public buildings by the use of imported stone. The Pantheon in Rome, for example, has exterior columns of red granite from Egypt and interior columns of yellow marble from Tunisia, and was adorned with statues of Greek marble. In Trajan's Forum, the huge complex that includes his famous column, there is marble from Greece, Tunisia, and Asia Minor as well as from the celebrated Carrara quarries in Italy. At Ostia, Rome's port at the mouth of the Tiber, the government maintained a storage depot for imported building stone; study of the pieces discovered there reveals that many had been quarried in Asia Minor or North Africa or Greece. So it is no surprise that divers have come upon a good number of wrecks of vessels that had been carrying loads of stone. These show that it was shipped in various forms—raw chunks, elements partially roughed out, fully finished pieces. Off the eastern coast of Sicily, for example, two cargoes of raw stone have been found. One consisted of thirty-nine blocks weighing overall some 350 tons; the biggest by itself weighs over 28 tons. The other had fifteen, totaling 172 tons, including a behemoth of 40 tons. Off southern Italy divers have discovered a wreck with a cargo of stone coffins; these had come, their sides roughly carved in preliminary fashion, from Asia Minor and were presumably headed for Rome, where the sculptures would be completed according to the buyers' desires. A ship that went down off the southeastern point of Sicily in the sixth century A.D. had in its hold the stone elements, fully finished, for a prefabricated church, right down to the altar, choir screen, and pulpit. And one of the very first wrecks to be investigated, the one found off Mahdia (Chapter 3), was carrying some sixty marble columns neatly stowed in five or six parallel lines in the hold.

Certain metals can survive under water. This has made possible, to the joy of all lovers of art, the recovery of a number of splendid bronze statues (Chapter 3). Of more interest to the historian is that it has also made possible the recovery of a whole range of metal objects: masses of copper, tin, and lead ingots (Pl. 8) that were being transported as cargo; fittings that belonged to the ship—anchor stocks of lead, sounding leads, lead tubing, tools, rigging rings; even objects belonging to the passengers or crew, such as coins they had dropped or left in the ship's strongbox. In one wreck divers found the bronze handles of a set of scalpels that must have come from the kit of a passenger who was a doctor.

One of the notable achievements of marine archaeology has been its discoveries in the field of ancient shipbuilding, a subject about which very little had been known hitherto. First and foremost, as we have already shown (Chapter 3), it has revealed that the ancient shipwright did not make a hull by fastening planks to a pre-erected skeleton of keel and ribs, the method we are familiar with, since European shipwrights have been assembling seagoing craft this way for hundreds of years. Instead he created a shell of planks, fastening each plank, edge to edge, to its neighbors by means of mortise and tenon joints and transfixing the joints with dowels to ensure that they did not come apart. Then, when the shell was partially or fully complete, he inserted frames as stiffening.

It so happens that, long before marine archaeology came into being, there were clear signposts that this was the ancient shipwright's method. Back in 1864 in the remains of the Roman harbor at Marseilles, part of a hull had been discovered—a hull built in this fashion. But no one took any notice either at the time or for long thereafter. Then, just short of seventy years later, a pair of striking examples came to light. For centuries it had been known that two big Roman barges were lying on the bottom of Lake Nemi some twenty miles south of Rome, very well preserved in the still waters. The Italian government, at the expenditure of a vast amount of money and energy, pumped out the lake until the vessels were visible, raised them, and put them in a museum specially built for the purpose on the shore; here they stayed until retreating German soldiers burned them when evacuating the area in 1944. The superstructures were gone but the hulls were in very good shape—and mighty hulls they were too, one measuring some 224 feet (68 meters) in length and 79 feet (24 meters) in beam, and the other just a shade smaller, 213 (65 meters) by 68 (21 meters). Enough miscellaneous items—bronze decorations, mosaic tesserae, chunks of marble veneering—were recovered to show that the barges were as elegant as they were large, veritable floating palaces. The hulls, it turned out, were put together by incredibly careful joinery: every plank all along its length was pinned to the ones above and below by a line of mortise and tenon joints set less than four inches apart, and every joint was transfixed by a dowel. Since the barges had been built for Emperor Caligula, a notorious spendthrift, it was assumed that this remarkable joinery was something special, reserved for Roman royalty who had an easy way with money.

It was the findings of marine archaeology that uncovered the truth of the matter, findings made possible, like so much else, by the ancients' use of amphoras. If a ship ends up on the seafloor with its load of amphoras still more or less in place over the bottom of the hold, these will act as a protective cover and keep the wood underneath from being destroyed (Pl. 37). Considerable parts of some thirty hulls have survived in this way, and they reveal that the joinery of Caligula's barges was not at all special but for many centuries the standard practice of antiquity. In an earlier chapter (Chapter 3) we dealt with the Ulu Burun wreck that proves how far back the building of seagoing vessels shell-first with edge-joined planking goes, to at least 1400 B.C. The remains of the thirty-odd hulls just mentioned not only show that the practice continued all through antiquity but reveal changes that took place over the years. Wrecks that date from the fourth century B.C. down to the first century A.D. are marked by topnotch workmanship: the joints are large, are set close to one another (at times so close that there is scarcely any space between), fit tightly, and are each transfixed by a dowel. Not infrequently, the planking is double, the planks in each layer joined with mortises and tenons. By the fourth century

A.D., the workmanship has become noticeably more lax: the joints are smaller, stand farther apart, fit loosely, and lack the transfixing dowels (Fig. 3). Moreover, there are hints of the skeleton-first method, which was eventually to become the standard method for seagoing ships in the Western world. In a wreck of the seventh century A.D., for example, the excavators have determined that the shipwright started with a shell of planks joined to each other—using very small mortises and tenons that fitted very loosely and were spaced very far apart—but continued building up the shell only to the waterline; at that point he inserted frames and finished off the hull by nailing the rest of the planks to these. Eventually shipwrights took the last step: completely abandoning the joining of planks to each other, they started with a skeleton of keel and frames and fastened all the planks to this, thereby initiating the method that ultimately produced the great sailing ships of the sixteenth and later centuries. Thanks to the thorough excavation of the wreck of a small coastal vessel found off Serçe Limani on the coast of Turkey opposite Rhodes, we now know that it had come into use by at least 1025 A.D. The vessel, whose demise can be pinpointed to that year, turns out to have been built totally skeleton-first—the earliest example so far of a seagoing craft made in this fashion.

The archaeologists have worked with such care and precision that they have been able to bring to light details about the arrangements aboard ancient craft, even about their crews. The wreck of the seventh century A.D. just mentioned was excavated so meticulously that it was possible to reconstruct the ship's galley and demonstrate that this modest vessel—it was only about 70 feet (20.52 meters) long and 17 feet (5.22 meters) in beam—had cooking facilities far more sophisticated than, for example, on Columbus' ships, which had no more than a firebox protected from the wind by a hood. Here there was a real galley, an enclosed space 11 feet by 4 feet and 6 feet high, covered by a tiled roof; it housed an ample firebox of tiles surmounted by an iron grill. In the wreck found off Kyrenia (p. 113), a small coaster, the recovery in what must have been the cabin area of four identical drinking cups, four spoons, and other utensils in sets of four makes it almost certain that this was the number of the crew.

Marine archaeology has come a long way from the time, as late as 1950, when the wreck at Albenga was ruthlessly ripped apart as a salvage vessel's huge steel grab raised samples of the cargo, to today's precise and painstaking procedures. It has made notable contributions to our knowledge of ancient maritime matters: it has revealed how the ancients constructed their vessels and in what general sizes;

what cargoes were loaded, and how, and in what volume; what some of the equipment carried was like; what facilities were aboard; even some idea of the size of the crews.

In recent years the archaeologists have varied their concentration on individual wrecks with other significant activities. They have measured the changes that took place in the shoreline over the centuries, explored the remains of ancient harbors, surveyed extended stretches of the seafloor to gather statistics on the numbers of wrecks and the nature of their cargoes. Such surveys have enabled them to select likely targets for full-scale investigation.

And, once a likely target turns up, the archaeological teams must get to work on it fast. For, unfortunately, they are in a race with looters, not merely amateurs, as in the early days, but professionals who are almost as well equipped as they and as adept in the techniques of raising finds to the surface. All too often they come upon a wreck that once had been a promising site but now is in disarray, a mere field of sherds despoiled of all objects that might conceivably have value on the art market.

Chapter 15

THE PIRATES OF CILICIA

IT CANNOT have been long after merchantmen first cleaved the waters of the Mediterranean that pirates began to dog their tracks. "Strangers, who are you?" asks the Cyclops of Odysseus and his men, "Are you here for trade? Or have you wandered recklessly over the sea like pirates who go about risking their necks to bring trouble on others?" In the age Homer was describing, piracy was a profession that energetic and adventurous men entered as a recognized way of making a living.

The profession lost some of its recognition as the centuries passed, but none of its attractions. It was so widespread that it actually affected the course of early Greek civilization: people moved their settlements away from the coast, where they were a target for raids, to points more inland and surrounded them with protective walls. The Athenians at one time had to set up a naval base on the Adriatic solely to protect their shipping from freebooters. Loss to pirates was one of the risks that moneylenders, shippers, and shipowners always reckoned in when they drew up contracts or fixed prices. The pirate even gained a place for himself in literature. A common scene in ancient comedy was the reunion of a long-lost child with its parents from whom pirates had snatched it as an infant to sell into slavery. Eventually the pirate wound up as wildly romantic as the Arab sheikhs of the drugstore novels who gallop off into desert sunsets with fair captives across their saddlebows. Readers of the Greek equivalent of this sort of fiction knew that hero and heroine, once aboard ship, would along the way be carted off by a gang of brigands, of whom some were bound to fall desperately in love with the girl.

Roving cutthroats who operated for their own profit weren't the only pirate menace. Any number of states considered piracy a legitimate form of maritime enterprise, and their flotillas were to be found ranging up and down the trade routes. When in 230 B.C. the Romans sent an embassy to Queen Teuta, who ruled the Illyrians of the Jugoslav coast, to complain about their attacks on Roman shipping, she pointed out with wide-eyed innocence that Illyrian sovereigns never interfered with what their subjects did on the seas. (Eighteen centuries later Queen Elizabeth I put on more or less the same act about Hawkins and Drake.) Moreover, it was as hard in those days as later to distinguish between pirates and privateers. In an age that had no international law, about the only way a government could force an alien into compliance with a given obligation was by indiscriminate reprisal, and even the most respectable Greek states didn't think twice about sending off their captains to attack the unsuspecting and innocent fellow citizens of a recalcitrant foreigner. Some captains, especially when their pay was in arrears, would interpret their orders liberally and attack any likely looking prize they came upon. As far as the victim was concerned, it made little difference whether a gang of freebooters boarded him for their own profit or the crew of an Athenian war galley because of some alleged offense on the part of one of his compatriots: he lost his vessel and cargo. Every now and then a state would use pirates as a temporary addition to its navy, thus throwing large-scale opportunities their way. Demetrius enlisted whole bands when he laid siege to Rhodes (Chapter 11), and Philip V quietly engaged the pirates of Crete to concentrate on Rhodian shipping (Chapter 12). Nineteen centuries later the Dutch and English were making the same sort of deals with Barbary corsairs.

The ancient pirate, like his later brethren, chased and boarded merchantmen. But his stock-in-trade was not that; it was slave-running. An attack on the high seas was hit-or-miss: a pirate chief could not tell from the look of an ordinary merchantman plodding along whether it was carrying a load of invaluable silks and spices or cheap noisome goat hides. But a swift swoop on any coastal town was bound to yield, even if the place was too poor for plunder, a catch of human beings, of whom the wealthy could be held for ransom and the rest sold for the going price on the nearest slave block. "Pirates came into our land at night," runs the inscription on a monument which the people of the island of Amorgos in the south Aegean set up in the second half of the third century B.C., "and carried off young girls and women and other souls, slave and free, in all over thirty in number. They cut loose the boats in our harbor [no doubt to forestall pursuit] and, seizing Dorieus' boat, escaped on it with their captives and whatever else they had taken." Amorgos was a small island, and the loss of even thirty people must have been a blow; luckily two brave and persuasive men among the thirty talked the pirate chief into holding them as hostages—the monument had been erected in their honor—and sending the rest back. An inscription that the people of Naxos, a large island nearby, set up at about the same time records a raid in which pirates seized no less than two hundred eighty people; they were all ransomed eventually, but it must have cut deeply into many a Naxian's savings. In landings of this sort, if the alarm was given in time the populace scampered off to safety or rounded up forces to drive the attackers off. It was not often that they captured any, for pirates, knowing what was in store for them, played it safe. There is a case on record of a Turkish corsair of the sixteenth century who, when caught, was roasted alive for three hours; it's very likely that ancient townspeople showed as little mercy to those who fell into their hands. When Caesar rounded up a gang, as we shall see in a moment, he sentenced them to crucifixion, as nasty and lingering a death as any.

Although no coastal town along the Mediterranean and no merchantman on it was totally safe from attack, there were certain areas that were especially dangerous. The "Tyrrhenians" very early got a reputation for buccaneering; the name was probably a catchall for the various groups that operated in the Tyrrhenian Sea west of Italy: Etruscans, Italians, Sardinians, Greeks from southern Italy. Dionysius I of Syracuse, that able and inventive general and admiral, managed to hold them down, but when he died they bounced back as strong as ever. The Illyrians of the Jugoslav coast were a particularly virulent breed, the only group who succeeded in making a contribution that outlived them: they designed a boat so light and fast—the liburnian—that the Romans paid them the compliment of adopting it as a standard naval unit (Chapter 16). The Illyrians had a field day in the Adriatic until Rome, between the two Punic wars, finally took some action; but since, in her usual fashion, she didn't follow up by establishing a permanent patrol in the area, they were quickly back in business. They worked in large packs—at their height they had a fleet of 220 ships—and frequently hired out to the neighboring kings of Macedon, especially after these had lost their own naval power. They met their end when they made the mistake of joining King Perseus in open war against Rome (p. 156). Farther to the east, the Cretans were notorious pirates as early as Homer's day (cf. p. 44). It was they who made the sail past Cape Malea, which every vessel plying between Greece and Italy had to go around, touch and go for even well-armed ships, and for years they were the chief targets of Rhodes' patrols. But neither the Tyrrhenians nor the Illyrians nor the Cretans matched for size, organization, and destructiveness the group that played out the last, lurid act in Mediterranean freebooting, the pirates of Cilicia.

Cilicia, on the southern coast of Asia Minor, has an inland portion that is a stretch of rugged mountains and a shoreline that is a serrated succession of precipitous headlands. This is a combination ideal for pirates: the trackless interior protects them from any attack by land forces against their back, and the coast offers a choice of lofty lookouts and well-hidden strongholds. Some time after the middle of the second century B.C., when Rome had defeated the Seleucid Empire, which bordered on Cilicia, and delivered her telling blow against Rhodes (p. 165), which used to police the waters round-about, this region became a spawning ground for a pirate movement that, within a half-century, managed to bring chaos into every corner of the Mediterranean.

The pirates of Cilicia made their headquarters in a town called Co-racesium, a miniature Gibraltar perched on a rock that dropped a sheer five or six hundred feet to the sea and was connected to the mainland by only a narrow isthmus. As word of their successes got about, there flocked here not only the riffraff of every nation in the area but even men of means and family eager to add the spice of danger to their lives. Eventually they had enough crews and ships to organize themselves on naval lines: they formed flotillas commanded by commodores, even fleets under admirals; to liburnians and hemiolias, the standard craft of the profession, they added men-of-war, even triremes. When Mithridates VI of Asia Minor began his bloody and long-drawn-out revolt against Rome in 89 B.C., the Cilician pirates joined him and thereby put at his disposal the best fleet available at the time in the Mediterranean. They had an efficient system of intelligence: agents would fraternize with the crews of merchantmen along the quays or in the waterfront saloons, discover their destinations, and relay the information to headquarters. But attacks on shipping were just a sideline. Their specialty was slave-running, and they raided the coasts with such ruthless efficiency that they actually depopulated certain areas. Numbers of cities were glad to get off by paying them protection money, and some entered into formal treaties permitting them access to their ports and markets. These brigands now supplied the bulk of the slaves sold at the great market on Delos, satisfying even the ever increasing demands of Roman plantation owners. Eventually they opened up a market of their own at Side, a convenient thirty-odd miles by water from their headquarters, which became second only to Delos.

By the early part of the first century B.C. the pirates of Cilicia literally controlled the seas. Rhodes had been forced to cut back her navy, the Seleucids had lost theirs to Rome, and Rome had given hers up. Very likely, when the pirates were first getting under way, rich Roman plantation owners who found their services so useful had discouraged talk of taking action against them. By now no aggregation of a few squadrons or even a fleet of standard size was going to do the job: the pirates commanded over a thousand ships; their arsenals were stocked with weapons and supplies; and, in concert with other miscellaneous packs, they were operating all over the Mediterranean—one group even helped a Spanish rebel to capture from Rome one of the Balearics, far off in the west.

Shortly before 70 B.C. their activity reached a crescendo. Landings were made on the shores of Italy itself, and noble Roman ladies, not remote provincials, were now carried off for ransom. One gang kidnapped the granddaughter of an admiral who had once led an antipirate campaign, and another hauled off two high-ranking Roman officials with their staffs. The Appian Way, Rome's chief highway, part of which skirted the coast, was no longer safe to travel on. A squadron broke into the port of Ostia and smashed a flotilla of Roman warships there. The Romans were the ultimate purchasers of most of the captives put on the block, but that did not deter the pirates from biting the hand that fed them. For Roman citizens they had specially worked up an ancient version of walking the plank. When one of these was captured and, in the hope that it might help, declared that he was a Roman, the pirates would go through a carefully rehearsed act. First they pretended to be thoroughly scared and humbly asked for pardon; next they solicitously dressed the victim in his toga (the mark of the Roman citizen), assuring him that it was to keep them from making the same error a second time; and then, once out at sea, they threw over the ship's ladder and prodded him down it with best wishes for a pleasant stroll home. On one occasion the jokes went the other way. A gang seized Julius Caesar when, as a young man, he was sailing from Rome to Rhodes to study law there, and made the mistake of not recognizing that their captive was something out of the ordinary, although he gave them plenty of clues. They set a ransom of twenty talents—an enormous figure—on his head, and Caesar genially pointed out that he was worth at least fifty. They accepted the revised figure with alacrity and willingly sent off some of his companions who had been seized with him to collect the cash. While awaiting their return, Caesar treated the cutthroats holding him as if they were a personal bodyguard: he would order them to keep quiet whenever he was ready for his siesta, commandeer an audience whenever he wanted to practice his oratory, and dress them down whenever he felt they failed to appreciate the finer points of his style and delivery. The pirates were amused no end by all this and made the slip of staying amused when Caesar good-humoredly promised that he would come back after his release and hang them all. The moment the ransom was paid he made his way to Miletus nearby, raised a fleet, returned, and did just what he said he would: he had as many as he could catch crucified. As a special favor for their rather decent treatment of him during his captivity, he allowed their throats to be slit before nailing them to the cross.

In 69 B.C. things came to a head. A pirate fleet sacked Delos for a second time, ending once and for all the island's commercial career. The seas became practically closed to shipping. It was this that finally goaded Rome into action: the city fed on imported grain, and the pirates had now hit it in its most sensitive spot, the belly. What ensued was one of the most remarkable operations in naval history.

Actually there had been some paving of the way. Since 77 B.C. Roman armies had been slowly slogging through the mountains of the hinterland behind the pirates' coastal strongholds. But this was only setting the stage: the coup de grace had to be delivered on the sea. The man who planned and executed it was Caesar's famous rival, Pompey the Great.

In 67 B.C., when the pirate menace had become a national crisis, the people of Rome handed Pompey a blank check to cope with it. The whole shoreline of the Mediterranean up to a point fifty miles inland, with all the resources therein, was turned over to him; he had the authority to requisition ships or men or money or whatever else he needed from any governor of any Roman province or from any king bound by allegiance to Rome. Pompey must have anticipated something like this, for the plan he put into action was too carefully thought out to have been made up on the spur of the moment. It was a masterpiece of strategy and it went off like clockwork.

He had to have ships. He got them, as Romans had ever since the Second Punic War, by commandeering the forces of such allies as Rhodes, the Phoenician cities, Marseilles, and so on. But the key to Pompey's success was not his ships alone—Roman admirals had gone after the Cilician pirates with powerful forces before and failed—but the scale and thoroughness of his planning: his strategy left nothing to chance and it embraced the whole of the Mediterranean. He divided the shoreline into thirteen sectors, each with its own commander and fleet. The essence of his plan was cooperation: each fleet was to attack the pirate nests in its sector simultaneously while Pompey, at the head of a mobile force of sixty vessels, swept from Gibraltar eastward, driving all before him either into the jaws of the forces along the shores or straight ahead into an ultimate cul-de-sac off Cilicia.

Within forty days Pompey had cleaned up the west and was ready for those who had fled headlong before him to the home base. As he approached, first individual ships then whole packs started to surrender. When he drew his siege lines around Coracesium, the last hard core gave up. It was a spectacular operation, brilliantly conceived and magnificently executed. In three months Pompey had accomplished what no power had been able to do for centuries. Except for a spasmodic outburst now and then, the age-old plague of the Mediterranean was ended for a long time to come. No doubt the job of keeping it that way got off with flying colors when Pompey, instead of butchering his captives and thereby building up a debt of hate, in a sociological experiment that seems startlingly modern carefully selected those he judged capable of reforming and resettled them in towns in the interior where they could start a new life away from the temptations of the sea.

Pompey did more than exterminate piracy. While he was about it he laid the foundation for a revival of the Roman navy, and provided the pattern for its organization. The squadrons he had activated were, in the next half-century, to grow into the fleets that fought in Rome's bloody civil wars and, when these had ended, to form the nucleus of the efficient force that turned the Mediterranean into a Roman lake.

Chapter 16

ROME RULES THE WAVES

ON 11 JANUARY 49 B.C. Julius Caesar crossed the Rubicon, and the fires of civil war blazed forth all over the Mediterranean. Not until two stormy decades had gone by were they stamped out, after tens of thousands of men had been killed and a thousand ships destroyed. And the nation that had once abandoned its navy saw the last round of its bitter internal strife fought out on the sea in a battle that pitted against each other two of the largest fleets ever assembled in ancient history.

When the curtain rose on the conflict in 49 B.C., Caesar held the west and Pompey the east with the ships and seamen that meant control of the water as well. Sea power, however, in those days had its limitations (p. 92), and Caesar, gambling shrewdly on them, was able to ferry an army from Italy through Pompey's blockade lines in the Adriatic to Greece, where he ultimately won complete victory. He now inherited some two hundred ships, all his opponent had left, but the daggers of Brutus and Cassius prevented his ever using them. And, although his grandnephew Octavian—or Augustus, to give him the more familiar name he adopted later—in a series of daring moves gathered into his hands the power his great-uncle once held, the fleet slipped through his fingers. Through the quirks of Roman politics and the irony of fate, most of it fell into the grasp of none other than Pompey's son, Sextus. He knew how to use it: he was as skillful a seaman as he was a political gambler.

By 42 B.C., a scant two years after Caesar's death, Sextus commanded one hundred and thirty ships and was ready to play his own hand. Almost immediately he got a windfall: Augustus and Mark Antony had joined forces to crush Brutus and Cassius, who, in what was by now a tradition, had commandeered the ships of the east; after their defeat, the remnants of their fleet joined Sextus. Augustus was faced with the job of consolidating his rule in Italy with barely a vessel to his name, while a wily and able opponent held the waters roundabout with a force of over two hundred. He sorely needed a navy and someone to head it; he created the one and found the other.

In 38 B.C., by exacting huge contributions and digging deep into his own pockets, Augustus managed to muster a fleet of three hundred and seventy ships, including units up to "sixes," the heaviest aggregation seen in over a century. He gave the command to his right-hand man Agrippa. Agrippa had already shown himself a skillful general; now he was to reveal equal gifts as an admiral, not only on the deck but at the planning table as well. He had a special base built just north of Naples, where he spent a winter putting the raw recruits Augustus handed him through a rigorous training. But there was still more to be done. Agrippa knew that he could not hope to win by ramming: his men, despite the winter's work, were still beginners compared with Sextus' crack crews, and, with their heavy ships, did not stand a chance of getting in a blow at the enemy's light fast craft. There remained only boarding, but boarding Sextus' slippery units posed a problem almost as difficult. Agrippa solved it by inventing a new weapon. His vessels were big enough to carry catapults. He mounted the arrow-shooting type but, instead of a shaft with the normal pointed head, he used one tipped with a grapnel and made fast at the other end to lengths of lines. It was a most ingenious device: not only did it have a much greater range than a hand-thrown grapnel, but it was far harder for the enemy to handle; to cut it away his axes had to bite through a stout pole instead of a slender rope. In September of 36 B.C., after several preliminary clashes, the two grand fleets, totaling, according to report, over six hundred ships, clashed off Naulochus just west of Sicily's northeastern tip. The fighting was savage, but Agrippa, helped no doubt by his catapult-grapnels, won a sweeping victory.

After destroying Caesar's assassins in 42 B.C., Augustus and Antony had divided the Mediterranean world between them, the one taking Italy and the west, the other the east. A showdown between them was inevitable. Augustus had had to delay it until Sextus was out of the way. Now he was ready. The fight came in 31 B.C., and the final round was fought on the second of September. The site was off the promontory of Actium, just north of the western end of the Gulf of Corinth and not far from the spot where, sixteen centuries later, another historic naval engagement was to take place, the Battle of Lepanto. Antony had started the campaign with over five hundred ships; however, when the decisive face-off took place, he could put in the line no more than two hundred and thirty, including an Egyptian squadron of sixty supplied by Cleopatra. It was a heavy fleet, reminiscent of the mighty aggregations that Demetrius and Ptolemy had led three hundred years earlier. Every size from trireme to "ten" was represented, and a great "ten" carried the flag. Agrippa had four hundred units, giving him a big advantage in numbers, but his largest were probably no more than "sixes," as in his fights against Sextus. Very likely, as there, his galleys carried catapult-grapnels. The engagment itself was anticlimactic. Months earlier Agrippa had seized bases from which his ships could intercept the grain freighters from Egypt that were supplying his enemies, and Antony found it harder and harder to feed the enormous masses of men in his army and crews. When his rowers took their places on the benches on September 2, they were underfed, sick, and discouraged. Nor did it help matters that, just before they shoved off, the unusual order came down to keep the sails on board (cf. p. 88); it may have been part of some subtle tactical plan, but to the men it smelled of flight. When the lines locked in conflict, Antony did not even wait for the finish: Cleopatra's squadron hoisted sail to make a run for it, and he ingloriously followed with a number of ships. Those that stayed fought bravely but hopelessly. A year later the lovers committed suicide, and for the first time in history the Mediterranean, from the Straits of Gibraltar to the Dardanelles, was in the control of one man. Augustus had ushered in the great era of the Roman Empire on the sea; it was to last for the next two hundred and fifty years.

Mastery of the Mediterranean was Augustus' first step. His next was just as important: to hold what he had won he created a finely organized navy. And for two centuries thereafter his successors maintained and improved upon what he had founded.

Following the trail blazed by Pompey in his whirlwind campaign against the pirates, Augustus divided the sea into sectors and apportioned them among two major and a number of minor fleets. On Misenum, the cape that stands at the seaward end of the northern arc of Naples' great bay, he erected a headquarters for his principal fleet: though its immediate job was the patrol of the waters westward, it had a general responsibility for all the waters both east and west. Here he maintained a force of some ten thousand men and fifty-odd ships of the larger types—mostly triremes, some quadriremes and quinqueremes, and a "six" as flagship—plus an appropriate number of smaller craft. Substations north along the Italian coast and on the islands of Corsica and Sardinia opposite served as convenient ports for patrols. The officer in charge, Prefect of the Misene Fleet as he was termed, became one of the more important government officials in the Roman state. His area of command was so widespread and complex that the bulk of his work was administrative, and most of those chosen were political career men who, attaining the post after a lifetime of public service, were more at home in an office than on the deck of a ship. Pliny the Elder, who was Prefect of the Misene Fleet in A.D. 79, the year Mount Vesuvius buried Pompeii under a rain of volcanic ash, is a case in point. He had previously served in the army as an officer, studied law, spent some years in practice, and put in a term as governor of the province of Spain. Though a conscientious administrator, his ruling passion was not his various offices—certainly not the navy— but the collecting of material for his famous encyclopedia. When

Vesuvius began its fateful eruption he ordered the ships out, primarily to get him near enough for a good look at the unique spectacle and,
as an afterthought, to pick up survivors. Whatever rescues there were
took place without him because, in his eagerness, he pressed too close
and lost his life.

A second major fleet, also made up chiefly of triremes, was located
at Ravenna far up the Adriatic. Its task was to patrol the Jugoslav coast
opposite, whose pirates had given so much trouble in earlier days. It
was less important than the fleet at Misenum and its prefect was subor-
dinate in rank. When required, its units cooperated with those of the
other.

The basic importance of these two squadrons was their very existence: so long as they stood by in watchful readiness, no potential rival
had a chance to build up and launch a force that could match them.
When the need arose, they ferried army units from place to place, and
at all times performed such useful functions as transporting important personnel and carrying dispatches. In addition to all this were two
duties only remotely related to the sea. To satisfy the Roman appetite
for public spectacles, Augustus and his successors varied the standard
fare of gladiatorial combats and horse races by occasionally putting on
mock naval engagements. They had artificial lakes dug out, surrounded them with seats—sometimes they just flooded regular amphitheaters—and staged on them full-scale sea battles: the crews were
condemned criminals and the fighting was to the death. It was the job
of the sailors of the navy to see to it that lake, ships, supplies, and the
like were all in proper order. A second responsibility assigned them
was the handling of the huge awnings that were spread over the seating areas of theaters and amphitheaters to shield spectators from the
sun; sailors were a natural choice for this work since they were the
most skilled in dealing with canvas and ropes. Special detachments
from Misenum and Ravenna were at times stationed at Rome just for
these extracurricular chores.

Augustus was fully aware that policing the Mediterranean meant
more than holding a powerful naval force at the ready. It also meant
running down sporadic pirates, patrolling harbor traffic, and ensuring
quick communications between ports, duties for which the two major
fleets were too far away and their units too heavy. So he began the
practice of building up small provincial squadrons, located at strategic
points like Alexandria and Seleucia, and equipped chiefly with light
fast craft. His successors followed his lead and, by the end of the first
century A.D., such groups were stationed not only about the Mediterranean but wherever Rome had shipping to protect: in the Black Sea,
on the Danube, near the mouth of the Rhine, by the English Channel.

The sailors and rowers and marines who manned the fleets came not from the Roman citizenry but from the various subject peoples of the Roman Empire. They were Greeks, Phoenicians, Syrians, Egyptians, Slavs—members for the most part of peoples that for centuries had gone down to the sea in ships. They entered the service generally between the ages of eighteen and twenty-three, signed up for a hitch that was no less than twenty-six years in length, and, if they lasted, were rewarded at discharge with Roman citizenship. When Augustus was desperately trying to build up his naval force to combat Sextus, he enlisted slaves as rowers—but he made certain to free them before sitting them on the benches; there were no slaves then or thereafter in the Roman navy. On shipboard things probably were run as they had been in the Hellenistic navies, for most of the officers were Greeks who would naturally tend to follow the traditions they had been brought up in, and the Romans for their part had little to add. Generally officers came up through the ranks: a man could work through the various grades to captain of a warship (*trierarchus*) or even leader of a squadron (*navarchus*). This last position was usually the end of the line inasmuch as the topmost ranks, certainly the prefectures of the fleets, were open most of the time only to Roman citizens.

We know the sailors of the Roman navy more intimately than those of its predecessors. For one, archaeologists have excavated their graveyards around Misenum and Ravenna and laid bare the inscriptions on their tombstones; from these we learn the countries they came from, their average span of service, a bit about their careers, and so on. For another, a good many came from Egypt; like servicemen in all times and places they wrote home, and excavators have recovered some of their letters from Egypt's dry sands (cf. p. 46). These are unique documents, for they provide what is so rare in ancient history, the warm light of personal experience.

The Roman army was the service with the long, honorable tradition. Since the navy was a newcomer and drew mostly upon the subject peoples of the empire for its personnel, it was a reluctant second choice for most boys. "God willing," wrote a young recruit who, around the beginning of the second century A.D., was a marine on a light galley attached to the provincial fleet stationed at Alexandria, "I hope to be transferred to the army; but nothing will be done around here without money, and letters of recommendation will be no good unless a man helps himself." The boy was especially bitter because his father had been a soldier who had served out his time and received an honorable discharge. The story has a happy ending, for a later letter reveals that he finally got what he wanted.

But other letters show that some boys were well satisfied with the navy. There is a particularly engaging one from a young boot, Apion, who, sometime in the second century A.D., had left his little village in Egypt, been shipped to Italy, and there received word that he was assigned to the fleet at Misenum. He writes to his father full of enthusiasm:

Dear Father,

First of all, I hope you are well and will always be well and happy, and my sister and her daughter and my brother. I thank the god Serapis that when I was in danger on the sea he quickly came to the rescue. When I arrived at Misenum I received from the government three gold pieces for my traveling expenses. I'm fine. Please write me, Father, first to tell me that you are well, second that my sister and brother are well, and third so that I can kiss your hand because you gave me a good education and on account of it I hope to get quick promotion if the gods are willing. Greetings to Capiton and my brother and sister and Serenilla and my friends. I've given Euctemon a picture of myself to bring to you. My name is Antonius Maximus, my ship the *Athenonikê*. Farewell.

P.S. Serenus, Agathodaemon's son, sends greetings, and so does Turbo, Gallonius' son.

Apion was fortunate: he had met a number of boys from his hometown; he had been given duty on a ship in the finest fleet; he saw— perhaps a bit overoptimistically—a chance of getting ahead. Like any young recruit in any age, he hungers for news from home and sends the family a picture of himself, no doubt showing him in his new uniform. In these pre-camera days it has to be a miniature, and in these pre-postal service days he must find someone heading for his hometown to deliver it. Now that Apion is in the Roman navy he drops his Egyptian name for a good Roman one. We do not know whether his rosy vision of quick promotion ever came to pass, but we do know that he prospered in other ways. A letter he wrote a number of years later is also preserved: Apion now uses only his Roman name; he had married a woman he met around the base, and he has three children, a boy and two girls.

The story revealed by this and similar letters is typical. All over the Mediterranean youngsters left their little villages, went overseas to Misenum or Ravenna, and there they settled down, married, raised families, and were buried. The process of recruiting had to be kept up continuously, for the children of these men did not often follow in their footsteps. If they could, they went into the army or some other more attractive way of life.

Augustus and the emperors who came after him were proud of the navy that kept the seas safe for them. They stamped pictures of its ships on the coins they minted or had them carved on the monuments they set up—and thereby provided for posterity an idea of what

Roman men-of-war looked like (Pl. 38; cf. Pls. 39, 40). These pictures reveal that the Romans, though they retained the basic types found in the fleets of their Hellenistic predecessors, introduced significant modifications. The rowing arrangements, from the triremes of the fifth century B.C. on, had included an outrigger for the topmost line of oarsmen (p. 83). The Romans eliminated this, making the hulls broad enough to accommodate all the levels of rowers, sometimes with the addition of an oar box for the topmost (Pl. 39); quite possibly such roomier galleys were better suited to the duties a largely peacetime navy had to perform. Aft they added a cabin for the commander in the form of an arched doghouse (Pls. 39, 40). Some of the ships are shown carrying the artemon (Pl. 39), but this, though attested now for the first time, may well go back to the Hellenistic period. The stempost ends in a big volute (Pl. 38), a feature that certainly goes back to that period.

One new type of warship does appear in the Roman navy, the liburnian (Pl. 39). It was a destroyer, a light, fast, highly maneuverable vessel ideal for pursuit of pirates or for quick communications. A piratical tribe of the Jugoslav coast had invented it, and the Romans found it useful enough to take over as a standard unit, particularly for the provincial fleets, which consisted almost exclusively of such craft. Liburnians had two banks of oars—they may have developed from the two-level *lembi* that were in use along the same coast in earlier centuries (p. 152)—and very likely did for the Romans what the triemiolia had for the Rhodians (p. 139). Though the latter was available for adoption, Roman admirals obviously preferred the liburnian. No doubt its two banks were easier to handle than the three of the other, and possibly its rig was too; its mast and sail, for example, perhaps could be lowered under way for a fight without disturbing the rowers. The liburnian achieved such popularity in the Roman navy that the term eventually came to mean warship in general.

The galleys were given names, but these were not inscribed on the hull as today. Instead, an illustrative carving was set on the bows, for example, a relief of a god if the ship was called after one (Pl. 38). As it happens, many were, with a preference for the major deities of the Roman pantheon: *Apollo, Ceres, Diana, Juno, Jupiter, Mars, Mercurius, Minerva, Neptunus*. A number of ships bore geographical names, and here there was a tendency, natural enough, to go in for rivers; at one time or another, all the great rivers of the ancient world—the Tigris, Euphrates, Nile, and Danube—were represented in the fleets. But quite a few ships were named after abstract qualities, and the fact that it was a peacetime navy seems reflected in the choice: alongside such appropriate names for men-of-war as *Armata, Triumphus*, or *Victoria*, the christeners went in for *Concordia*, *Iustitia*, *Libertas*, *Pax*, *Pietas*, and the like.

One of this navy's key duties was to guard the trade routes. During the first two hundred years after the beginning of the Christian Era, these were traversed by the mightiest merchant marine the Mediterranean had even seen or was to see for over a dozen centuries. The various types of craft that made it up are the best known of the ancient world, for even more representations of them are extant than of the contemporary war galleys (Pls. 41–45, 48). Shipwrights had their tombs decorated with a picture of a vessel they had built (Pl. 46), shippers with a picture of one of their freighters coming safely into harbor (Pl. 41), and Roman emperors would issue coins stamped with a boat or harbor scene to commemorate acts of theirs that had benefited commerce. After a gap of centuries we can again see what merchantmen looked like, observe the form and fittings of their hulls, make out the details of their rigging, even watch them in action.

Some of the features of the ships so illustrated appear for the first time, but this does not prove that they were innovations, and certainly not that the Romans had a hand in them. Though Rome now ruled the Mediterranean world, the people who took care of its commerce were still Greeks and Phoenicians and Syrians and others who had made their living this way for centuries. The craft they sailed in were, in all likelihood, basically the same as their fathers had; seamen by and large are a conservative lot. Whatever looks new may have been invented years earlier, and most of it probably goes back to Hellenistic times, when marine architects were called upon to meet the needs of a great expansion of trade (Chapter 13).

One thing is clear: there were many more big merchantmen afloat now than ever before. The freighters that carried government cargoes were commonly 340 tons burden, and those of the crack grain fleet (Chapter 17) ran to 1,200 tons; seventeen centuries were to pass before merchant fleets of such tonnage again sailed the seas. Circumstances occasionally called for even greater ships. The best examples are the leviathans that were specially built to haul from Egypt the obelisks the Romans had a penchant for setting up as monuments in their capital. The shaft and pedestal now in front of St. Peter's stands about 130 feet high and weighs just under 500 tons; the Emperor Caligula had it brought over about A.D. 40 and the vessel he constructed to carry it was ballasted with 800 tons of lentils—a total load of 1,300 tons. When Pope Sixtus V's architect, Domenico Fontana, in 1585 moved the obelisk from its original location in Nero's circus to where it now stands, he used 800 men, 140 horses, and 40 rollers, and the whole contemporary world broke into applause at the feat. But

Caligula's seamen and engineers had taken the monument from Heliopolis near Cairo, barged it down the Nile, loaded it on its ship, sailed it—undoubtedly against foul winds—from Alexandria to Rome, transferred it again to a barge to get it up the Tiber, and re-erected it at the point where Fontana found it.

Mediterranean merchantmen had always carried a handful of oars for emergency or auxiliary work. In the pictures of this age, merchant galleys make their appearance, freighters specifically designed to be driven by both sail and rowers (Pl. 44). They unquestionably go back to earlier times; the horse transports that formed part of the Athenian fleets (p. 92) were in effect the same sort of ship. Most were small, for plying between nearby coastal points, but many were of fair size, particularly useful for longer voyages where foul winds or calms were to be encountered or when speed was essential. There must have been a good many of these engaged in the transport from Africa and Asia of the wild animals that were in continuous demand at Rome for the gladiatorial games (Pl. 47); the trip was hard on the beasts and had to be made as rapidly as possible. Those merchant galleys that were light and fast enough could, when the occasion called, be pressed into service with the navy.

As far back as the second millennium B.C. Minoan shipwrights had designed a hull for their sailing vessels that was well rounded and had stemposts and sternposts that curved upward in graceful arcs (Pls. 4, 10). And, since the ancient mariner was as resistant to change as his later brethren, it remained the commonest type in the Mediterranean throughout antiquity (Pls. 42, 43, 45). A variant was also in existence, one in which the prow curves inward, as on a fighting galley, and ends in a projecting forefoot. It is at least as old as the other, for it occurs on some representations of skiffs dating to Minoan times. Now it appears, and very frequently, not only on skiffs and similar small craft (Pls. 46, 50) but on large-sized merchantmen as well (Pl. 43). The forefoot often extends far enough to look for all the world like a ram, yet to explain it as such makes no sense, since a ram has no place either on a heavy freighter, powered only by sail, or on a tiny rowboat. Whatever the purpose, this form of prow did not live on after the end of the ancient world; it is not to be found on the wooden vessels of Europe in subsequent centuries.

The merchantmen of this age were beamy; their length–to–beam ratio was commonly three or four to one. Larger types intended for longer trips had a cabin aft (Pls. 42, 45), but it was big enough to house only the captain, occasional VIPs, and the like. The ships were first and foremost for carrying cargo, and they took on passengers only incidentally; hence, although they commonly had some aboard—for the ordinary voyager headed overseas, freighters were the sole form of transportation available—they supplied no services. Travelers booked deck passage, sleeping either in the open or under little tent-like shelters that their servants put up in the evening and took down in the morning. They brought their own food, which their servants prepared in the ship's galley. This, as we have seen (p. 175), could be relatively spacious and fitted with an ample hearth; though intended primarily for the crew, at certain times the galley was at the disposal of passengers' servants. The ships did supply water, which was stored in a large wooden tank in the hold.

Behind the cabin rose the sternpost, which was most often carried up high, brought downward in a graceful curve, and finished off with the figure of a goose head; the stem, by contrast, was equally often blunt and squarish (Pls. 42, 43). On vessels with the ramlike bow, stems were less severe, ending in an ornamental volute or a goose head (Pls. 43, 45). The stempost frequently bears a relief illustrating the vessel's name; the ship to the left in Pl. 42, for example, has one portraying Liber, the Roman god of wine, and very likely the L on the sail is his initial. On larger ships a gallery sometimes girdles the stern (Pls. 42, 48).

Shipwrights preferred fir, pine, and cedar for planking, frames, and keel, but, since cypress, elm, alder, and other woods saw service as well, they no doubt contented themselves with whatever was locally available. Oak was freely used for frames and false keel, very frequently for tenons and treenails, and every now and then for strakes. Pine and fir were the favored woods for yards and masts. Sails were chiefly of linen, usually of oblong blocks of cloth sewn together (Pls. 42, 45); the edges were secured by a boltrope (Pl. 42) and the corners reinforced by leather patches. Ropes were of flax, hemp, papyrus, or esparto grass. Ballast was most often sand or stone—stone of any kind: rocks, old building blocks, even inscribed slabs that had been discarded; divers found a number of these in the wreck off Mahdia (Chapter 3).

The hulls, with their planks so painstakingly joined to each other, required scant caulking; where it was necessary, the material was generally tow. It was customary to smear the seams or even the whole exterior hull with pitch or pitch and wax, and to spread a layer of pitch on the interior. Many ships, small as well as big, had their underwater surface protected by a sheathing of thin lead plates nailed over a layer of tarred fabric; this practice seems to have been given up by the end of the second century A.D. Ship's paint was encaustic, that is, wax melted to a consistency that could be applied with a brush and to which color had been added. The colors available, mostly mineral derivatives, were purple, white, blue, yellow, brown, green, red. Reconnaissance vessels and pirate ships could be painted a shade that matched seawater to serve as a sort of camouflage. A colored mosaic of a large Roman freighter shows how gaily vessels could be decorated: the hull is done in bands of red and dark blue, the stern galley and trim and steering oars in yellow, and the stern ornament is gilded.

The pictures of this age are invaluable when it comes to rigging: they portray not only the types in vogue but individual features as well. The standard rig is still the squaresail. Most ships are equipped with an artemon, while the larger types carry a topsail above the main, the only superimposed sail found in the ancient world. It was a triangular piece of canvas that had its base spread along the upper surface of the yard and its apex hauled up to the truck of the mast (Pl. 42). The very biggest freighters were rigged with all these sails plus a mizzen (Pl. 43). A relief carved on a stone plaque that was found in the harbor of Rome illustrates in detail the complicated tackle that a seagoing sailing vessel carried (Pl. 42). Projecting over the bows is the artemon mast. An extremely heavy forestay running from the top of the mast to the base of the artemon mast and an elaborate cluster of shrouds, with tackles for adjustment, steady the mast. The mainsail, broader than it is high, is made up of square and rectangular pieces sewn together and protected along the edges by a boltrope; figured on it is a picture of the she-wolf suckling Romulus and Remus, the legendary founders of Rome. A dozen brails for shortening sail run from the foot up through fairleads to the head and then, probably rove through blocks on the yard, down to the deck. Above the main is the topsail, split in the middle to allow the forestay to pass through. One of the two massive steering oars is visible; socketed to the handle at right angles to the blade is a long tiller which the helmsman pulls toward him or pushes away to twist the blade in the water and thereby direct the ship's course. The plaque illustrates two phases of action. On the left the vessel has just entered port and is sailing at reduced speed past the lighthouse at the mouth: the ship's boat, which had been in tow at the end of a long line, is being brought up short to the starboard quarter; the mainsail is being shortened; the artemon has been removed and its halyard made fast to a bumper whose forward end bulges with some cushioning material; a hand stands by, and, as soon as the ship noses up to the stone quay, he will lower it in order to hold the prow a safe distance away; two men and a woman, probably VIPs who were passengers aboard, cluster about an altar set up on the poop to offer sacrifice in thanks for a safe return. On the right a vessel—either the same one or a sister ship—has made fast to the quay; sailors are aloft securing the canvas (they have stripped off the topsail and are furling the main); a gangplank has been thrown over to the

quay, and a stevedore walks along it bent under the weight of an amphora on his shoulder—the discharging of the cargo, either wine or
oil, has already begun.

It was long assumed that the square–rig was the only type the ancient mariner used. This was a mistake: he not only knew the fore-
and-aft rig but several versions of it. He knew both the triangular
lateen and the lateen that, having a short luff, is strictly speaking quad-
rilateral rather than triangular (Pl. 49). He knew as well the sprit-rig,
the rig that consists of a sail more or less square in shape supported by
a spar—the sprit—that runs from a point near the base of the mast
diagonally to the peak of the sail. It was favored for small craft, fishing
smacks or the like (Pl. 50; cf. Pls. 52, 53), but there is at least one instance of a much larger vessel so rigged. A carving on the side of a
sarcophagus, a stone coffin, done sometime in the third century A.D.
(Pl. 45), pictures three ships that neatly illustrate different types afloat
at the time. The two on the outside are square-rigged: the one on the
left has the rounded prow, that on the right the prow with projecting
forefoot. The one in the center, with a rounded prow, is the same size
as the other two but carries a sprit-rig: the mast is stepped far up in the
bows and the sail made fast to it by the luff, very loosely, as was the
practice on occasion centuries later; the sprit runs diagonally across
the windward side of the sail to the peak, and a double-ended vang
made fast to its tip permits trimming of the peak (Pl. 51).

The skipper of a merchantman of this age, in addition to the "coast
pilots" that had long been known (pp. 114–15), may have had charts to
plot courses on. He had a lead line to test depths, and the lead had on
the bottom a cuplike depression for tallow so that he could bring up
samples of the bottom. He was able to send messages to other ships or
to shore with signal flags. He had a ship's boat for emergencies or use
in harbor that was towed astern with a hand stationed in it at all times
(Pl. 42). He had no compass, but, in the Mediterranean where distances over open water are usually not too great and where visibility is
exceptionally good, this lack was not as serious as it might have been
elsewhere. One reason he limited his sailing to the season between
April and November (p. 40) was less the fact that winter brought
storms than that it brought frequent cloudy weather, which, obscuring
sun and stars and landmarks, increased the hazards of voyaging.

We noted earlier that slaves were admitted into the crews of warships only under very exceptional circumstances (p. 87; cf. p. 188).
The opposite was true of the merchant marine. In Roman times, just
as in Greek (p. 114), it was not uncommon for merchantmen to be
manned entirely by slaves, the captain and mates as well as the ordinary seamen. A shipowner, if he had sufficient capital, might own both

vessel and crew; if not, he would probably own the captain, perhaps the mates, and hire the rest from slave owners who specialized in the renting out of labor. The Greeks and Romans, throughout most of their history, preferred to use slave labor, whether owned or rented, for both white-collar and blue-collar work rather than free men paid a wage.

The merchantmen of this age carried less canvas than they could have and they carried it low; this made them slow but at the same time safe. When the breeze was favorable they could average between four and six knots, when foul much less, since their square rig did not allow them to sail efficiently against such winds; craft that were sprit-rigged or lateen-rigged presumably did better. The carving on the sarcophagus mentioned a moment ago nicely illustrates the ancient skipper's sailing skills. It is remarkable for being the earliest detailed representation of a crisis at sea. The coffin held the remains of a boy—or man—who had drowned, and the coffin maker decorated it with the dramatic story of how he met his end. The scene is the mouth of the harbor at Rome. Here, on a windy day when the waves were running high, the boy had fallen out of a tiny skiff in which he had been rowing, perhaps in the very sight of his parents standing at the end of a mole. Two vessels race to the rescue from inside the port, one slightly ahead of the other. At the critical moment the one in the lead finds itself in imminent peril of colliding with a ship heading into the harbor. It is this moment that the artist chose to portray, and his portrayal is detailed enough to enable us to work out precisely what happened. The two rescue ships, facing right, are traveling with the wind on the port quarter. The one heading in, facing left, is on a starboard tack. Clearly there is a strong wind blowing, for the square-riggers have shortened sail by taking up on the brails, and the sprit-rigger by tricing up the tack of the mainsail. The latter, though in the lead, suddenly finding itself in danger, has had to give up all thought of making the rescue. The one behind has taken over that task, and one of the crew is leaning anxiously over the bow ready to reach out a hand to the boy in the water. Apparently he is not aware of help from this quarter: his attention is riveted depairingly on the ship nearest him which, confronted by its own peril, can no longer bother with him. The two vessels in the collision zone are maneuvering swiftly to avoid disaster. Both have excellent skippers; they are doing precisely what is called for. On the square-rigger the skipper has backed the mainsail. This will slow his forward motion. The artemon is still drawing, which will throw his bow to port and carry him past on the outside of the other ship (Fig. 7). Very likely he wants the artemon trimmed, but he is getting somewhat less than perfect cooperation: his hand forward has

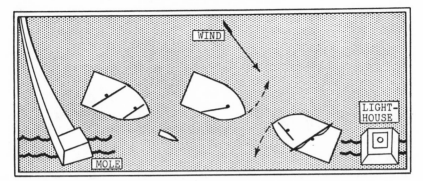

FIG. 7. Reconstruction of the sailing maneuvers pictured in Pl. 45.

given up in fright, rushed amidships, and settled down to pray. On the other vessel the skipper is working to swing his bow to port and pass on the inside. This will bring him from a broad to a close reach, and his hands accordingly are busy trimming sail: the one aft has grabbed the leech to get the sail inboard in a hurry. Another minute will tell the story. We know the rescue attempt was unsuccessful; let us hope that at least the collision was avoided.

The nation that had entered the First Punic War with a squadron of twenty vessels had come a long way. The triremes and liburnians of its fleets ringed the Mediterranean, and the multifarious craft of its merchant marine thronged its waters. The one guarded, and the other carried, a far-flung and intensely active commerce—but that is a story that needs a chapter for itself.

Chapter 17

ALL ROUTES LEAD TO ROME

"I BUILT MYSELF five ships, loaded them with wine—worth its weight in gold at the time—and sent them to Rome. . . . Every single one of them was wrecked, that's the god's honest truth; in one day Neptune gulped down thirty million. You think I was licked? No, by god! To me this loss was a drop in the bucket, practically nothing. I built some more ships . . . , loaded another cargo of wine plus lard, beans, perfume, slaves. Then the little woman did the right thing by me: sold all her jewels and clothes and put a bundle of cash in my hands. That's what sparked my fortune: when God's on your side, things go fast. I netted a round ten million on that one voyage." The speaker is Trimalchio, Petronius' famous character, the ex-slave who became a multimillionaire. Petronius, of course, is exaggerating for comic effect but not too much. There was a fortune to be made in maritime commerce in Roman times. One of the family of the Calpurnii, wealthy shippers based at Pozzuoli with connections in Africa and Syria and Asia Minor, made enough money to underwrite the cost of building a temple for his hometown. Sextus Fadius Musa, a wealthy shipper of Spanish olive oil to Rome who was based at Narbonne in France, set up a fund to enable a local social organization to celebrate his birthday forever. Successful traders like these were to be found from Spain to Syria. Augustus had launched and his successors maintained two centuries of peace; in this favorable climate commerce burgeoned, outstripping in extent, volume, and velocity anything that had gone on before. It was more than just the total of what the Hellenistic world had carried on earlier in the east and of what Carthage had in the west. One of its great new components was something which, growing steadily since the middle of the second century B.C., now reached maturity: filling the needs of the one million or so souls who lived in the city of Rome.

The Roman man in the street ate bread baked with grain grown in North Africa or Egypt, and fish that had been caught and dried near Gibraltar. He cooked with oil from North Africa in pots and pans of copper mined in Spain, ate off dishware fired in French kilns, and drank wine from Spain or France. The Romans of wealth dressed in garments of wool from Miletus or of linen from Egypt or even silk from China, and had them cleaned with fuller's earth from an island in the Aegean. They adorned themselves with gems and pearls from India, and scented themselves with aromatics from eastern Africa and southern Arabia. They seasoned their food with Indian pepper and sweetened it with Athenian honey, had it served in dishes of Spanish silver on tables of African citrus wood, and washed it down with Sicilian wine poured from decanters of Syrian glass. They lived in houses whose walls were veneered with colored marble quarried in Asia Minor, and their rooms were filled with statues imported from Greece. Staples and luxuries, from as near as France and as far as China, poured into the capital, enough of the one to feed a million people, and of the other to satisfy the extravagances of the political, social, and economic rulers of the Western world.

Until the middle of the first century A.D., the bulk of this trade was channeled through Pozzuoli, the port of Naples. It had a fine natural harbor capable of handling large ships, while the only port near Rome, Ostia at the mouth of the Tiber, had nothing better than an open roadstead that was constantly being encumbered by the silt the river carried down every year. This meant that all cargoes had to be transferred to smaller craft to be carried up the coast, a procedure involving trouble, delay, and expense. The Emperor Claudius finally decided to do something about the matter and in A.D. 42 began to build in the marshy plains north of the Tiber's mouth a big, completely man-made harbor to which was given the matter-of-fact name of Portus, "the port." Two long curving moles embraced a vast anchorage one-third of a square mile in extent. At the tip of one of them Claudius's work gangs sunk and filled with concrete the great ship his predecessor had built a few years earlier to carry the Vatican obelisk to Rome (p. 191). On the massive foundation so formed they set a lighthouse that rose in four diminishing stages, three square topped by a round (it is pictured in Pls. 42, 43). It was modeled on the famed lighthouse at Alexandria and soon became famous enough on its own to serve as a pattern for beacons elsewhere. A canal connected the new port with the Tiber. An incoming vessel either discharged its cargo onto barges that were drawn by teams of men or mules or oxen, trudging along a towpath, through the canal and up the Tiber to the great docks of the city, or transferred the cargo onto special craft equipped for both sailing and towing, which sailed round to the Tiber's mouth and were then towed upstream (Pl. 52). Even the new harbor wasn't enough to handle Rome's ever increasing traffic. Consequently, between A.D. 101 and 104, the Emperor Trajan dug out a hexagonal inner basin behind Claudius' port to add an eighth of a square mile of additional anchorage, lined it on all sides with warehouses, and widened the canal that led to the Tiber.

As a result of all this, Ostia boomed. Streets in the business section were lined with shops; in the residential areas apartment houses went up to take care of the expanding population. Members of the various trades and business enterprises in the time of the Roman Empire liked to band together in social and burial societies; the list of those at Ostia is practically an index to the activities of a busy port in any time or place. There were half a dozen for the different categories of boat-men: riverboatmen and bargemen to carry cargoes up the Tiber; fer-rymen to transport passengers; tugboatmen to man the stout skiffs that warped vessels into and out of the harbor (Pl. 53). There were societies of shipwrights, caulkers, riggers, "sandmen" (to handle the sand commonly used as ballast), divers (to salvage goods dropped overboard), stevedores (Pls. 35, 52), warehousemen, watchmen, and of dealers of various kinds—grain, wine, olive oil, hides. Agents of the towns, big and small, that did business with Rome maintained offices at Ostia. A line of such offices was located in the colonnade behind the theater; by walking along it, one could conveniently check on arrivals from, or departures for, various ports in North Africa, France, Sar-dinia, and other areas.

The vast flow of goods to Rome was merely the most notable aspect of the commerce of the age. Italy sold abroad pottery and metalware and, up to the end of the first century A.D., quantities of wine; by then her best customers, the provinces, began not only to produce for themselves but to export to their former supplier. All of Rome's prov-inces traded with one another as well as with the capital. Spain sent garum to France and dried fish to Greece; colored marbles from Asia Minor went into buildings in North Africa; statuary from Athens' workshops adorned the houses of the well-to-do throughout the west; Egypt shipped its papyri all around the Mediterranean. In the east, ports of long standing such as Ephesus and Miletus, which had been slowly dying in the confusion and confiscations of Rome's civil wars, came to life. In the west, along the coasts of North Africa and Spain, the construction of moles, quays, and warehouses gave once primitive harbors a new look. Emperor Nero undertook no less a project than cutting a canal across the Isthmus of Corinth. It was one of his bravura gestures of generosity toward Greece, of help almost solely to its com-merce because the major sea routes now bypassed it. As it happened, political difficulties made him give up the project and the isthmus re-mained uncut until 1893.

Thus the commerce of the Roman Empire embraced hundreds of places and products, all of what had gone on in earlier ages plus all that was brought into being by the new world Rome created. Within this far-flung and complex network two lines of trade stand out con-

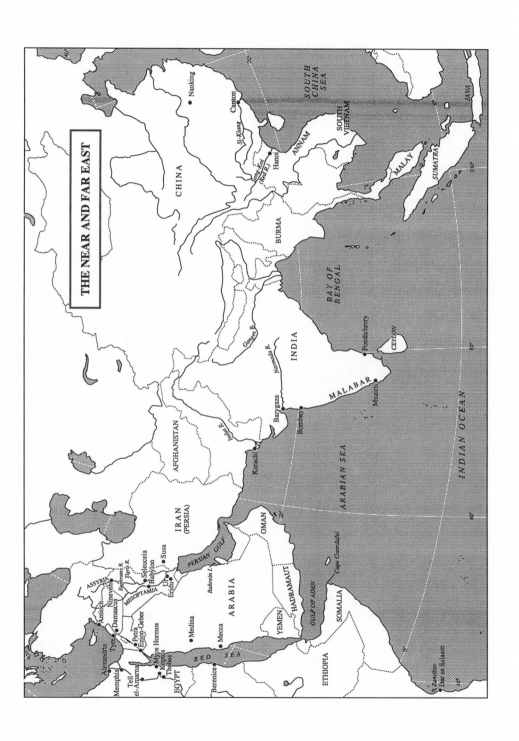

THE NEAR AND FAR EAST

spicuously above all others, one for the distances it spanned and the
exotic nature of the imports it dealt with, the other for the vast bulk of
its shipments and the mighty organization it required: Rome's trade in
the Indian Ocean, and the Alexandria-Rome grain service.

"The beautiful vessels, the masterpieces of the Yavanas, stir white
foam on the Periyar river . . . , arriving with gold and departing with
pepper." So wrote an Indian poet sometime in the second century A.D.
On the river stood Muziris, the port on the southwestern coast of India
that was the major exporter of the region's cash crop, pepper. The
"Yavanas" were, strictly speaking, men from any part of the West, but
in a context such as this it meant the Westerners who, sailing out of the
Red Sea ports of Roman Egypt, carried on trade with India. Their
ships lined the quays of Muziris and other Indian ports, and their sailors haunted the waterfront dives. In the residential areas behind, their
agents established little foreign colonies, anticipating by a millennium
and a half the employees of Britain's East India Company.

Many an official embassy made its way from the East to the West.
India sent several during the reign of Augustus, one from Ceylon visited the Emperor Claudius, and they kept coming as late as the reign
of Constantine the Great. Chinese records contain a long and flatter-
ing account of how people lived in Rome's eastern provinces based in
part on the report of an ambassador who had gotten as far as Mesopotamia in A.D. 97. (It has the surprising observation that the people "are
honest in their transactions, and there are no double prices," something not often said about Near Eastern tradesmen.) One group of
Westerners made their way almost to the borders of China, for the
same account notes that in "the ninth year of the Yen-hsi period during the emperor Huan-ti's reign [A.D. 166] . . . the king of Ta-ts'in,
An-tun, sent an embassy who, from the frontier of Jih-nan [Annam]
offered ivory, rhinoceros' horns, and tortoise shell. From that time
dates the [direct] intercourse with this country." Ta-ts'in is the Chinese name for the Roman Empire, and An-tun is Antoninus, the family name of Marcus Aurelius. The account goes on to comment on the
very ordinary quality of what was offered; there were, for example, no
jewels. Most likely it wasn't an official body at all but a group of traders
who, to get one jump ahead of their competitors, were trying to buy
their silk directly from China instead of going through the usual middlemen.

What came from India to the West via Egypt in the days of the
Ptolemies (Chapter 13) was a trickle compared with what flowed in
after Augustus brought peace to the Mediterranean world. The ultimate consumer of most of it was the city of Rome. Pepper and other

spices arrived in such quantities that Emperor Domitian sectioned off part of a colonnade in the heart of the city, the *horrea piperataria*, "pepper sheds," for the exclusive use of spice merchants; when Alaric the Goth in A.D. 408 agreed not to sack Rome, part of the price paid was three thousand pounds of pepper. Silks and gems poured in so profusely that there was concern about the drain on Rome's financial resources. "Thanks to women and their jewels, our money is being transferred to foreigners," grumbled Emperor Tiberius, and Pliny the Elder worried about how imports from India cost Rome fifty million sesterces annually.

In Augustus's day over a hundred ships set out each year for India from Myos Hormos or Berenice, the major ports on the northwestern shore of the Red Sea, six times as many as under the last Ptolemies. Troops of archers were carried as guards against pirate attack, and vessels of the Roman navy may have patrolled parts of the Red Sea. The ships sailed, as under the later Ptolemies, either with the southwest monsoon almost astern to the mouth of the Indus River near Karachi, or with it on the starboard quarter to the southwestern coast of India, the heart of the pepper country. They generally left in July, the height of the southwest monsoon season, and returned with the northwest monsoon any time between November and April. The items they loaded aboard for export had come from Alexandria by boat down the Nile to Koptos (the riverside town where the Nile, making a great swing to the east, comes nearest to the Red Sea), and from there by camel or donkey across the desert to the ports of departure. The imports they brought from India did the journey in reverse.

The Rome-India run was the most remote trade route of the age, yet it is the one about which we have the most information. An anonymous merchant or skipper who knew it firsthand sometime around the middle of the first century A.D. compiled a *Periplus Maris Erythraei*, "Guidebook of the Erythraean Sea," a term that embraced what is today the Red Sea, Gulf of Aden, Persian Gulf, and parts of the Indian Ocean. There may have been similar manuals covering other sea lanes of the Roman Empire, but this is the only one that has survived. It was written both for skippers and shippers: it was a "coast pilot" for the eastern shore of Africa as far south as Dar es Salaam and for the shores of Arabia and India, and at the same time a merchant's guide to what could be bought and sold at each point along the way. It has hardly more literary merit than a United States Hydrographic Office publication and it is a scant twenty or so pages long, but it is a mine of priceless information.

The author deals first with the African coast. On this leg, he reports, the important items a trader can pick up are tortoise shell, ivory, and aromatics such as frankincense and myrrh, and they are to be had in exchange for clothes, metals, tools, tableware. He warns against unfriendly natives; it's wise, he notes at one point, to take "in considerable quantity wine and grain, not for trade but as an expenditure for the goodwill of the locals."

But the heart of the book is the trip to India, and for that the author returns to the starting bases of Myos Hormos and Berenice. First he describes the passage down the Red Sea and along the southern shore of Arabia. The harbors are few and mostly poor, and, because of treacherous waters and pirates, the coastal voyage along Arabia is particularly dangerous. The products par excellence of the region are frankincense and myrrh, and the items one can sell there are chiefly staples: clothing and textiles, copper and tin, grain and olive oil and wine, certain drugs and cosmetics. However, one also took along a number of expensive luxuries for the courts of the king and the local governors: horses, pack mules, silverware, goldware, de luxe clothing. After a very brief look at the Persian Gulf—apparently its trade was in the hands of Arab, Persian, and Indian shippers—the author gets to India.

He reaches it at the mouth of the Indus. Here was a market where clothing, fabrics, glassware, and silverware could be exchanged for semiprecious stones, cottons, and silks. The place was obviously a terminus for transit trade because few of these products were local; the stones came from Afghanistan and Iran and the silks all the way from China. Farther down the coast at Barygaza—Broach today—about two hundred miles north of Bombay, all these items were available plus some pepper; among the things the locals would take in return was "wine, principally Italian." The rajah here was interested in strictly top-of-the-line luxuries: "precious silverware, slave musicians, beautiful girls for concubinage, fine wine, expensive clothing, choice unguent." Navigation along this coast from the Indus to Barygaza was tricky, and the author describes the hazards with vivid detail. One of the worst was getting into the ports, particularly difficult because of the poor visibility, sandbars, and steep rise and fall of the tides. His bald style even takes on color and drive as he tells of one place where "so much power is generated at the inrush of the sea even during the dark of the moon, particularly if the flood arrives at night, that when the tide is just beginning to come in and the sea is still at rest, there is carried from it to people at the mouth something like the rumble of an army heard from afar, and after a short while the sea itself races over the shoals with a hiss." The rajah of the area helped out by furnishing native fishing boats not only to guide but even to tow arriving vessels in.

Finally, the author reaches the Malabar coast, which, as the source of pepper and gems, was the most important trading area. Here in

Muziris especially, on the site of what is today Cranganore, the biggest freighters were found, those that had made the voyage straight across the ocean from the Gulf of Aden. They came

> because of the volume and quantity of pepper and malabathron [a form of cinnamon]. They [the ports of southwestern India] offer a market for: mainly a great amount of money . . . ; clothing with no adornment, in limited quantity; multicolored textiles; sulphide of antimony; coral; raw glass; copper, tin, lead; wine, in limited quantity. . . . They export pepper . . . ; good supplies of fine quality pearls; ivory; Chinese cloth [i.e., silk]; nard from the Ganges area; malabathron, brought from the interior; all kinds of transparent gems; diamonds; sapphires; tortoise shell.

One of the most interesting bits of information in this passage is that the products here were paid for primarily by "a great amount of money." Tiberius had grumbled about this, Pliny the Elder had given statistics—and the past century has furnished the concrete proof: a striking number of Roman coins have been unearthed in southern India, all silver and gold, no copper. In commercial exchanges they were treated as bullion: the medium of exchange was not the face value of the coins but a miscellaneous batch totaling a given weight. Those that have turned up date from the reign of Augustus to Nero, but this doesn't mean that trade ended abruptly at that time. Nero and his successors issued debased money which the Indians refused to accept; merchants thenceforth had to pay in the older coins or some equivalent.

The trade route did not stop at the southern tip but continued up the east coast. Archaeologists have uncovered near Pondicherry the remains of a Western trading station that was active from the second century B.C. to the end of the second A.D. The author of the guide-book is familiar with this coast but only as far as the Ganges. At this point his information peters out: he knows about regions farther east but only vaguely. And to the north he tells of a land where "there is a very great inland city called Thina from which silk floss, yarn, and cloth are shipped by land. . . . It is not easy to get to this Thina; for rarely do people come from it, and only a few."

This is where this unique manual ends—but not where the ancient mariners stopped. By the second half of the second century A.D., as we have seen, they had pushed as far as Annam (Vietnam today). A skipper about whom nothing else is known except that he was called Alexander led the way farther east, getting as far perhaps as Canton. In his wake came merchants who traded with Malaya and Java. For at least a hundred years more they kept coming: Chinese records mention a Western merchant who reached South Vietnam by sea in A.D. 226 and was sent on to the emperor at Nanking, and a large and expensive gift that a group from the West brought the emperor in 284.

This, then, is the general picture of one of Rome's great lines of trade, the far-flung one that linked it with Africa, Arabia, India, and the Far East. A hasty glimpse gives the impression of tremendous complexity: the author of the handbook that provides so much of the available information drops the names of dozens of ports and of a bewildering variety of objects of trade. But a closer look reveals a pattern. There were, basically, half a dozen key products that Rome imported, and they came from distinct areas: from Africa and Arabia, frankincense and myrrh; from Africa and India, ivory; from India, pepper and certain other spices, certain drugs, cottons, and silks, the last an import from China. Frankincense was virtually a necessity, something ancient religion could not do without. The others were mostly luxuries, things wealthy Romans insisted on having to improve the taste of their food, enhance their looks or dress, and add elegance to their furnishings, though they had to pay for them in hard cash.

And they paid great amounts of hard cash, for these luxuries were all costly. The Greek merchants who made Athens into a center of overseas commerce in the fourth century B.C., an age with smaller horizons and simpler tastes, had all been small-scale operators (Chapter 9), men of relatively modest means. A century later, when the great Hellenistic empires had replaced the Greek city-states, the size of commercial endeavors inevitably increased, and merchants, such as those who carried on trade under the Ptolemies, consequently worked on a much larger scale than their Athenian predecessors. But the shippers of the Roman Empire who traded with India had to be financiers on the grand scale, men in a position to put up, or borrow, major sums. A papyrus document from Egypt, dating to the mid-second century A.D., reveals graphically how much could be involved. It deals with a shipment from southwestern India to Roman Egypt. The preserved portion—the document is unfortunately incomplete—lists quantities of nard, ivory, and textiles, and what they are worth. The figures indicate that a cargo of such items—even the cargo of a Roman merchantman of but standard size—must have cost a monumental amount of money.

Rome's second great line of trade is precisely the opposite in every respect: instead of exotic luxuries intended for the rich, it involved a bulky and cheap commodity essential for the daily existence of a million people—grain. And much of it didn't cost Rome a cent.

The city of Rome posed a problem in supply that was unique. Starting out as a mere village, it had grown by Augustus' time into a sprawling metropolis with a huge population, much too big to look to the surrounding country for its food. As a matter of fact, long before it reached this size, it had begun to draw its grain from overseas, and the government found itself obliged, like the Greek cities (pp. 109-10), to assume the responsibility for seeing to it that supplies were adequate. The vagaries of politics compelled it to expand the role it played. Around the end of the second century B.C. large quantities of grain were flowing in as taxes in kind from some of the provinces Rome now ruled. To curry favor, political leaders started the practice of first selling grain to the citizens at below the market price and then of distributing it to them free. During the first three centuries A.D., an average of 200,000 people were receiving such handouts. To complicate matters further, the city by this time was getting most of its wine and olive oil from abroad. Between what was needed for the dole and for the open market, every emperor from Augustus to the last to sit on the throne found the *annona*, as the supply of food for the city was called, one of his most pressing problems. It grew even worse in the third century A.D. when handouts, first of oil and then of wine and pork, were added to the traditional one of grain. The *praefectus annonae*, "minister of supply," became one of the most harried officials in the government. It wasn't the cost of the commodities involved that caused the trouble: much of these came to Rome free of charge as taxes in kind. The problem was transportation, getting the cargoes moved from overseas to the capital.

One of the rare statistics preserved from the ancient world is the figure for the amount of grain shipped yearly from Egypt to Rome— 20 million *modii*, or about 135,000 tons. And this satisfied merely a third of the city's requirements; the rest came from North Africa. On the outskirts of modern Rome, near the point on the Tiber where the ancient docks used to be, is a fair-sized hill today called Monte Testaccio, "Mount Potsherd." It is composed, from foot to summit, of broken pieces of pottery, remains of the containers in which over the years millions of gallons of olive oil had been shipped mostly from Spain, some from North Africa. Now, the run from North Africa was a matter of three days and from Spain of little more than a week. But Egypt was something else again.

Egypt lies to the southeast of Rome. The winds that prevail over the waters between, during the summer months when the ancient mariners sailed, are northwesterly. This meant that freighters raced downhill from Ostia or Pozzuoli to Alexandria with the wind on their heels in ten days to two weeks. Everything added up to a quick voyage: the direction of the wind made possible a voyage straight to the destination, the wind itself was strong and steady, and the vessels most often traveled in ballast since the city had a lopsided balance of trade, taking in far more than it shipped out. But the skippers paid heavily for this on the return: it was uphill work against foul winds all the way. The northwesterlies dictated a course that was a third again as long as the voyage out. Following the preferred route, the ships, now fully laden, headed for the southern coast of Asia Minor on a port tack, there turned west and, on a starboard tack, coasted along to Rhodes. From here they worked south of Crete and then, tacking continuously, beat their way to Syracuse in Sicily, with perhaps a stop at Malta en route. Here they could wait, if they had the time, for a southerly to carry them through the Strait of Messina and north; otherwise they headed into the northwesterlies once again and slogged it out the rest of the way. The voyage took at least a month and on occasion two or more. A vessel could count on only a single round-trip or, at most, a trip and a half during the sailing season.

Whatever the winds, the grain consigned to Rome had to reach the docks on the Tiber or the city went hungry. During the bitter combat for the throne in A.D. 69, Vespasian, who held the east, planned to starve Rome into submission by cutting off the grain shipments from Egypt. Once when supplies in the city were running low, Emperor Claudius offered special rewards to skippers who were willing to sail during winter, or to those whose ships were undersized, holding no more than seventy tons. Hardly an economical way of doing things, but he had no choice.

There was only one way to meet the problem: see to it that enough big ships were available and shuttle them between Rome and Alexandria. Augustus took the first step—he probably started with a group of Alexandrian shipowners who had hauled grain for the Ptolemies—and his successors followed his lead in this as in so many other things. The result was the crack fleet of Rome-Alexandria grain "clippers."

By luck we happen to know what the ships on this run looked like. One day sometime in the second century A.D., one of them met up with a particularly bad stretch of weather, was blown far off course, and wound up in, of all places, Athens' port, the Piraeus. This was a far cry from what it had been formerly: Athens was now a sleepy university town and its once great harbor handled little more than local traffic. The arrival of a ship from the famous grain fleet created a sensation; the *Queen Elizabeth* or any of the Atlantic superliners wouldn't cause more had they suddenly appeared at a dock in Charleston or Savannah. The whole town turned out to see it—including, fortunately for posterity, Lucian, one of the most famous and prolific writers of the age. He and a group of friends walked the five miles from Athens to the Piraeus to get a look at what was causing all the excitement. He was astonished. He wrote:

> What a size the ship was! One hundred and eighty feet in length, the
> ship's carpenter told me, the beam more than a quarter of that, and forty-

four feet from the deck to the bottom, the deepest point in the bilge. What a mast it had, what a yard it carried, what a forestay held it up! The way the sternpost rose in a gradual curve with a gilded goose-head set on the tip of it, matched at the opposite end by the forward, more flattened, rise of the prow with the figure of Isis, the goddess the ship was named after, on each side! And the rest of the decoration, the paintings, the red pennant on the main yard, the anchors and capstans and winches on the foredeck, the accommodations toward the stern—it all seemed like marvels to me! The crew must have been as big as an army. They told me she carried so much grain that it would be enough to feed every mouth in Athens for a year. And it all depends for its safety on one little old man who turns those great steering oars with just a skinny tiller. They pointed him out to me; woolly-haired, half-bald fellow. Heron was his name, I think.

A length of one hundred and eighty feet, beam of more than forty-five, forty-four feet deep—it was a mighty vessel, able to carry between 1,200 and 1,300 tons of grain. It was as big as our *Constitution*, the famous frigate now in Boston Harbor. The ships that plied between Europe and America did not reach this size until the beginning of the nineteenth century. If all the grain ships on the Rome-Alexandria run were like it, an aggregation of about eighty would have been sufficient to ferry the 135,000 tons that Egypt supplied. If any were smaller, a correspondingly larger number would have been required.

There were no such things as passenger ships in the ancient world. The traveler boarded whatever trading vessel turned up that was headed in the direction of his destination, hopping from port to port if he could find none that would take him all the way. If he happened to be going from Rome to Alexandria, he got a break: the great grain ships provided an excellent passenger service. When the Jewish princeling Agrippa was planning to leave Rome for Palestine, Emperor Caligula advised him not to take the coastal route but to make the direct sailing; "the ships," he added, "are crack sailing craft and their skippers the most experienced there are; they drive their vessels like race horses on an unswerving course that goes straight as a die." Even the Roman emperors used them. When Vespasian was ready to return from Egypt to Rome in the spring of A.D. 70, he had at his disposal any galley in the navy, but he preferred to do the first leg on a grain clipper. The big vessels, keeping to the open sea, didn't waste time in daily stops along the way, and—a point that Vespasian very likely had in mind as he contemplated the long voyage that faced him—they offered accommodations that were luxury itself compared with cramped quarters on the poop of a man-of-war. There was plenty of room aboard: when Josephus, the Jewish historian, crossed in A.D. 64 he had no less than six hundred fellow passengers.

A traveler from Italy would board at Pozzuoli or, after Claudius and Trajan had finished their work, at Portus in the spring when those ships that had lain over there set sail, generally in ballast, for Alexandria; they would arrive in a few weeks and thus have practically the whole summer before them for a round-trip from Egypt. Those that had wintered in Alexandria had a much harder schedule. They left there, fully loaded with grain and passengers, just as soon as the sailing season opened, and made port in late May or June. They were easy to spot as they neared the harbor, and their arrival was a great event. An eyewitness at Pozzuoli recounts:

> Today the Alexandrian ships suddenly came into view, the ones that are usually sent ahead to announce that the fleet [i.e., of big grain ships] is behind and will be arriving; they are called "dispatch boats." They are a welcome sight to the country. The whole mob from Pozzuoli stands on the dock, and, even in a big crowd of ships, they can pick out those from Alexandria by their sails, since these are the only ones allowed to keep the topsails raised, although all use them on the open sea. . . . All other vessels, when they have gotten to Capri . . . , have orders to make do with the mainsail, so the topsails on those from Alexandria stand out conspicuously.

Once arrived at Pozzuoli or Portus, the ships had to hope for a quick turnaround since they had a full circuit, to Alexandria and back again to Rome, to fit in before the sailing season ended. This, however, couldn't always be counted on. Much was involved: the vessel had to be checked into port, it had to shift its load to barges or small freighters, and then it had to wait around until it got clearance from the authorities to leave. All this could take more than a month. There is a letter preserved which a hand on one of the grain ships wrote to his brother in Egypt sometime in the second or third century A.D.; it survived intact in Egypt's protecting sands until it was dug up at the end of the nineteenth century. It speaks for itself:

> Dear Apollinarius,
>   Many greetings. I pray continuously for your health; I am well. I'm writing to let you know that I reached land on Epeiph 6 [June 30] and that we unloaded on the 18th of the same month [July 12]. I went up to Rome on the 21st of the same month [July 19] and the place welcomed us as the god willed. We are daily expecting our discharge; up to today not one of the grain fleet has been released. Best regards to your wife, and Serenus, and every one of your dear friends. Farewell.
>
>   Your brother Irenaeus
>   Mesore 9 [August 2]

Irenaeus' ship clearly would not be getting back to Alexandria until late in August, and squeezing in a return to Rome before the sailing season closed down was going to be nip and tuck. But the pressure was such that the skippers had little choice: they had to shove off even though they ran the risk of being forced to winter at some harbor along the way. As a matter of fact, this is precisely what happened during one of the most celebrated voyages in ancient history, St. Paul's to Rome in A.D. 62.

At Myra, a port on the southern coast of Asia Minor, the Roman centurion who was escorting the group of prisoners that included Paul "found a ship of Alexandria sailing into Italy, and he put us therein. And when we had sailed slowly many days, and scarce were come over against Cnidus, the wind not suffering us, we sailed under Crete." Although it may have seemed so to the passengers, this was nothing unusual: their skipper would have been surprised had he picked up a fair wind on this leg. But Paul was soon to face far worse. The ship he had boarded was one of those that had already completed a round-trip that year and was now trying to cram in a second run to Rome; the passenger list was consequently light—there were only 276 aboard, counting the crew. By the time his vessel made Crete it was dangerously late in the season, so, on arrival at some small haven on the southern coast, Paul urged that they stay there for the winter. Just then a favorable breeze sprang up, and the captain, owner, and others favored taking advantage of it to reach a harbor a little farther along the coast that was more secure. They put to sea and, very soon after, an east-north-east gale struck them. Centuries before Paul's time the same wind had blown Colaeus to fame and fortune (p. 73), and sailors today still keep a weather eye out for the *gregale*, as they call it. For fourteen days the vessel rode helplessly before it under bare poles; the crew kept the seams from opening by passing girding cables from one side underneath the hull to the other, they cut away part of the rigging, and they jettisoned some of the cargo to lighten ship. Colaeus had been driven all the way to Spain, but Paul was luckier: at midnight of the fourteenth day the seamen suddenly sensed that land was near. The leadsman was ordered to take soundings. He reported first twenty fathoms, then, very soon after, fifteen; the water was shoaling dangerously fast. The skipper gave the command to drop four anchors astern in order to hold the ship in place until day broke. As soon as there was some light, he saw that there was only one thing to do: try to run his vessel ashore. He ordered the artemon raised, the anchors cut away, and the helmsman to head for the beach. The gamble worked: everyone aboard was rescued, although the hull broke in two. The land turned out to be Malta, and Paul spent three months there until another grain clipper, one that had started from Alexandria a little ahead of his ship but had prudently put in at the island for the winter, took him on the last leg of the journey when the sailing season reopened the following spring.

The Apostle's voyage graphically points up the hazards that faced the ships on the Rome-Alexandria grain run. The creation and maintenance of this aggregation was an outstanding maritime achievement, at once a great passenger and a great freight service. The vessels, like practically all other merchantmen, were owned, commanded, and manned by Greek or Phoenician or Syrian or other maritime-minded subjects of the empire; but it was the Roman government that welded them into a regular service and the Roman talent for organization and administration that assured its efficient operation. Year in and year out the great ships kept sailing until, in A.D. 330, Constantine the Great finished building another city, Constantinople, to serve as the capital of the empire, on the site of the ancient Greek town of Byzantium. He took the ships over to bring the grain of Egypt to his new foundation and left the population that remained at Rome to be fed by the quick shuttle service from North Africa.

Chapter 18

AN END AND A BEGINNING

IN A.D. 269 a horde of Goths ripped up and down the Aegean, spreading havoc among the islands. Goths on the warpath were nothing new: the movement of barbarian peoples that was to tear huge rents in the fabric of the Roman Empire was well under way by this time. What was new was to find them on the sea. After over two centuries of easy living, carrying out peacetime maneuvers and ferrying troops, Rome's great navy, like so much else in the empire, had gone soft. By A.D. 230 the plague of piracy had erupted again; between 253 and 267 mobs of Goths were using the waterways, the Black Sea and the Aegean, to get to the scene of their maraudings; by 285, when Diocletian was crowned emperor, the provincial squadrons had vanished from the Mediterranean and the big Italian fleets had shrunk to mere skeletons; and in 324, when Constantine the Great fought it out with one of his rivals, both sides had to commandeer ships from the maritime cities of the east. A full circle had been traversed: Rome was again virtually without a navy.

In A.D. 395 the Roman Empire broke into two parts, an eastern and a western; whatever warships were left moved to the east—and the Vandals had a field day in the western Mediterranean. They were a Germanic tribe that had spilled over into North Africa. From there, practically without breaking stride, they took to the sea, captured Corsica and Sardinia and other strategic islands, and in 455 even succeeded in sacking Rome. There was no one to stop them; matters were worse than in the worst days of the pirates of Cilicia (Chapter 15). But when their leader, Gaiseric, died in 477, their plunderings came to a halt. Gradually another fleet arose to restore and maintain some order on the water. The credit goes to those most able of the ancient mariners, the Greeks of the eastern Mediterranean; it was the last contribution they were to make, and it was a notable one.

The western part of the Roman Empire little by little fell into the hands of invaders from Germany. But the eastern was made of sterner stuff: the Byzantine Empire, as the nation that took root here is called, did not come to an end until 1453, when the Turks finally took Constantinople, its capital. One of the chief reasons for this long life is sea power. Shortly after A.D. 500 the empire launched a navy that managed to fill the gap left by Rome's collapse on the sea. In the

214 CHAPTER EIGHTEEN

seventh century a dangerous enemy unexpectedly appeared on the scene: in 636 the Arabs embarked on their meteoric career by conquering Syria; a few years later they added Egypt and, by the end of the century, all of North Africa. To meet the new menace, the empire built up its navy into a powerful force, big enough to be divided, like its predecessor, into a home fleet and a number of provincial detachments. Until the eleventh century it was the strongest in the eastern Mediterranean, although it had to fight some bitter battles against the squadrons of Islam to hold the distinction. The new navy was no warmed-over version of what the Romans had used: the ships were of a different design and, from A.D. 678 on, they mounted a new and effective type of weapon. Its introduction came at a dramatic and timely moment.

In 673 the Arabs began an all-out attack by water against Constantinople. Every summer for the next five years their ships sailed from an advanced base on the island of Cyzicus in the Sea of Marmora to harry and blockade the Byzantine capital. A sack seemed just a matter of time—and would have been were it not for one man. Callinicus, an engineer, had fled to Constantinople from his native town when the Arabs flooded into Syria. At one and the same time he paid off those who had driven him out and those who had taken him in: he saved the city by coming up, in the nick of time, with a new way of using an old weapon, fire.

The Greeks and the Romans for centuries had tried fire in one form or another. On the sea, back in the second century B.C., the Rhodians had won some spectacular victories by hanging blazing fire pots in front of their galleys (pp. 139, 156). The key ingredient in almost all the formulas for "Greek fire," as the various inflammable mixtures came to be called in later times, was what the ancients referred to as naphtha, crude oil which, throughout the oil-rich areas of the Near East, could be scooped up at dozens of points where it seeped out of the ground. Although it was inflammable enough in its simple state, the usual practice was to lace it with sulphur or pitch or quicklime. Then came a revolutionary discovery: if saltpeter were included, a mixture resulted that was capable of spontaneous combustion. Callinicus has been given the credit for having been the first to have hit upon this. If he wasn't, he may at least have developed a formula vastly more effective than any hitherto known: it not only saved the Byzantines at the time, but provided them with their chief weapon for the future; merely by keeping it a secret from the Arabs they were able to hold a clean advantage on the sea for centuries.

Callinicus' phenomenal success turned fighting with fire into one of the major modes of warfare of the age, and a whole arsenal of new

weapons came into being. Ships were now fitted with two types of incendiary artillery. One was the catapult, now loaded not only with ar-
rows and stones but with clay jars filled with the latest, most improved
version of Callinicus' self-igniting mixture; on impact they shattered
and the contents, splattered about, burst everywhere into flame. Another seems to have been an incendiary rocket and a mechanism to
launch it. A bronze tube was mounted on deck and into it was slipped
a reed that had been filled with Greek fire and stoppered. The tube
was aimed and a fuse was lit; it ignited the reed, which burst into
flame; the gases that were released shot it out of the tube, and a shaft
of fire streaked through the air toward the target. But it was fighting
at close quarters rather than at a distance that called into play the
Byzantines' fire weapon par excellence, the one that became standard
equipment on all their warships. This was a great long tube, of wood
lined with bronze, that was set on the foredeck with its mouth trained
outward. Its other end was coupled to an air pump. It was loaded with
Greek fire; this was ignited, the pump was worked—and a shaft of
flame belched forth from the mouth (Pl. 54). It was the world's first
flamethrower, and a highly effective one. There was even a miniature
model, small enough to hold in the hand, which marines used; they
kept it hidden behind their shield and, at the appropriate moment,
fired it at the enemy.

The naval arms of the age were new and so were the ships that
carried them. The Romans had gone in for two-level galleys to some
extent, but the backbone of their navy was the trireme. In the Byzantine fleets the ships of the line all were two-level; triremes and other
three-level types were things of the past. Unfortunately we have no
information about their size and shape; a clue lies in the name they
were known by, *dromon,* "runner," a name that points to an emphasis
on speed in the design. It was used in both a strict and a loose sense. In
the first it referred solely to the largest type of war galley, one with at
least one hundred oars and sometimes as many as one hundred and
twenty, normally with one man on each oar, although sometimes there
were two, probably on the oars in the upper level. But dromon was
also loosely used of the smaller ships of the line as well, whose levels
had fewer oars. None of these types had outriggers; both levels were
worked, as in the warships of the Roman navy, through ports in the
hull. All ships had two masts, a mainmast and a foremast, and the
largest type might have a mizzen as well. In the later centuries at least,
these were fitted with lateen sails. The sails were carried during battle
and not left ashore as had been the practice heretofore.

The dromons had a foredeck and poop deck but were otherwise
open, with merely gangways along the sides and a catwalk down the

middle offering passage from one end to the other. To protect the rowers, a light frame was rigged along the gangways on which shields were hung. At first dromons were fitted with rams like all previous war craft. But more important were the new fire weapons and the armament connected with boarding and fighting at close quarters, and, as a result, the ram was eventually eliminated. In the bows was a fighting platform from which marines could sweep an enemy's deck with missiles. The dromons strictly so called, the largest warships, added a second platform amidships with long overhangs projecting laterally over the gunwales; on each a heavy weight was suspended and, when an enemy came so close that these were poised over his rowers, the lashings that held the weights were loosed or cut away. Every ship carried a flamethrower in the bows; larger units mounted rocketlaunchers and catapults; and the largest had all this plus an extra pair of flamethrowers, one amidships and one at the stern. Since the enemy also used fire in some form, vulnerable parts of the vessel were protected with stretched hides which, in battle, because water was ineffectual against Greek fire, were saturated with vinegar.

The dromon was the ship of the line not only of the Byzantine navy but, with some modifications, of its principal rival as well. The Arabs who overran Syria and Egypt were a people far more at home on the desert than on the water, and the keels of their first squadrons were laid down in the dockyards of Alexandria by Greeks and Egyptians who shortly before had been building ships for the Byzantine fleet. For centuries afterward the new rulers drew on their conquered subjects not only for shipwrights but also for crews. In the first and second centuries A.D. Egyptian youngsters had rowed the vessels of Rome's Misene fleet (cf. p. 188); in the seventh and eighth and even later, they manned the benches of the caliph's Egyptian squadron, while Arab marines fought from its decks.

Constantinople's fleet was a worthy replacement for Rome's. It had to be: without a first-rate fighting force the Byzantines would have lost their commerce to Arab raiders and their capital to the Arab grand fleet. In the field of merchant shipping, however, though they carried on an active and widespread commerce, they produced nothing to match the achievements of their predecessors. Rome's greatest efforts had been called forth by her trade in the Indian Ocean and by the challenge of the run from Alexandria to the Tiber; the one played only a short-lived part, and the other none, in the commerce of her successors.

In the second century B.C. the Ptolemies had broken the age-old monopoly of the Indians and Arabs in the trade with India (Chapter

13). In the first two centuries A.D., the great age of the Roman Empire, the merchants working out of Roman Egypt monopolized it. In the third century, so full of unrest throughout the empire, Persians and Abyssinians took it over. In 641 the Arabs captured Egypt, and from that time on Arab, Persian, and Indian shippers shared the commerce of the Indian Ocean until Vasco da Gama sailed his squadron into the harbor of Calicut on May 20, 1498.

The Arab conquest of Egypt meant, too, that the Nile's harvest now went down the Red Sea to Mecca and Medina instead of across the Mediterranean to Europe. But it was not this that brought about the end of Rome's great fleet of grain carriers; that had taken place hundreds of years before. Soon after Constantine had founded his new capital, the huge cargoes of Egyptian grain that used to go to the Tiber were diverted northward to the Bosporus. Getting it to the new destination was far simpler than to the old; there was no need for a fleet of superfreighters. The run was so much shorter and easier that vessels could make two or even three round-trips during a season. The only difficulty was navigating the Dardanelles (cf. p. 70), and Emperor Justinian, in the early part of the sixth century, solved this by building a big granary on the island of Tenedos near the mouth of the strait. It was 280 feet long, 90 wide, and quite tall, large enough to hold the combined cargoes of all the vessels on the run. When the wind in the strait was foul, ships unloaded here and hustled back to Egypt, leaving it to small craft to carry the grain the rest of the way as soon as a favorable breeze came along. The Arab conquest of Egypt in 641 brought even this service to an end. From then on the capital depended on the supplies it could shuttle in from the Balkans and southern Russia.

All this does not mean that the Byzantine Empire abandoned maritime commerce once Egypt was lost to it. For over a hundred years thereafter its traders were still to be found in every major port from Italy to the Black Sea, and its fleet not only guaranteed safe passage for their freighters but, in certain areas, ensured a monopoly by keeping those of competitors away. Persians and Arabs brought the products of the East to the Mediterranean, but it was the Byzantine merchant who forwarded them to the West. As time went on, however, Constantinople's economic practices worked to deprive its own merchants of their share, and cargoes traveled more and more in Armenian, Arab, and, above all, in Italian ships. The empire's merchant marine gradually dwindled away; Constantinople remained a great commercial center, but the transport of that commerce was being taken over by others. By A.D. 1100 the Byzantines had completely relinquished their old role: the energetic traders of Pisa and Genoa and

Venice now held the commerce of the Mediterranean in their grasp, and Italian fleets were in control of its waters.

A century or so later came the great contributions of the Middle Ages to the arts of the sailor: helmsmen could now steer by the compass as well as by the stars or sun or wind, and with the handier stern rudder instead of the old steering oars. Moreover, the time was drawing near when the ram and the flamethrower were to make way for naval cannon. The day of the ancient mariner was truly ended.

TABLE OF DATES

(Dates in round numbers are approximate)

B.C.

3500–3400	Invention of sails
3100	Earliest pictures of sails
3000–2500	Trade between Mesopotamia and India
2600	Pharaoh Snefru imports timber from Lebanon
	Earliest contacts between Egypt and Crete
2450	Pharaoh Sahure ferries troops
2250	Pharaoh Pepi ferries troops
2000	Pharaoh Mentuhotep III sends a ship down the Red Sea
2000–1500	Heyday of Minoan maritime activity
1500–1100	Mainland Greece foremost in the Aegean
1504–1450	Thutmose III
	Rekhmire
1500	Queen Hatshepsut's expedition to Punt
1417–1379	Amenhotep III
	Kenamum
1379–1362	Akhenaten
	The Tell-el-Amarna letters
1300–1000	Age of the Sea Raiders
1190	Ramses III defeats the "invaders from the north"
1184	Traditional date of the fall of Troy
1100	Wenamon's voyage
	Dorian Greeks migrate into the Greek peninsula
	Voyage of the Argo
1000–700	Phoenicians colonize the west
970	Phoenicians supply timber to Solomon
	Phoenician trade with India
800–550	Age of Greek colonization
800	Invention of the ram and penteconter
700	Invention of two-banked galleys
700–600	Invention of the trireme
600	Necho's expedition circumnavigates Africa
500	Hanno's voyage
490–479	Wars between the Greeks and Persians
480	Battles of Artemisium and Salamis
480–322	Athens controls the Aegean
431–404	The Peloponnesian War

429	Battle of Rhion
415–413	Syracusan expedition
406	Battle of Arginusae
405	Battle of Aegospotami
398	Invention of the quinquereme
384–322	Demosthenes
336–323	Alexander the Great
323–31	The Hellenistic Age
322	Battle of Amorgos
310 (?)	Pytheas' voyage
305–282	Ptolemy I (Soter)
	Antigonus the One-Eyed
	Demetrius Poliorcetes
306	Battle of Salamis (in Cyprus)
305	Siege of Rhodes
282–246	Ptolemy II (Philadelphus)
283–239	Antigonus Gonatas
264–241	First Punic War
260	Battle of Mylae
256	Battle of Ecnomus
255	Battle of Cape Hermaeum
241	Battle of the Aegates Islands
246–222	Ptolemy III (Evergetes)
222–205	Ptolemy IV (Philopator)
221–179	Philip V
218–202	Second Punic War
201	Rhodian embassy to Rome
200–197	Rome defeats Philip V
192–190	Rome defeats Antiochus III (the Great)
191	Battle of Corycus
190	Battle of Side
	Battle of Myonnesus
171–167	Rome defeats Perseus
167	Delos becomes a free port
146	Destruction of Carthage
120 (?)	Eudoxus sails to India
89–85	Rome's first war with Mithridates VI (Eupator)
88	First sack of Delos
69	Second sack of Delos
67	Pompey destroys the pirates of Cilicia
48	Caesar defeats Pompey
44	Assassination of Caesar
42	Defeat of Brutus and Cassius
36	Battle of Naulochus
31	Battle of Actium

27 B.C.– A.D. 180	Heyday of the Roman Empire
27 B.C.–A.D. 14	Augustus
14–37	Tiberius
37–41	Caligula (Gaius)
41–54	Claudius
54–68	Nero
62	St. Paul's voyage to Rome
69–79	Vespasian
79–81	Titus
81–96	Domitian
96–98	Nerva
98–117	Trajan
117–138	Hadrian
131–161	Antoninus Pius
161–180	Marcus Aurelius
253–269	Goths in the Aegean
284–305	Diocletian
311–337	Constantine
330	Founding of Constantinople
395	Division of the Roman Empire
455	Vandals sack Rome
527–565	Justinian
636	Arabs conquer Syria
641	Arabs conquer Egypt
673–678	Arabs besiege Constantinople

NOTES

ABBREVIATIONS USED

ANET   J. Pritchard, *Ancient Near Eastern Texts Relating to the Old Testament*, 2d ed. (Princeton 1955)
AJA   *American Journal of Archaeology*
Ath. Mitt. *Mitteilungen des deutschen archäologischen Instituts, Athenische Abteilung*
CAH   *Cambridge Ancient History*
ESAR   T. Frank and others, *An Economic Survey of Ancient Rome* (Baltimore 1933–1940)
GOS   J. Morrison and R. Williams, *Greek Oared Ships* (Cambridge, Eng. 1968)
IG   *Inscriptiones graecae*
IJNA   *International Journal of Nautical Archaeology*
JEA   *Journal of Egyptian Archaeology*
JHS   *Journal of Hellenic Studies*
RE   *Paulys Real-Encyclopädie der classischen Altertumswissenschaft*
SSAW   L. Casson, *Ships and Seamanship in the Ancient World*, 2d ed. (Princeton 1986)
TAPA   *Transactions of the American Philological Association*

CHAPTER 1
DOWN TO THE SEA IN SHIPS

3–5   Primitive craft, *SSAW* chaps. 1–2. Obsidian from Melos, C. Renfrew and M. Wagstaff, *An Island Polity: The archaeology of exploitation in Melos* (Cambridge, Eng. 1982) 24. Egyptian and Mycenaean contacts with Britain, C. Renfrew, *Before Civilization* (London 1973) 215; R. Atkinson, *Stonehenge* (London 1956) 84–85. Early tin trade, J. Muhly, *Copper and Tin. The Distribution of Mineral Resources and the Nature of the Metals Trade in the Bronze Age* (Hamden, Conn. 1976) 271–88.

CHAPTER 2
INTERNATIONAL TRADE BEGINS

6–9   "Bringing of forty ships," *ANET* 227. Early contacts between Egypt and the Levant, *CAH*³ i.2.45–47, 345–51. "No one really sails," *ANET* 441. Mesopotamian trade in the fourth millennium B.C., J. Oates in *Antiquity* 51 (1977) 221–34. Magan, Meluhha, Mesopotamia–Indus Valley trade,

W. Leemans, *Foreign Trade in the Old Babylonian Period* (Leiden 1960) 159–66; Muhly, *Copper and Tin* (Chap. 1) 288–330; S. Ratnagar, *Encounters. The Westerly Trade of the Harappa Civilization* (Oxford University Press, Delhi 1981) 68–148. Indian chank, J. Hornell in *Antiquity* 15 (1941) 239–40; Ratnagar 147–48. Mesopotamian businessmen, A. Oppenheim in *Journal of the American Oriental Society* 74 (1954) 6–17. "Who am I," Oppenheim 10–11.

10–13 Location of Punt, K. Kitchen in *Orientalia* 40 (1971) 184–207. Henu, J. Breasted, *Ancient Records of Egypt* (Chicago 1906) i §§ 429–32. Shipwrecked sailor, A. Erman, *The Literature of the Ancient Egyptians* (London 1927) 29–35. Hatshepsut's inscription, Breasted ii §§ 246–95. Her expedition, Kitchen *ibid.*; *CAH*[3] ii.1.329–33; T. Säve-Söderbergh, *The Navy of the Eighteenth Egyptian Dynasty* (Uppsala 1946) 8–30.

13–17 Egyptian ships, *SSAW* 11–22. Egyptian trade, *CAH*[3] ii.1.385–90. King of Cyprus' letters, S. Mercer, *The Tell El-Amarna Tablets* (Toronto 1939) No. 34. Kenamun's tomb, R. Faulkner in *JEA* 33 (1947) 40–46. Rekhmire's tomb, N. de G. Davies, *The Tomb of Rekh-mi-Re at Thebes* (New York 1943).

17–19 "Minos is the first," Thucydides 1.4. Minoan trade, *CAH*[3] ii.1.577–81; K. Branigan, *The Foundations of Palatial Crete* (London 1970) 179–95 (in error, however, in suggesting that Crete imported tin from the west). Libyan plant (silphium), ostrich feather, A. Evans, *The Palace of Minos at Knossos*, ii (London 1928) 54, 174, 764.

20–22 Thera frieze, L. Casson in *IJNA* 4 (1975) 3–10; L. Morgan, *The Miniature Wall Paintings of Thera* (Cambridge, Eng. 1988) 121–45. Minoan influence on Greece, *CAH*[3] ii.1.642–44. Mycenaean conquest of Crete, ii.1.654–55. Mycenaean trade, ii.2.136, 181–86.

CHAPTER 3
EXCAVATING UNDER WATER

23–25 Antikythera wreck, G. Weinberg, ed., *The Antikythera Shipwreck Reconsidered* (Transactions of the American Philosophical Society, New Series, Vol. 55, Part 3, Philadelphia 1965); J. du Plat Taylor, *Marine Archaeology* (London 1965) 35–39. Jacques Cousteau conducted dives on the site in 1985 and recovered more statuary and, most important, coins that proved to have been issued at Pergamum in 86 B.C. Orrery, D. de Solla Price, *Gears from the Greeks: The Antikythera Mechanism* (Transactions of the American Philosophical Society, New Series, Vol. 64, Part 7, Philadelphia 1974). Mahdia, Taylor 39–53. Albenga, 53–66. Early finds along the French and Italian Riviera, N. Lamboglia and F. Benoit, *Scavi sottomarini in Liguria e in Provenza* (Bordighera 1953); L. Casson in *Archaeology* 6 (1953) 221–28.

25–27 Grand Congloué wreck, F. Benoit, *l'Épave du Grand Congloué à Marseille* (xive supplément à "Gallia," Paris 1961); H. Frost, *Under the Mediterranean* (London 1963) 240–53; L. Long in A. McCann, *The Roman Port and Fishery of Cosa* (Princeton 1987) 164–66. Modern marine archaeology, cf. G. Bass, ed., *A History of Seafaring Based on Underwater Archaeology* (London 1972) 52, 63, 83, 147–49, 151. Cape Gelidonya wreck, G. Bass, *Cape Gelidonya: A Bronze Age Shipwreck* (Transactions of the American Philosophical Society, New Series 57, Part 8, Philadelphia 1967); Bass, *Hist. of Seaf.* 23–24. Ulu Burun wreck, Bass *et al.* in *AJA* 90 (1986) 269–96, 92 (1988) 1–37, 93 (1989) 1–29; Bass in *National Geographic* 172.6 (Dec. 1987) 693–732.

27–29 Shipbuilding, *SSAW* 201–208. Levantine merchantmen, 35–36. Half-ton anchors, *IJNA* 13 (1984) 169–70 and fig. 2. Minoan merchantmen, *SSAW* 32–34; L. Basch, *Le musée imaginaire de la marine antique* (Athens 1987) 93–138.

CHAPTER 4
WAR ON THE SEA

31–33 Uni, Thutmose's use of sea power, Säve-Söderbergh, *The Navy* (Chap. 2) 31–41. "Every port town," *ANET* 241. Letters of Rib-Addi, Mercer, *The Tell El-Amarna Tablets* (Chap. 2) Nos. 85, 98, 101, 105, 113, 114. Letter of king of Cyprus, No. 38. Mycenaean occupation of Crete, cf. *CAH*[3] ii.1.579–81.

33–35 "The northern countries," *ANET* 263. Ramses III's illustrated inscription, H. Nelson in *Journal of Near Eastern Studies* 2 (1943) 40–55; an earlier picture of a sea battle, a scene in the Thera frieze, is but a fragment (Pl. 5). "No land could stand," *ANET* 262. "The net was made ready," Breasted, *Ancient Records* (Chap. 2) iv § 77. Tjeker and Peleset to Palestine, *CAH*[3] ii.2.377–78.

36–38 Troy and the Trojan War, *CAH*[3] ii.2.342–50; M. Mellink, ed., *Troy and the Trojan War* (Bryn Mawr, Penn. 1986); cf. the interesting debate on the war's historicity in *JHS* 84 (1964) 1–20.

38–43 Homer's ships, *SSAW* 43–48; T. Seymour, *Life in the Homeric Age* (London 1907) chap. xi. Sailing season, *SSAW* 270–72. Odysseus' boat, *Odyssey* 5.244–61 and cf. *SSAW* 217–19. Early Greek craft, 30–32, 38–39.

CHAPTER 5
RAIDERS AND TRADERS

44–46 "I spent only," Odyssey 14.244–72. Piracy in this age, H. Ormerod, *Piracy in the Ancient World* (Liverpool 1924) 88–96. "Ah, yes . . . I wandered," *Odyssey* 4.81–85. "Sacked the city," 9.40–42. "In ancient times," Thucydides 1.5–7.

47–54 Wenamon's narrative, *ANET* 25–29.

CHAPTER 6
THE DAWN OF MARITIME EXPLORATION

55–60 Myth of Jason, A. Burn, *Minoans, Philistines, and Greeks* (London 1930) 189–97. "Precipitous cliffs," *Odyssey* 12.59–60.

CHAPTER 7
WESTWARD HO!

61–62 Greek "dark age," V. Desborough, *The Greek Dark Ages* (London 1972) 352–55.

62–66 The Phoenicians in the west, D. Harden, *The Phoenicians* (London 1962) 57–75, 157–65; G. Bunnens, *l'Éxpansion phénicienne en Méditerranée* (Brussels 1979). Etymology of the name, Harden 21–22. Dyeing industry, J. Huxley, *From an Antique Land* (New York 1954) 73–76. Deliberate shipwreck, Strabo 3.5.11 (175–76). Dido's bargain, Vergil 1.365–68. "Unload their wares," Herodotus 4.196. Odysseus' swineherd, *Odyssey* 15.403–84. "Now therefore command," I Kings 5.6–11. "And King Solomon," 9.26–28. Ophir, V. Christides in *Revue Biblique* 77 (1970) 240–47 (either Africa or India). Alphabet, *CAH*² iii.1.811–33. Western exploration and the metals trade, Muhly, *Copper and Tin* (Chap. 1) 262–71.

66–74 Colonization, *CAH*² iii.3.83–195; for discussion of some of the legal problems, cf. R. Littman, *The Greek Experiment* (New York 1974) 58–62. "Frogs on a pond," Plato, *Phaedo* 109B. "Sons of virgins," Strabo 6.3.2 (278). Syracusan colonist's swap, Archilochus cited in Athenaeus 4.167d. Ancient version of the Pocahontas legend, A. Burn, *The Lyric Age of Greece* (London 1960) 146. Relations with natives, *CAH*² iii.3.155–57. Abdera, Burn 97, 316. Miletus, H. Michell, *The Economics of Ancient Greece*, 2d ed. (New York 1957) 238–42. "City of the blind," Burn 114. Corinthian trade, T. Dunbabin, *The Western Greeks* (Oxford 1948) 224–50. Ship-hauling road, N. Verdelis in *Ath. Mitt.* 71 (1956) 51–59; B. MacDonald in *JHS* 106 (1986) 191–95. Colaeus, Herodotus 4.152. Phocaeans, Burn 144–49. Phocaean skippers in the Atlantic (Midacritus and Euthymenes), M. Cary and E. Warmington, *The Ancient Explorers*, 2d ed. (Penguin 1963) 45, 61–62.

75–79 Warships of the age, *SSAW* 49–65. Earliest representation of a ram, F. van Doorninck in *IJNA* 11 (1982) 277–86. Two-masted warship, L. Casson in *IJNA* 9 (1980) 68–69. Dousing sail before battle, *SSAW* 235–36. The *hemiolia*, 128–29, 445–46. Architect from Corinth, Thucydides 1.13.3. Merchantmen, *SSAW* 65–70. Hebrew seal, N. Avigad in *Bulletin of the American Schools of Oriental Research* 246 (1982) 59–62. Few quays, Herodotus 6.116 (as late as 490 B.C. Athens used the open roadstead off Phaleron).

CHAPTER 8
THE WOODEN WALLS

81–83 Battle of Salamis, Herodotus 8.75–96, but his account has aroused much controversy; see, e.g., W. Pritchett, *Studies in Ancient Greek Topography* (Berkeley 1965) 94–102; GOS 139–43.

83–89 Triremes, *SSAW* 77–96; J. Morrison and J. Coates, *The Athenian Trireme* (Cambridge, Eng. 1986) 128–79. Trireme slips, GOS 181–92. Replica,

Morrison and Coates 192–228; Morrison and Coates, eds., *An Athenian Trireme Reconstructed: The British sea trials of Olympias, 1987* (BAR International Series 486, 1989); P. Lipke in *Archaeology* (March/April 1988) 22–29, (November/December 1988) 88; J. Coates in *Scientific American* 260.4 (April 1989) 96–103. Lashing to a thalamite thwart, Herodotus 5.33.2. Crews, *SSAW* 300–306. Recruiting, Morrison and Coates (1986) 114–27. Haphazard supply system, A. Gomme, *Essays in Greek History and Literature* (Oxford 1937) 190–203. Training, *SSAW* 278–80. Rig and gear, 224–38, 245–51, 256. Age and classification, 90, 92. War surplus sale, Isaeus 11.48 (the ship must have been a discard, or near discard, since the purchaser was no very rich man); for damaged rams sold as scrap bronze, see W. Murray in *Greek, Roman, and Byzantine Studies* 26 (1985) 141–150.

89–96   Tactics, *GOS* 313–20; H. Wallinga, *The Boarding-Bridge of the Romans* (Historische Studies uitgegeven vanwege het Instituut voor Geschiedenis der Rijksuniversiteit te Utrecht 6, Groningen 1956) 26–57. *Diekplus* and *periplus*, Wallinga 32–35; *GOS* 137–39, 314–19; J. Lazenby in *Greece & Rome* 34 (1987) 167–77 and I. Whitehead, ibid. 178–85. Circular formation at Artemisium, Herodotus 8.11; cf. Morrison and Coates (1986) 52–54. Phormio, Thucydides 2.83–84, 90–92; cf. *GOS* 315–16. Syracuse, Thucydides 7.59–71; cf. *GOS* 317–20. Arginusae and Aegospotami, Xenophon, *Hell.* 1.6.24–38, 2.1.20–30; cf. Wallinga 29–31.

CHAPTER 9
THE MERCHANTS OF ATHENS

97–108   Pasion and Phormio, T. Glover, *From Pericles to Philip* 4th ed. (London 1926) chap. x. Athens' harbor, R. Garland, *The Piraeus* (Ithaca, N.Y. 1987) 150–56. Athens' commerce, Athenaeus 1.27e–28a (far-ranging list of imported items). Ships headed for the Aegean, Herodotus 7.147. Athens' grain trade, Michell, *The Economics* (Chap. 7) 258–78. Maritime loans, L. Casson, *Ancient Trade and Society* (Detroit 1984) 27–28, 44–45. Zenothemis and Hegestratus, Demosthenes 32. Two Lycians, 35. Use of coin, Casson 32.

108–12   Metics and aliens, L. Casson in *TAPA* 106 (1976) 44–45 = Casson 44–46. Legal accommodation for non-Athenians, E. Cohen, *Ancient Athenian Maritime Courts* (Princeton 1973) 9–10, 23–40, 76. Heracleides, W. Dittenberger, *Sylloge inscriptionum graecarum*, 3d ed. (Leipzig 1915) 1.304. Trade in naval supplies, Michell 281–83. Ceos' ruddle, *IG* ii2.1128.

112–15   "Many of my crew," Demosthenes 50.14–16. Triremes, quadriremes, and quinqueremes in Athens' navy, *SSAW* 97. Merchantmen, 169–84. Kyrenia ship, J. Steffy, in *AJA* 89 (1985) 71–101; M. Katzev in *Institute of Nautical Archaeology Newsletter* 16.1 (March 1989) 4–10. Merchant galleys, *SSAW* 157–68. Sailing speed, 281–91; cf. Katzev 8, 10. Amorgos, Diodorus 18.15.8–9. Scylax, *RE* s.v. *Scylax* 635–46 (1929); J. Thomson, *History of Ancient Geography* (Cambridge, Eng. 1948) 88.

CHAPTER 10
BEYOND THE PILLARS OF HERCULES

116–21   Ancient conception of Africa, Thomson, *History of Ancient Geography*
(Chap. 9) 99, 135, 137. "Africa, except where it borders," Herodotus 4.42;
cf. Cary and Warmington, *Ancient Explorers* (Chap. 7) 111–21, Thomson
71–72, J. Desanges, *Recherches sur l'activité des Méditerranéens aux confins de
l'Afrique* (Coll. de l'École française de Rome, Rome 1978) 7–16. Polybius'
doubts, Polybius 3.38. "Sataspes went to Egypt," Herodotus 4.43; cf. Cary
and Warmington 120–21, Thomson 73, Desanges 29–33, W. Hyde, *Ancient
Greek Mariners* (New York 1947) 240–44.

121–23   "The Carthaginians commissioned Hanno," text, ed. W. Aly, in *Her-
mes* 62 (1927) 321–24, reprinted in Desanges 393–97; discussed in Cary
and Warmington 63–68 (convinced), Hyde 141–48 (convinced), Thomson
73–76 (convinced but cautious), Desanges 39–85 (who, after a review of
subsequent references to the voyage in ancient literature, is skeptical).
Cerne, see Pseudo–Scylax 112 (C. Müller, *Geographi graeci minores* [Paris
1855] i.94) for a fuller description, and cf. Desanges 115–19 (who locates it
on the site of Mogador).

124–26   Pytheas, Cary and Warmington 47–56, Thomson 143–51, Hyde
124–34. "In fact there is no star," Hipparchus, *In Arati et Eudoxi phaenomena
commentarii* 1.4.1. Irish customs, Strabo 4.5.4 (201).

CHAPTER 11
THE AGE OF TITANS

127–36   "I just got rid," Plutarch, *Demetrius* 19.5. "Demetrius will rescue
me," 29.4–5. Naval arms race, *SSAW* 137–40. Oarage of Hellenistic warships, 99–116. Size of fleets, W. Tarn, *Antigonus Gonatas* (Oxford 1913) 454–
58. Demetrius' naval artillery, Diodorus 20.83.1; on naval artillery in general, see *SSAW* 121–22. Apollodotus' letter, A. Hunt and C. Edgar, *Select
Papyri* ii (Loeb Classical Library, Cambridge, Mass. 1934) No. 410. Trireme
tax: the trierarchema; cf., e.g., C. Edgar, Zenon Papyri in the University
of Michigan Collection (Ann Arbor, Mich. 1931) No. 100.2. Athlit ram,
J. Steffy and L. Casson, *The Athlit Ram* (College Station, Texas 1991). Actium
monument, W. Murray, *Octavian's Campsite Memorial for the Actian War*
(Transactions of the American Philosophical Society, Vol. 79, Part 4, Philadelphia, 1989).

136–42   For the naval history of the period, see CAH vi, chap. xv; vii,
chaps. iii, xxii. Salamis, Diodorus 20.49–52; cf. Wallinga, *Boarding-Bridge*
(Chap. 8) 46–48. The "sixteen" a fossil, *SSAW* 139. Rhodes, W. Tarn and
G. Griffith, *Hellenistic Civilisation*, 3d ed. (London 1952) 174–76; R. Berthold, *Rhodes in the Hellenistic Age* (Ithaca, N.Y. 1984) esp. 91–99. Fire containers, *SSAW* 123. *Triemiolia*, *SSAW* 129–31. Rhodes' security system,
Strabo 14.2.5 (653). Siege of Rhodes, Diodorus 20.82–88, 91–99. Rhodian
crews, *SSAW* 306–309. Enemy commanded by Rhodians, e.g. Polyxenidas

(pp. 153–156). Three brothers, M. Segre in *Rivista di filologia* 60 (1932) 446–61. Malea, Strabo 8.6.20 (378); cf. Ormerod, *Piracy* (Chap. 5) 22, note 2.

CHAPTER 12

LANDLUBBERS TO SEA LORDS

143–51   First Punic War, *CAH* vii, chap. xxi. Second Punic War, viii, chaps. ii–iv. Development of Roman sea power, J. Thiel, *A History of Roman Sea-Power Before the Second Punic War* (Amsterdam 1954); W. Tarn in J. Sandys, *A Companion to Latin Studies*, 3d ed. (Cambridge, Eng. 1921) 489–501. "From the tree," Pliny the Elder 16.192. Complement of a quinquereme, *SSAW* 105. Training on land, 278. The *corvus*, Wallinga, *Boarding-Bridge* (Chap. 8). 120 marines, *SSAW* 105. Mylae, Thiel 184–87. "Was the first Roman," E. Warmington, *Remains of Old Latin* iv (Loeb Classical Library, Cambridge, Mass. 1940) 128–31. Fleet numbers, G. Tipps in *Historia* 34 (1985) 437–45. Ecnomus, 445–64.

152–56   Wars with Philip and Antiochus, *CAH* viii, chaps. v–vii. Roman sea power in this period, J. Thiel, *Studies on the History of Roman Sea-Power in Republican Times* (Amsterdam 1946). Philip's use of pirates and sabotage, Polybius 13.4–5; Polyaenus 5.17; cf. M. Rostovtzeff, *The Social and Economic History of the Hellenistic World* (Oxford 1941) 607–608 and Ormerod, *Piracy* (Chap. 5) 147–48. Rhodes' and Philip's fleets, Polybius 16.2–8. *Lembi, SSAW* 125–27.

CHAPTER 13

EAST MEETS WEST

157–58   Contract, text, ed. U. Wilcken, in *Zeitschrift für ägyptische Sprache und Altertumskunde* 60 (1925) 90; cf. Rostovtzeff, *Social and Economic History* (Chap. 12) 922, 1555. Hellenistic merchantmen, *SSAW* 172–73. The leviathan, 185–86, 191–99. Elephantine houseboat, 341–42. Rig, 240. Harbors, 366. Eratosthenes, Thomson, *History of Ancient Geography* (Chap. 9) 158–66. Maps, 98, 205–208.

158–62   Egypt's economy, Rostovtzeff 255–422; Tarn and Griffith, *Hellenistic Civilisation* (Chap. 11) 189–96; *CAH*² vii.1.133–67. Control of Alexandria's harbor, Strabo 2.3.5 (101); cf. *ESAR* ii.593–94 (a document dated 246 A.D., but the practice it reflects must have been in use in Ptolemaic times), 715 (Nos. 64, 66). Cargo manifest, C. Edgar, *Zenon Papyri* i (Cairo 1925) No. 59012. Pepper, Athenaeus 2.66e–f; Plutarch, *Sulla* 13. Red Sea and Indian Ocean trade, Rostovtzeff 1243–48; Tarn and Griffith 241–49; P. Fraser, *Ptolemaic Alexandria* (Oxford 1972) 179–81. Lighthouse, Fraser 17–20. Souvenir of the lighthouse, J. Hackin, *Recherches archéologiques à Begram* (Mémoires de la délégation archéologique française en Afghanistan ix, Paris 1939) 43 and figs. 38, 39.

163–64   Rhodes, Berthold, *Rhodes* (Chap. 11) esp. 47–54, 206–209; Rostovtzeff 676–93. Rhodes' place in the grain trade, L. Casson in *TAPA* 85

(1954) 171–74 = Casson, *Ancient Trade* (Chap. 9) 73–75. Rhodian jars, Rostovtzeff 680. Rhodian bankers, Casson in *TAPA* 172 = Casson 75. Working
through a Rhodian agent, 175 = 76–77. Earthquake relief, Polybius 5.88–
89. Rhodes' harbor revenues, Polybius 30.31.12. Rhodian law, Rostovtzeff
680. Colossus of Rhodes, Tarn and Griffith 318–19; H. Maryon in *JHS* 76
(1956) 68–86. Ephesus, Sidon, Tyre, etc., Tarn and Griffith 251, 255, 257–
58, 260.

165–67   Slave trade, Rostovtzeff 1259. Art trade, 744–45. Delos, 787–99.
Drop in Rhodes' revenues, Polybius 30.31.10–12 and cf. Casson in *TAPA*
179 = Casson 78. Delos' trade transient, 179–80 = 78–79. "Merchant, sail
in," Strabo 14.5.2 (668).

167–69   The monsoons and Eudoxus, Strabo 2.3.4 (98–99); cf. Rostovtzeff
926–29, Tarn and Griffith 247–49, J. Thiel, *Eudoxus of Cyzicus* (Historische
Studies uitgegeven vanwege het Instituut voor Geschiedenis der Rijksuniversiteit te Utrecht 23, Groningen 1966), Fraser 182–84. Arab craft and
seafaring and the India trade, G. Hourani, *Arab Seafaring in the Indian Ocean
in Ancient and Early Medieval Times* (Princeton 1951) 6–28.

CHAPTER 14
NEW LIGHT ON ANCIENT SHIPS AND SHIPPING

170–71   Amphoras: a short but authoritative treatment, particularly of
Greek amphoras, in V. Grace, *Amphoras and the Ancient Wine Trade*, Excavations of the Athenian Agora, Picture Book No. 6, 2d ed. (Princeton 1979);
a full treatment of Roman amphoras with a masterly introduction dealing
tersely with all phases of the subject in D. Peacock and D. Williams, *Amphorae
and the Roman economy: an introductory guide* (London 1986); amphoras in
wrecks, P. Gianfrotta and P. Pomey, *Archeologia subacquea* (Milan 1981) 143–
66. Wooden containers, Herodotus 4.2 (used by the Scythians); Strabo
5.1.12 (218) (used by the Celts). Rhodes' logo, cf. Grace fig. 23. Sestius,
McCann, *Roman Port* (Chap. 3) 33, 171–77.

171–73   Shipping of grain, *SSAW* 200. Garum, R. Curtis in *Classical Journal*
78 (1983) 232–40. Shipments of garum, E. Will in McCann 202. Wreck off
Toulon, P. Pomey in "L'épave romaine de la Madrague de Giens (Var),"
xxxiv᷉ supplément à "Gallia" (Paris 1978) 103. Albenga, Gianfrotta and
Pomey 283–84. Building stone 210–22; Bass, *History of Seafaring* (Chap. 3)
75–76, 83, 152–53. Storage depot, Gianfrotta and Pomey 212–14. Cargoes
of stone off Sicily, *SSAW* 370 note 40; Gianfrotta and Pomey 218. Stone
coffins, Gianfrotta and Pomey 215–17. Church, 217, 219; Bass 136–37,
152–53. Metal ingots, *SSAW* 199–200; Gianfrotta and Pomey 183–89. Fittings, *SSAW* 246 n. 85, 252–56; Gianfrotta and Pomey 285–96; Bass 60, 139.
Coins, Bass 52; G. Bass and F. van Doorninck, Jr., *Yassi Ada*. i, *A Seventh-
Century Byzantine Shipwreck* (College Station, Texas 1982) 92. Medical instruments, D. Gibbins in *Antiquity* 62 (1988) 294–97.

173–74   Marseilles hull, M. Clerc, *Massalia: Histoire de Marseille dans l'antiquité*

(Marseilles 1927–29) ii.172–76. Nemi barges, G. Ucelli, *Le navi di Nemi*, 2d ed. (Rome 1950).

174–76   Preservation of hulls, cf. Bass 53, 79, 82, 148–49. Thirty-odd hulls, Gianfrotta and Pomey 235. Changes, J. Steffy in *IJNA* 11 (1982) 26–28. Effect of switch to skeleton-first, B. Greenhill, *Archaeology of the Boat* (London 1976) 286–88. Serçe Limani wreck, Steffy 28–32. Construction of seventh–century wreck, Bass and van Doorninck 69–81. Size, 86. Galley, 87–120. Kyrenia crew, M. Katzev in Bass 50. Harbors, J. Shaw in Bass 88–112. Looters, P. Throckmorton, *Shipwrecks and Archaeology* (Boston 1970) 210–29.

CHAPTER 15
THE PIRATES OF CILICIA

177–79   "Strangers, who are you?" *Odyssey* 9.252–54. Settlements away from the sea, Thucydides 1.7. Naval base on the Adriatic, Dittenberger, *Sylloge* (Chap. 9) 1.305. Scenes in Greek comedy, Plautus, *The Rope*. Greek novels, Ormerod, *Piracy* (Chap. 5) 266–70. Teuta's reply, Polybius 2.8.8; cf. Ormerod 172. Reprisal, Ormerod 62–67; *CAH*[2] vii.1.287. Demetrius' use of pirates, Diodorus 20.82.4. "Pirates came into," Dittenberger 1.521. Naxos inscription, 1.520. Turkish corsair, Ormerod 55.

179–83   "Tyrrhenians," Ormerod 152–62; *CAH*[2] vii.1.285–86. Illyrians, Ormerod 166–84. Cretans, 142–50. Cilicians, 190–247. Naval organization and ships, Plutarch, *Pompey* 24. Slave market at Side, Strabo 14.3.2 (664). Capture of the Balearics, Plutarch, *Sertorius* 7. Landings on Italy, Plutarch, *Pompey* 24; Cicero, *Pro lege Manilia* 32; cf. Ormerod 231. Treatment of Roman citizens, Plutarch, *Pompey* 24. Caesar and the pirates, Plutarch, *Caesar* 1–2. Pompey's campaign, *Pompey* 26–28; cf. Ormerod 233–41.

CHAPTER 16
ROME RULES THE WAVES

184–86   Sextus Pompey, C. Starr, *The Roman Imperial Navy 31 B.C.–A.D. 324*, 2d ed. (Cambridge, Eng. 1960) 5-7. Agrippa's catapult–grapnel, *SSAW* 122. Battle of Actium, Starr 7–8; Murray, *Octavian's Campsite* (Chap. 11) 131–51. Sails kept aboard, Plutarch, *Antony* 64.2.

186–89   Augustus founds a navy, Starr 11–13, 106. Fleets of Misenum and Ravenna, 13–38. Awnings, R. Graefe, VELA ERUNT. *Die Zeltdächer der römischen Theater und ähnlicher Anlagen* (Mainz 1979). Provincial squadrons, Starr 106–20. Nationality of crews and length of service, 75–81. Augustus' use of slaves, *SSAW* 326. Officers, Starr 38–45. "God willing," H. Youtie and J. Winter, *Papyri and Ostraca from Karanis*, Second Series = *Michigan Papyri* viii (Ann Arbor, Mich. 1951) No. 468. "First of all," Hunt and Edgar, *Select Papyri* (Chap. 11) i (1932) No. 112. Apion's later letter, *Aegyptische Urkunden aus den königlichen Museen zu Berlin, Griechische Urkunden* ii (Berlin 1898) No.

632 and cf. F. Preisigke, *Berichtigungsliste der griechischen Papyrusurkunden aus Ägypten* i (Berlin 1922) 58. Sailors' children prefer the army, Starr 95.

189–91 Warships on coins, *SSAW* figs. 122–23. Broad hulls, 143–45. Cabin, artemon, stempost, 146–47. Liburnians, 141–42. Names, 355–58.

191–92 Merchant ships on coins, H. Mattingly and E. Sydenham, *The Roman Imperial Coinage* iii (London 1930) 422 and pl. xvi.331. Harbors on coins, i (1923) 151–52 and pl. x.168. Size of merchantmen, *SSAW* 170–73. Vatican obelisk, 188–89. Merchant galleys, 157–68. Projecting forefoot, 35, 158, 174, 331.

192–96 Cabins, *SSAW* 179–81. Passengers, L. Casson, *Travel in the Ancient World* (London 1974) 153–54. Water supply, *SSAW* 177. Stempost, gallery, 174–75. Ship timber, 212–13. Rope and sailcloth, 231, 234. Ballast, 176. Caulking, pitching, 209; Gianfrotta and Pomey, *Archeologia* (Chap. 14) 260. Lead sheathing, *SSAW* 209–10; Gianfrotta and Pomey 258–59. Paint, SSAW 211–12. Colored mosaic, fig. 154; color plate in L. Casson, *Illustrated History of Ships and Boats* (New York 1964) fig. 62. Rig, *SSAW* 229–45. Lead line, flags, ship's boat, 246–49. Slaves, 328. Speed, 281–91; M. Katzev in *INA [Institute of Nautical Archaeology] Newsletter* 16.1 (March 1989) 7–10.

CHAPTER 17
ALL ROUTES LEAD TO ROME

198–200 "I built myself," Petronius, *Satyricon* 76. Calpurnii, C. Dubois, *Pouzzoles antique* (Paris 1907) 46. Sextius Fadius Musa, *ESAR* v.271–72; R. Meiggs, *Roman Ostia*, 2d ed. (Oxford 1973) 289. Rome's population, *ESAR* v.218. Rome's imports, M. Rostovtzeff, *The Social and Economic History of the Roman Empire*, 2d ed. (Oxford 1957) 66–67, 153–58. Portus, *SSAW* 367–69; Meiggs 51–62, 149–71. Ostia's expansion, Meiggs 62–78. The societies, 311–36. Italy's change to importer, Rostovtzeff 162. Spanish garum, *ESAR* v.292. Asia Minor marble, iv.624. Athenian statuary, i.353–54. Egyptian papyri, ii.328. Prosperity of Ephesus and Miletus, iv.719–20. Corinthian canal, Suetonius, *Nero* 19.

202–203 "The beautiful vessels," L. Casson, *The* Periplus Maris Erythraei, *Text with Introduction, Translation, and Commentary* (Princeton 1989) 296. Rome's trade with India, 21–27. Indian embassies to Rome, 38. "Are honest in their transactions," "the ninth year," F. Hirth, *China and the Roman Orient* (Shanghai 1885; repr. Chicago 1967) 42. Not an official body, 173–76. Pepper sheds, E. Nash, *Pictorial Dictionary of Ancient Rome*, 2d ed. (New York 1968) i.485. Alaric's price, J. Bury, *History of the Later Roman Empire* i (London 1923) 177. "Thanks to women," Tacitus, *Annals* 3.53. 50,000,000 sesterces, Pliny the Elder 6.101. Over one hundred ships, Strabo 2.5.12 (118). Security on the Red Sea, Pliny the Elder 6.101; Starr, *Roman Imperial Navy* (Chap. 16) 113. Time of departure, Casson 15. Routing in Egypt, 13.

203–206 *Periplus Maris Erythraei*, text in Casson 49–93. African coast, *Periplus* 1–18 (= Casson 51–61). "In considerable quantity," 17 (= 61). Red

Sea, Arabia, 19–33 (= 61–71). Mouth of Indus, Barygaza, 38–49 (= 73–81). "Wine," "precious silverware," 49 (= 81). "So much power," 46 (= 79–81). "Because of the volume," 56 (= 85). Roman coins in India, M. Wheeler, *Rome Beyond the Imperial Frontiers* (London 1954) 137–43. Pondicherry, 145–50. "There is a very great," *Periplus* 64 (= Casson 91). Alexander, Ptolemy, *Geography* 1.14.1 (Kattigara = Canton?). Third century A.D. contacts with China, Hirth 16, 272–75, 306–308. Size of investment, Casson 35.

206–209   Tribute in grain, *ESAR* v.218–20. Grain subsidies and distributions, D. van Bercham, *Les distributions de blé et d'argent à la plèbe romaine sous l'empire* (Geneva 1939) 15–116. 200,000 recipients, 27–31. Wine and pork added, *CAH* xii.308. 20,000,000 modii, Aurelius Victor, *De Caesaribus* 1.6. Monte Testaccio, *ESAR* v.272–73; E. Rodríguez Almeida, *Il Monte Testaccio* (Rome 1984). Rome–Alexandria run, *SSAW* 297–99. Rome-Alexandria in ballast, Strabo 17.1.7 (793). Vespasian's plan, *CAH* x.829. Claudius' rewards, Suetonius, *Claudius* 18; Gaius, *Institutes* 1.32c; cf. L. Casson in *Memoirs of the American Academy in Rome* 36 (1980) 24–25. "What a size," Lucian, *Navigium* 5. Size of the Isis, *SSAW* 186–88. Size of fleet of grain carriers, 188.

209–212   Booking passage, Casson, *Travel* (Chap. 16) 152–53. Caligula's advice, Philo, *Against Flaccus* 26. Vespasian's return, Josephus, *Bellum Judaicum* 7.21. Josephus' crossing, Josephus, *Vita* 15. "Today the Alexandrian ships," Seneca, *Epistles* 77.1–2. Apollonarius, Hunt and Edgar, *Select Papyri* (Chap. 11) No. 113. St. Paul's trip to Rome, Acts 27. "Found a ship," Acts 27.6.

CHAPTER 18
AN END AND A BEGINNING

213–16   Gothic seaborne invasion, Starr, *Roman Imperial Navy* (Chap. 16) 194–96. Commandeering of ships, 197. Byzantine–Arab conflict, A. Lewis, *Naval Power and Trade in the Mediterranean, A.D. 500–1100* (Princeton 1951). Callinicus, M. Mercier, *Le feu grégeois, les feus de guerre depuis l'antiquité, le poudre à canon* (Paris 1952) 13–14. Greek fire, 24–40, 123–25. Byzantine warships, *SSAW* 148–54. Arabs' use of Egyptian rowers, 326–27. Arab navies, Hourani, *Arab Seafaring* (Chap. 13) 53–61.

217–18   Persians and Arabs take over Far East trade, Hourani 36–50, 61–79. Alexandria–Constantinople run, granary on Tenedos, A. Johnson and L. West, *Byzantine Egypt: Economic Studies* (Princeton 1949) 156. Byzantine commerce diminishes, Lewis 120–21, 245–49.

INDEX

Abdera, 69

Abdi-Ashirta, 32

Abyssinia, 217. *See also* Ethiopia

Achilles, 36

Actium, 136, 185

Adalia, Gulf of, 154

Aden, 162

Aden, Gulf of, 119, 203, 205

Adriatic, 22, 113, 151, 152, 177, 179, 184, 187

Aea, 55, 56, 57, 59

Aeetes, 55, 56

Aegates Islands, 151

Aegean, 17, 25, 27, 42, 64, 66, 71, 73, 87, 96, 101, 115, 116, 127, 137, 138, 139, 160, 163, 165, 199, 213

Aegina, 100

Aegospotami, 95, 96

Aeneas, 62

Afghanistan, 8, 161, 204

Africa, 19, 27, 64, 65, 72, 73, 116, 118–21, 123, 144, 148–51, 160, 161, 168, 172, 192, 198–200, 203, 206, 207, 212–14

Agamemnon, 21, 36, 37, 38

Agrippa, 185

Agrippa (Prince of Judaea), 209

Ajax, 38

Akaiwasha, 34

Akhenaten, 21, 31, 32, 34

Alaric, 203

Alashiya, 53

Albenga, 24, 25, 172, 175

Alexander (explorer), 205

Alexander the Great, 101, 102, 115, 127–29, 153, 157

Alexandria, 128, 157–66, 168, 172, 187, 188, 192, 199, 202, 203, 207–12, 216

Alexidamus, 140, 141

Algeria, 163

Algiers, 65

alphabet, 64

Alps, 151

Amber, 19, 126

Amenemhet, II 18

Amenhotep, III 15

Amon, 47–53

Amorgos, 115, 129, 178

Amphitrite, 60

amphoras, 24, 25, 27, 29, 170–72, 174; classification, 171; for garum, 172; Rhodian, 163; of Sestius, 171; size, 170; stamps, 171; weight, 170

amulets, 72

Amurri, 32

Anaximander, 70

anchors, 29, 40, 89, 173, 209, 211

Androcles, 106

Andros, 137

Annam, 202, 205

annona, 207

Antigonus Gonatas, 137, 139, 142, 152

Antigonus the One-Eyed, 127, 128, 129, 134, 136, 138

Antikythera, 23

Antioch, 128, 161, 164

Antiochus (father of Seleucus), 128

Antiochus III, 142, 153–56, 167

Antipater, 135

Antisthenes, 97

Antoninus, 202

Antony, 184–86

aphract, 90, 140

Apion, 188, 189

Apollo, 68, 165, 166

Apollodorus, 106, 108

Apollodotus, 134, 135

Apollonius, 135, 160

Appian Way, 180

Arabia, 9, 15, 62, 64, 128, 160–62, 164, 165, 167, 199, 203, 204, 206

Arabian Sea, 167

Arabs, 116, 161, 162, 166–68, 204, 214, 216

archers (as marines), 86, 141, 203

Archestratus, 97

Archimedes, 146

Arginusae, 91

Argo, 55–60

Argonauts, 55–60, 70

Armenia, Armenians, 217

olive oil, 8, 16, 71, 72, 99–101, 114, 159,
160, 164, 167, 171, 198, 200, 204, 207
Oman, 8
Ophir, 64
Oran, 65
Orca, 125
Orkney Islands, 125
Orpheus, 58
Ostia, 146, 172, 181, 199, 200, 207
ostriches, 19
outrigger, 83, 85, 90, 94, 131, 190

paddles, 3, 20
paint, ship's, 193
Palermo, 66
Palestine, 4, 6, 15, 19, 30, 34, 35, 209
Pantelleria, 66
Pantheon, 172
papyrus, 15, 19, 22, 46, 47, 51, 53, 100,
134, 157, 159, 200, 206
Paralos, 92
parchment, 159
parexeresia, 83
Pasion, 97, 98, 102, 109
passenger service, 192, 193, 209, 210, 212
Paul (Apostle), 211, 212
pearls, 161, 199, 205
Peleset, 34, 35
Pelias, 56
Peloponnese, 71, 72
Peloponnesian War, 92, 97, 101, 112, 154
penteconter, 74, 77, 80, 83, 84, 86, 89, 91,
121
pentekontarchos, 86, 141
Pepi, 30
pepper, 160, 161, 199, 202–206
perfume, 64, 72, 128, 161, 166, 198
Pergamum, 152, 156, 159, 167
Periander, 72
Pericles, 99
periplus (coast pilot), 91, 92, 95
Periplus Maris Erythraei, 203
Periyar river, 202
Perseus, 156, 179
Persia, Persians, 68, 74, 81–83, 91, 92, 100,
101, 127, 128, 204, 217
Persian Gulf, 4, 8, 9, 64, 162, 167, 203, 204
Petra, 161, 166
Petronius, 198
Pharos, 162

Phaselis, 106
Philip II, 101
Philip V, 142, 152, 156, 178
Philistines, 34
Phocaea, Phocaeans, 74, 75, 79, 88, 124
Phoenicia, Phoenicians, 6, 9, 15–19, 30, 33,
34, 46, 54, 61–67, 70, 73, 74, 76, 78, 80,
82, 84, 116, 118–20, 122, 123, 129, 137,
140, 154, 161, 164, 166–68, 182, 188,
191, 212
Phoinikes, 62
Phormio (admiral), 92, 93, 94, 102
Phormio (merchant), 98, 109
pigs, 100
Pillars of Hercules, 116, 118, 121
pillows, 100
Pindar, 59
pine. *See* timber
Piraeus, 97–105, 108, 109, 111–14, 115,
208
piracy, pirates, 10, 31, 32, 44–46, 53, 57,
61, 75, 78, 91, 92, 103, 106, 113, 114,
138–40, 142–44, 152, 156, 161, 165,
166, 169, 177–83, 187, 190, 203, 204,
21; of Cilicia, 177–83; of Crete, 152,
178, 179; of Illyria, 152, 177, 179, 187;
in literature, 177; in navies, 140, 152,
178, 179; punishment of, 179, 181–83;
of the Red Sea, 10, 161; Tyrrhenian,
144, 179
Pisa, 217
pitch, 100, 112, 159, 193, 214
Plato, 67
Pliny the Elder, 186, 203, 205
Po, 80
Polybius, 118
Polycles, 140, 141
Polyxenidas, 153, 155, 156
Pompeii, 186
Pompey, 182–84, 186
Portus, 199, 210
Poseidon, 24
pottery. *See* tableware
Po Valley, 143
Pozzuoli, 167, 198, 199, 207, 210
praefectus annonae, 207
precious stones, 8. *See also* gems
Prefect of the Misene Fleet, 186
privateers, 178
prorates, 86, 140–42